CASE-BASED REASONING IN DESIGN

Case-Based Reasoning in Design

MARY LOU MAHER
University of Sydney, Australia

M. BALA BALACHANDRAN
University of Wollongong, Australia

DONG MEI ZHANG
CSIRO, Sydney Laboratory, Australia

Ψ Psychology Press
Taylor & Francis Group

New York   London

First Published by
Lawrence Erlbaum Associates, Inc., Publishers
10 Industrial Avenue
Mahwah, New Jersey 07630

Transferred to Digital Printing 2009 by Psychology Press
270 Madison Ave, New York NY 10016
27 Church Road, Hove, East Sussex, BN3 2FA

Library of Congress Cataloging-in-Publication Data

Maher, Mary Lou.
    Case-based reasoning in design / Mary Lou Maher, M. Bala
Balachandran, Dong Mei Zhang.
        p.   cm.
    Includes bibliographical references and index.
    ISBN 0-8058-1831-6 — ISBN 0-8058-1832-4 (pbk)
    1. Computer-aided design. 2. Engineering design—Case stud-
ies. I. Balachandran, M. (Muthaukumar), 1953–. II. Zhang,
Dong Mei. III. Title.
TA174.M335 1995
620'.0042'0285—dc20   95-17344
                                              CIP

Publisher's Note
The publisher has gone to great lengths to ensure the quality of this
reprint but points out that some imperfections in the original may
be apparent.

Contents

Preface

Computer support for design has gone through many generations and philosophical perspectives. In the early days, it was thought that computer-based design support should take the form of a sophisticated calculator that could handle complex analytical problems and make fewer errors than people. Similarly, there was a strong push toward CAD and computer support for generating production drawings. As the CAD systems improved and included more and more functionality, the analysis programs became capable of solving more and more complex problems with better accuracy. However, the idea of computer-based design support still eluded us.

In the late 1970s and early 1980s, there was a new approach introduced for computer-based design support: the artificial intelligence (AI) approach. Both logic and rule-based systems looked promising because they could address the aspect of design reasoning that was hard to do with numbers. Several expert systems were developed across a broad range of applications, some of which touched on the area of design. Still, these expert systems for design seemed to fall short of their promises. They needed more rules to cover more situations, they didn't learn as people did, and they were good at inferring new facts from known facts but not at synthesizing new designs. There are many reasons why the expert system approach has had limited success in providing computer-based support for design, but the point is that the research community is still looking for that elusive "computer-based design support." Professional designers are only interested if the system gets it right and saves them money.

One of the recent developments in problem solving paradigms in AI is the idea of case-based reasoning. In case-based reasoning, some aspect of a new problem provides a reminder of a previous experience and that experience can be the basis for a new solution. This approach shows great potential for computer-based design support. It combines the best of AI and expert systems, using symbolic reasoning and experience, and does not appear to have some of the pitfalls, such as the use of deduction to generate solutions, the difficulty in updating to reflect new experience, and so on. However, the use of case-based reasoning in design is in its early days, and there is some confusion about what role this new paradigm can play and how such systems are implemented.

Let's look at what case-based reasoning in design means. Assume you are a structural engineer on a design project for a new hotel that has water views on both sides of its main axis. You may recall a similar project that your firm worked on a few years ago because it was also a hotel with a narrow floor plan. In order to reuse some of the ideas in the previous design you need to find the drawings or the reports filed after the building was completed. Or, you may contact the design engineer for the project, if he is still employed by the firm. Ultimately, in order to benefit from the previous experience of yours or of the firm that employs you, first, someone needs to remember a relevant previous project and, second, someone needs to be able to locate the information related to the relevant project.

This use of case-based reasoning, that is, to support designers when generating a new design solution, is concerned with the recall and the reuse of relevant design experience. In general, case-based reasoning can take on many faces to provide different answers to various problem solving needs. For example, case-based reasoning has been used to help generate explanations or to present experience in such a way that it teaches a lesson. In this book, the focus is on the use of case-based reasoning to support a designer in recalling a relevant design and in the reuse of that design to help generate a solution to a new design problem. In this sense the focus is oriented toward the design process view of case-based reasoning. This is a fairly strong bias and must be recognized as such. Case-based reasoning can be much more broadly defined and has been applied to demonstrate other perspectives on this problem solving paradigm.

This book has been written for academics and professionals who would like to use case-based reasoning to support designers and are looking for a specification of the process of case-based reasoning in design and alternatives for representation and implementation. The book should appeal to researchers who are considering:

- The unresolved issues of design research.
- Applications of case-based reasoning to complex problems.
- Representations of design knowledge and design experience.
- Process models of design.

From the professional perspective, this book should appeal to people involved in the development and/or use of computers during the design process. Such professionals will find the book provides a set of alternatives for the representation of design cases and examples of their implementation, a broad coverage of the issues in implementing a case-based reasoning system for design, and the advantages and disadvantages of different implementation decisions.

The book is organized into two major parts. The first part includes Chapters 1 through 5 and gives an introduction to the issues and alternatives in using case-based reasoning in design. Chapter 1 is an overview of case-based reasoning. This chapter introduces the authors' bias on the definition of case-based reasoning and introduces the terminology that will help the reader understand the rest of the book. Chapter 2 focuses on design, design processes, and the applications of case-based reasoning to support the recall and reuse of previous designs. Chapter 3 presents the considerations and alternatives for representing design cases.

Chapter 4 deals with recalling previous design cases, Chapter 5 with adapting design cases. These chapters provide a general discussion of case-based reasoning in design with examples along the way.

The second part of the book is about specific implementations of case-based reasoning in design. Rather than survey all such implementations to date, we have decided to present in detail two applications we have implemented. We present all the things we found hard to determine given the current literature on case-based design. We found many descriptions of how to represent design case memory, but found very little on how to translate this to a computer program. Hopefully, in these two chapters there are enough examples of implementations that the reader could confidently implement his or her own system. In a way, these two chapters are cases in themselves that could provide the basis for a new case-based design system. Chapter 6 presents CASECAD, focusing on the representation of design cases using a variety of representation paradigms and the strategies for recalling a similar case. Appendix A includes the actual Lisp code for CASECAD and Appendix B presents an entire design case as represented in CASECAD. Chapter 7 presents CADSYN, focusing on the contents of case memory to support design case adaptation and the implementation of a constraint satisfaction approach to adapting design cases.

In summary, the purpose of the book is to present the issues in taking a paradigm from AI, specifically case-based reasoning, showing how it is relevant in supporting designers in generating new designs, and presenting some of the implementation issues and their resolution. The book does not present an exhaustive account of how case-based reasoning can be used in design, that would take too long and be too hard. The book, therefore, focuses on something that can be done well, showing how case-based reasoning can help a designer recall a relevant previous design and reuse the design in a new design situation.

Acknowledgments. This book was written after several years of successful collaboration among the authors. The collaboration occurred at the Key Centre of Design Computing, University of Sydney. Firstly, we would like to thank the many people, including researchers, students, and staff at the Key Centre that provided useful comments and assistance in the development of the case-based reasoning projects. We acknowledge the support from the Australian Research Council and the Australian Postgraduate Research Awards Program. We thank Rita Villamayor for her assistance in collecting case data, and especially, the engineers at Acer Wargon Chapman for giving us their time and information. Special thanks to Alex Wargon for introducing us to his colleagues and persuading them to participate in this project. We thank our reviewers, including Ashok Goel and Gerhard Schmitt, for providing comments that improved the quality of the book. Finally, we thank Fay Sudweeks for producing the final copy of the book who, through her skill and patience, makes all our efforts look better.

About the Authors

Mary Lou Maher is Co-Director of the Key Centre of Design Computing and Associate Professor in the Department of Architectural and Design Science at the University of Sydney. She joined the University of Sydney in 1990 after 5 years on the Faculty of the Department of Civil Engineering at Carnegie Mellon University and working with the Engineering Design Research Centre. She teaches and does research in computer-aided design and knowledge-based systems. She is a Fellow of the Australian Institution of Engineers, and a member of the American Society of Civil Engineers' Expert Systems and Artificial Intelligence Committee, the American Association of Artificial Intelligence, and the IEEE Computer Society. She is the editor or co-author of six books on knowledge-based systems and over eighty papers.

M. Bala Balachandran is a Lecturer in computer science at the University of Wollongong in Australia. He received a B.S. in engineering from the University of Sri Lanka and a Graduate Diploma and a Ph.D. in design computing from the University of Sydney in 1984 and 1989, respectively. Previously, he spent five years as a research associate in the Key Centre of Design Computing at the University of Sydney. His research interests include hybrid expert system, case-based reasoning, fuzzy logic, and AI-based design. He has authored or co-authored two books and more than twenty papers on knowledge-based systems and computer-aided design. He is a member of the Institution of Engineers, Australia, the Australian Computer Society, and the IEEE Computer Society. He currently teaches primarily in the area of artificial intelligence and expert systems.

Dong Mei Zhang is a Knowledge Engineer in the CSIRO Division of Information Technology, Sydney Laboratory. She obtained B.S. and M.S. degrees in Computer Science from the Northeast University of Technology in China in 1985 and 1988, respectively. She worked as a software engineer in the China Academy of Building Research before commencing her Ph.D. at the University of Sydney. She completed a Ph.D. at the Key Centre of Design Computing in 1994 on a hybrid approach to case-based reasoning in design. Her interests include artificial intelligence in design, database development for design, and case-based design systems.

1 Overview of Case-Based Reasoning

Case-based reasoning promises to provide a way to support design by reminding designers of previous experiences that can help with new situations. As designers, we learn to design by experiencing design situations. For example, generating a design for a bridge requires not only an understanding of the analysis of bridges, but exposure to examples of several bridge designs. We learn to analyze through the use of formal methods, but creating a new design requires previous experience, or at least, exposure to another's design experiences. Case-based reasoning addresses this type of reminding and reuse of experience with computational models and guidelines for their implementation. In order to appreciate the role case-based reasoning can play in design, this chapter provides an overview of case-based reasoning as a computational model. In this chapter, case-based reasoning is presented simply, maybe even simplistically, in order to introduce the terminology used in the remainder of the book. For a more detailed presentation and discussion of case-based reasoning, the reader is referred to Kolodner (1993).

Case-based reasoning is an approach to problem solving that falls under the more general category of reasoning by analogy. Analogical reasoning is based on the idea that problems or experiences outside the one we are currently dealing with may provide some insight or assistance. Through analogy, we may be reminded of a window design when designing a door to a balcony with a view. Analogy is a way of recognizing something that has not been encountered before by associating it with something that has. We often use analogy to explain a concept or our reason for making decisions. Analogy can help us to search for an answer to a problem, or to explain how or why we make certain decisions, or to provide examples for teaching concepts. Even when we are not "problem solving", analogy plays an important role in understanding the world around us.

Because people are familiar with the use of analogy, it is an idea that can be studied, applied, and extended for the development of computer support for human problem solving. Analogy can be used in common situations, where the previous experience is directly applicable, or in unique or creative situations, where the previous situation shares something with the new situation, but the differences are just as interesting as the similarities. By studying the use of analogy, we can develop formal models of problem solving.

The development of formal models of analogical reasoning has been studied by researchers in AI. An early model of analogical reasoning for problem solving is reported in Carbonell (1981). The development of this model has led to new approaches to machine learning (Carbonell, 1983), and to the distinction between derivational analogy and transformational analogy (Carbonell, 1983, 1986). Derivational analogy learns from the problem solving *process* performed in the previous experience; transformational analogy learns from the *solution* for the previous experience. The research in analogical reasoning as a means of learning new concepts from past experience has focused on the learning process and the representation of the analogy operators (Prieditis, 1988; Russell, 1989; Keane, 1988).

The application of these ideas to engineering design domains has led to the concept of structure-mapping (Falkenhainer, Forbus, and Gentner, 1990), and to the application of analogy and mutation for creative design (Zhao, 1991), providing operational definitions of analogical reasoning. Now we can consider whether the analogy draws on previous experience in the same domain or previous experience from another domain, referred to as *within-domain* or *cross-domain* analogy. The representation of previous experience determines how useful it can be in a new situation. Many of these ideas have been studied as research projects to further our understanding of how analogy can be modeled and how to operationalize the various approaches to analogical reasoning.

Seeing analogy from the perspective of memory and reminding has developed somewhat independently of analogical reasoning and has led to the concept of memory organization (Schank, 1982) as a guideline for computer representations. Continuing with the study of memory and its use as a basis for new problem solving, generating explanations, and identifying the reasons for failure has led to models for representing experience in computers (Kolodner and Riesbeck, 1986). This work has been extended, applied, and developed into an entire area of AI-based problem solving called *case-based reasoning* (Riesbeck and Schank, 1989; Kolodner, 1993). Case-based reasoning has continued as a research area within AI but has also been applied and used in real-world situations.

Case-based reasoning is a formalization for the development of a computational model of problem solving that is based on memory organization and reminding. Case-based reasoning has been developed as a process model with specific stages and knowledge resources that reflects the research in analogical reasoning. The relevance to designers is to apply the research in memory organization for defining a case memory of previous designs and to apply the process of analogical reasoning for the reuse of previous design experiences.

This chapter presents a view of case-based reasoning as an operational model of problem solving that supports a designer in generating a new design concept. Two extreme views of case-based design are:

1. To provide a resource of previous experience to aid a designer, called a *design aiding system.*
2. To provide a computational approach to the design process, called a *design automation system.*

Because most applications of case-based reasoning tend to fall somewhere between the two extremes, the focus of the presentation in this book is *design support*. In order to understand how case-based reasoning can support design, we first overview case-based reasoning and its application more generally. Then from this common base, we can build the concepts and issues related to case-based design in subsequent chapters.

CASE-BASED REASONING AS A COMPUTATIONAL PROCESS

Case-based reasoning is an approach to problem solving that makes use of a database, or case base, of previously solved problems when solving a new problem, where a database is a collection of data stored in the computer, and a case base implies that the data represent previous problem solving episodes. This approach is used as a model to guide the development of computer programs that assist in problem solving by accessing the case base directly. The concerns of case-based reasoning then become recalling the relevant case or cases and reusing or adapting the relevant cases.

Case-based reasoning as a computational model of problem solving is contrasted with the expert systems approach. Both approaches rely on the explicit symbolic representation of knowledge based on experience to solve a new problem. Expert systems (Jackson, 1990; Buchanan and Shortliffe, 1984) use past experience stored in a knowledge base of generalized heuristics to assist in solving a new problem. The generalized heuristics can be stored as rules of thumb or as logical inferences. Case-based reasoning uses a representation of specific episodes of problem solving to learn to solve a new problem. Both case-based reasoning and expert systems use the experience of past problem solving when solving a new problem. Case-based reasoning systems store past experience as individual problem solving episodes, and expert systems store past experience as generalized rules and/or objects.

For example, the development of a computer program that assists in the design of a new pedestrian bridge over a busy street could be based on an expert systems approach or a case-based reasoning approach. An expert systems approach would encode heuristics about the types of bridges and their appropriateness for the span and width of the crossing, among other relevant information about bridges. A case-based reasoning approach would have a case base of previously designed bridges, among which one or more would be selected as the starting point for the new bridge design. Using the expert system approach, a new bridge design would be generated by applying the relevant rules to define the parameters of the new bridge. Using the case-based reasoning approach, a relevant previous bridge design would be recalled and adapted to the new design situation.

In many ways, a case-based reasoning approach mimics the way a person may solve a problem by recalling a previously solved similar problem. The person is reminded of the previously solved problem because it has some relevance to the new problem. In the bridge design example, the person may recall another pedestrian bridge, or maybe a bridge over the same span. After the person recalls a previously solved problem, certain aspects of the previous problem's solution are used in the new context and others are not. In the bridge design example, a pedestrian bridge with a span of 15 meters may be recalled, but the new design requires a span of 18 meters. The same design for the superstructure, such as the steel arch, may be used, but the span and sizes of the steel members will change.

The two major considerations in case-based reasoning are:

1. Identifying a relevant previous experience.
2. Determining what changes and what stays the same.

Identifying a relevant previous experience can be considered as searching the case base for a match with some predefined features or attributes of the new problem. For example, the pedestrian bridge design problem may use a search for other pedestrian bridges of a specified length. Determining what changes and what stays the same can be considered as adapting some of the attributes of the retrieved case to fit the new problem. For example, adapting a pedestrian bridge in case memory with a length of 15 meters for a new bridge with a length of 18 meters requires changing the length and other related attributes.

Modeling these two parts of case-based reasoning as a computational model is illustrated in Figure 1.1. The two major considerations are referred to as *recall* and *adapt*, where during recall the case base is searched for a relevant previous experience, and during adapt the decisions of which aspects to change and which to retain are made. Using this model for problem solving, the system can learn from its own experience, as well as the experience of the people who supply the cases. Each new solution can be added to the case base, making it available in a new problem solving session.

Looking more closely at the model of case-based reasoning illustrated in Figure 1.1, the two processes, recall and adapt, can be defined in more detail. The recall process can be decomposed into indexing, retrieval, and selection. Indexing is concerned with the identification of the attributes that a previous problem should have in order to be relevant to the new problem. Retrieval is a process of identifying which cases that have all or a subset of those attributes should be retrieved for further consideration. Finally, selection is a process of evaluating the retrieved cases so they may be ranked. The "best" case is then selected for adaptation.

The adapt process includes a recognition of the differences between the selected case and the new problem and decisions regarding what aspects of the case are changed to fit the new problem. This process can be decomposed into *modify* and *evaluate*. Modifying a selected case is a process of changing parts of the case description. Evaluating the modified case is a process of checking the new case description for feasibility. The elaborated case-based reasoning process is illustrated in Figure 1.2.

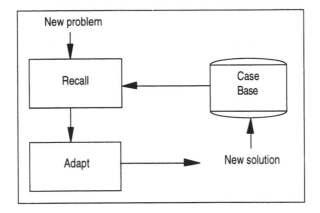

Figure 1.1. A simple model of case-based reasoning.

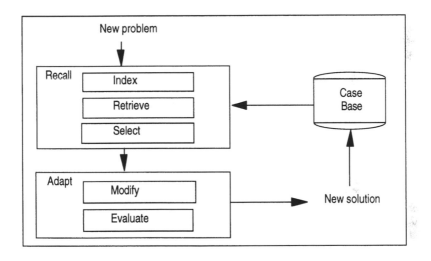

Figure 1.2. An elaborated model of case-based reasoning.

Implementing a case-based reasoning approach as a computer program follows the models already described, where each component of the model is an algorithm or database. The overall algorithm for case-based reasoning (CBR) can be summarized as:

```
begin
     get new problem specifications;
     identify indexing attributes;
          retrieve a set of cases that match attributes;
          select one case;
          repeat
               modify case;
               evaluate solution;
          until solution is satisfactory;
end
```

There are several approaches to implementing this algorithm. For example, to get new problem specifications, the program may simply ask the user to type in a set of specifications and use the specifications directly as the indexing attributes, or it may reason about the user's unstructured specification to identify key attributes for searching case memory. Another example of the different ways CBR can be implemented is to *select one case* that has the largest number of attributes with the same values as the new problem or the case that has the highest ranking in a weighted count of matching attributes. Alternatively, recall could be less structured, as the user navigates through a case base without providing the new problem specifications or selecting one case to consider further.

The use of a CBR approach requires the definition of a representation of the case base, or *case memory organization*. This representation defines how the reasoning can be implemented. The content and organization of cases determines their reuse in a new situation. A very simple example of this is in the bridge design problem: If the case base does not include the attribute for the length of the bridge, then the new problem cannot be matched against this attribute. However, for adaptation purposes, if case memory does not include knowledge about how a change in length affects the size of the bridge components, then the change in length to match the new problem cannot be evaluated.

CASE MEMORY

Case memory, or the case base, includes a representation of a set of previously solved problems. This representation provides the basis for their use by the CBR system and by the person using the CBR system. The importance of determining what is in case memory and how this is represented cannot be overemphasized. The computational process of CBR assumes an adequate and useful case base. The development of case memory is an ill-defined process that can be as difficult as the knowledge acquisition stage in developing an expert system. In fact, the case base is the equivalent of a knowledge base for CBR.

This section provides a brief overview of the issues and alternatives in developing case memory. These issues and others are considered in more detail in subsequent chapters, with special consideration to design. Developing a case memory includes a definition of:

- The content of each case.
- The representation of the contents of each case.
- The organization of the set of cases in case memory.

The content of each case is basically a description of the previously solved problem. The difficulty in translating this into a representation of case memory in the computer lies in the identification of relevant information to include in the description. The problem solving episode to be recorded in case memory may have well-defined problem specification and solution attributes or a well-defined process by which it was solved. Formalizing this aspect of CBR requires an analysis of the problems for which the CBR system will be used, as illustrated in Figure 1.3.

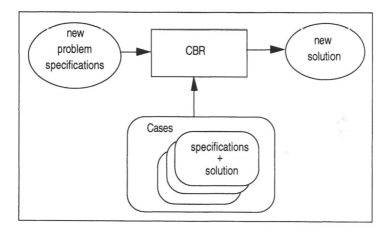

Figure 1.3. Analyzing the contents of case memory.

In order for there to be some commonality between the specifications to the new problem and the individual cases in case memory, a description of a case should include a representation of the initial specifications. In order for the cases to be useful in solving the new problem, a description of a case should include a representation of the solution. This is the most simplistic analysis needed for defining the content of case memory. In addition to the basic specifications + solution descriptions, case memory will also need to include knowledge for identifying a similar situation when the new problem specification is incomplete. This could take the form of indexing features and priorities. Case memory may also include a description of intermediate stages in the development of the solution, and possibly assumptions and justifications associated with decisions in the previous problem.

The representation of the contents of each case defines how the information about a case is organized, as a set of attribute-value pairs, as part-subpart relationships, or as a network of attributes. These three alternatives are illustrated in Figure 1.4. Representing a case as attribute-value pairs represents the relevant decisions in the previous case and the specific values associated with each decision. Representing a case as a hierarchy of part-subpart relationships facilitates representation and reasoning about large and/or complex cases. The hierarchical representation includes more content than the attribute-value pairs representation because it includes relationship knowledge. The network-based representation of cases can build on the hierarchical representation with multiple attribute-value pairs at each node and allow additional types of relationships to be represented, or it can be similar to a semantic network, where the nodes in the network represent a single feature of the case.

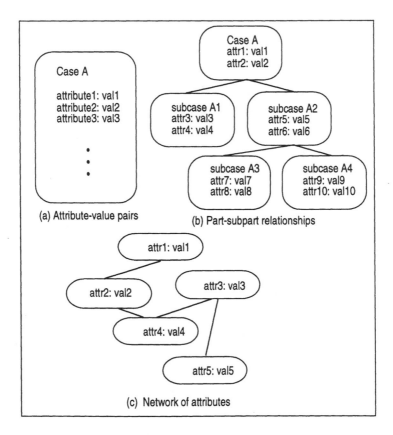

Figure 1.4. Organization of a case in case memory.

The representation of a case is usually generalized for all cases in case memory, so that all cases are described by the same set of attributes or part-subpart relationships, or all cases are described as networks of attributes. In this way, the organization of cases in case memory provides a template or model for defining the content of a case and for adding new cases to an existing case memory. This stage in the development of a CBR system results in a clearer definition of the contents of case memory and the representation schemes relevant to a CBR solution to a class of problems.

The organization of the set of cases in case memory provides mechanisms for locating one case or a part of a case in case memory. The cases may be clustered or accessed by common attributes. Organizing cases in a structured way allows the CBR system to quickly and accurately search for similar cases. As case memory becomes very large, the need for an organizational structure becomes more important. The simplest way to organize case memory is to store the name of each case in a list with a pointer to the content of the case. As case memory gets larger, the use of an indexing tree, where each node in the tree is an attribute-value pair of one or more cases, reduces the space that needs to be searched. These two approaches to organizing case memory are illustrated in Figure 1.5. In Figure 1.5 (b), cases B and C both have attr4: val4, attr1: val1, and attr2: val2.

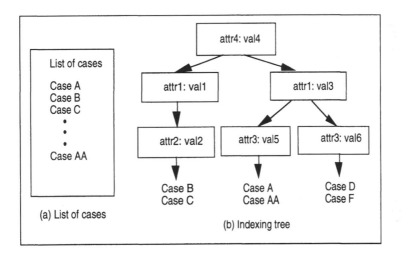

Figure 1.5. Organizing a set of cases in case memory.

The organization of case memory for access to an individual case is referred to as the *indexing scheme*. The development of an indexing scheme is dependent on the size of case memory and how a new problem is specified. If case memory is not large, with less than 50 cases, the indexing scheme that uses a list of cases is sufficient. Retrieving a case from a larger case memory would be too slow with the list of cases scheme. In Figure 1.5, the indexing scheme illustrated in part (a) assumes that all cases will be retrieved by name and that each case will be compared separately to the new problem specifications. The indexing scheme illustrated in part (b) assumes that the attributes in the nodes of the indexing tree will be part of the specification of the new problem. If these attributes are not part of the new problem specification, then the relevant set of cases cannot be identified.

RECALLING CASES

Recalling a case from case memory is a pattern-matching problem that is based on the specification of a new problem. For example, the specification for the design of a new building is recorded in a document called a *brief*. A subset of the brief may be useful in recalling one or more similar building designs. A new problem may be specified as a set of attribute-value pairs, as a set of constraints or conditions on the values of each attribute, or as a network of attributes. Given a specification, the recall process can be decomposed into three tasks:

1. Index.
2. Retrieve.
3. Select.

In order to index cases in case memory, the specification of a new problem is transformed into a pattern to be matched. The pattern may be taken directly as the user input specification or it may be modified, for example, to include an order of importance of the attributes. A general approach to determining a pattern to match for indexing case memory for a specific new problem is given below.

```
begin
    identify features of specification;
    organize features;
        begin
            identify critical features;
            assign weights to features;
            group features;
        end
    output pattern for matching;
end
```

The retrieval task in CBR searches case memory for matches between individual cases and the pattern that serves to index the cases. Each case in case memory may be compared to the pattern, or the pattern may provide a set of indices to partition case memory, so only a relevant subset of cases are compared with the pattern. Retrieval can be based on a perfect match, where the pattern is found exactly, or on partial matches. If partial matches are retrieved, a threshold may be set to determine when a partial match is close enough. A general approach to case retrieval is given below.

```
begin
    get pattern for matching;
    determine relevant cases for comparison;
```

```
repeat for all relevant cases
    determine how close the case matches the pattern;
    if case match above threshold
        then add case to retrieved list;
    output list of retrieved cases;
end
```

The selection task in CBR orders the retrieved cases to determine which case is the best match. The selection process depends on the pattern used to index case memory. If the pattern is a set of weighted features and each retrieved case is ranked according to the weight of the matching features, selection is based on the retrieved case with the highest ranking. If the pattern is simply a set of features, then selection is based on the case with the most features in common with the indexing pattern. Selection is the result of ranking the retrieved cases, where there are various methods for determining the ranking.

ADAPTING CASES

In some problems, a selected case provides a solution to the new problem. For example, when using a CBR approach to determine if a loan should be approved, the retrieved case provides a solution: approve or disapprove. In most problem solving, however, the selected case needs to be modified to be appropriate as a solution to the new problem. For example, a CBR approach to designing a bridge may recall a similar bridge, but the recalled bridge design cannot be used without modification for the new site. This modification is referred to as *adapting a case*.

Adapting a case from case memory to solve a new problem requires additional knowledge. The form this knowledge takes depends on how adaptation is done. One approach to adaptation is to identify those attributes of a case that can be changed and associate a formula with each adaptable attribute to be evaluated during adaptation. Another approach to adaptation is to associate a set of constraints with case memory that must be satisfied when adapting a case. These two approaches are broadly defined as *parametric adaptation* and *constraint satisfaction*.

Parametric adaptation adapts a previous case for a new problem solving episode by associating formulas with the attributes, or parameters, that can be changed. When defining the content of case memory, certain attributes are identified as adaptable attributes. Each of these attributes has a formula or procedure to be evaluated during case adaptation. The general approach to parametric adaptation is given below.

```
begin
    repeat for each adaptable attribute
        evaluate associated formula;
end
```

This approach to case adaptation assumes that the adaptable attributes are the same for each case retrieved and for each new problem encountered. The parametric adaptation considers each attribute in isolation from the others, so the change in value of the attribute is not dependent on other adaptable attributes. The consistency of the solution as a collection of attributes is not checked.

The constraint satisfaction approach to case adaptation requires a set of constraints to be associated with case memory. Once a case is selected as the basis for the new solution, the constraints provide the knowledge needed to check for inconsistencies between the selected case and the new problem. A domain of possible values for each attribute is needed when changing the values of attributes to satisfy constraints. The approach to constraint satisfaction is given below.

```
begin
    propose new solution;
    check constraints;
    repeat
        change values of attributes of proposed solution;
    until all constraints are satisfied;
end
```

Adapting cases is a potentially complex task that has not been fully explored. When possible, a simple approach to adaptation is used to automate the adaptation process. Otherwise, the user of the CBR system assists, or even performs, case adaptation.

APPLICATIONS OF CBR

CBR technology has been applied to a wide range of problems. CBR systems have been demonstrated in such varied domains as law, medicine, cooking, dispute resolution, customer service, labor mediation, process control, and engineering design, especially in the past several years, yielding significantly improved performance and cost savings. CBR provides the potential for developing knowledge-based systems more easily than generalized knowledge-based approaches. The assumption is that it is easier to produce specific examples of problem solving than to generalize across a class of problems to suit all new problems encountered.

Some case-based systems have been developed to solve problems automatically, whereas others have been built only to aid human problem solvers. CBR systems deployed in the field of industrial and commercial applications have delivered a number of benefits, including reduced cost, reduced errors, faster system development, reduced training time, decreased personnel required, improved decisions, and improved customer service. Although a wide range of potential applications have been explored, commercial CBR applications have focused, for the most part, on case retrieval for decision support.

CBR, in general, provides a set of specific advantages compared to other knowledge-based techniques.

- Case-based reasoning allows the reasoner to suggest solutions to problems quickly, avoiding the time necessary to create those answers from scratch.
- Case-based systems are easier to develop because the knowledge acquisition process is reduced to the task of collecting and recording cases from the domain expert. Adding knowledge is as easy as inserting new cases into case memory.
- Case-based reasoning provides a natural way for humans and computers to interact to solve problems. In many circumstances, case-based systems have been developed to help human problem solvers, rather than to automate problem solving.
- Case-based systems can easily be made to learn by continuing to collect cases and to insert them into the case memory. In other words, the CBR methodology provides a suitable framework for learning from experience.

In this section, we describe a number of major application areas of CBR: planning, diagnosis, help-desks, classification, configuration, and design. For each area of application, we describe sample case-based systems and their domains and reasoning tasks.

Case-Based Planning

Planning is the process of producing a sequence of actions for achieving a specified goal in a problem solving task. Case-based planning is the idea of planning as remembering. A case-based planner builds a new plan using an old plan as a starting point.

CHEF is a case-based planner whose primary domain is Szechwan cooking (Hammond, 1986). Its input is a set of subgoals that it needs to achieve, such as "achieve taste hot" or "use method stir fry," and its output is a new recipe plan. CHEF has to build one plan that satisfies a number of goals simultaneously. CHEF creates its plans by retrieving relevant old plans from case memory and by modifying the retrieved plan to fit new goals. One major advantage of using CBR for planning is that CBR can find old plans that satisfy multiple goals simultaneously, thus significantly reducing the time required to solve the problem. CHEF indexes its recipe plans by the conjunction of goals they achieve and by the problems they avoid. For example, the plan Broccoli and Tofu is indexed by several goals, such as "include tofu," "use method stir fry," and "achieve taste hot." CHEF employs a similarity metric for judging the similarity of goals required for determining partial matches. Another interesting feature of CHEF is that it anticipates problems beforehand by learning from problematic experiences.

The adaptation process of CHEF involves two steps. The first step is the reinstantiation of the old plan. It creates an instance of the retrieved plan after substituting new objects for the ones used in the old plan. In the second step, CHEF employs a set of special modification procedures called *object critics* to repair the old plan to satisfy the current goals. CHEF stores the result of planning in its plan memory for future use.

Other planning systems that use CBR include PLEXUS (Alterman, 1986) in the domain of subway riding and PRIAR (Kambhampati and Hendler, 1992) in the domain of automated manufacturing.

Case-Based Diagnosis

In diagnosis, a problem solver is given a set of symptoms and asked to explain them. Just as in planning, a case-based diagnostic problem solver often needs to adapt an old diagnosis to fit a new situation. A case-based diagnostician uses past cases to suggest appropriate explanations to new symptoms and to warn of explanations that have been found inappropriate in the past.

CASEY (Koton, 1988) is a case-based system developed to diagnose heart failures. CASEY integrates both CBR and model-based reasoning for diagnosis. The input to the system is a description of a patient's symptoms. The output is a causal network of possible internal states that could lead to those symptoms. CASEY is built on top of the Heart Failure Program, which is the source of the seed case base of diagnoses. When given the symptoms of a new patient, first, CASEY looks for cases of patients in the case library with similar, but not necessarily identical, symptoms. It uses model-based evidence rules to determine which of the partially matching cases that are retrieved are sufficiently similar to suggest an accurate diagnosis. If it finds a good match, CASEY then performs adaptation using model-guided repair strategies to diagnose the new patient. If it has no similar case, it passes the case to the Heart Failure Program, which diagnoses it and returns it to CASEY for future use.

Case-Based Help Desks

The ability to quickly and effectively assist customers with their problems is very important for a company's success. Customers often seek assistance from knowledgeable technicians, so-called *help desks*. Help desks give customers advice and solutions. Many help desk applications using CBR have been developed by a number of commercial companies over the past few years. The fact that front-line technicians use experience with previous problems to solve new problems makes CBR particularly appropriate for help desk systems. Case-based help desk applications. in general, look like smart database systems. The help desk user describes a problem to the system, and the system retrieves the closest matching similar cases, which suggest one or more solutions.

An example of a deployed CBR customer service application is Compaq Computer's SMART system (Acorn and Walden, 1992). SMART is an integrated call tracking and problem resolution system that contains hundreds of cases related to diagnostic problems arising in the use of Compaq products. Its input is the description of a customer's problem. SMART retrieves the most similar cases from its case base and presents them to the customer service analyst, who then uses the retrieved cases to solve the problem.

Another help desk system that uses CBR technology is CASCADE, developed by Digital Equipment Corporation (Simoudis, 1992). CASCADE uses CBR and validated retrieval to suggest solutions when a customer's VMS operating system crashes. The help desk user describes a problem to the system, and CASCADE finds and presents to the user those cases that are appropriate to the current problem. CASCADE allows the engineers to recognize and deal with problems without aid from other personnel and has demonstrated how CBR and a fairly large case base can be used for fault recovery.

Case-Based Classification

Classification is the process of identifying a given object or situation by type. A case-based classification system classifies an object or situation by finding the object or situation from case memory that is the closest match to the new object. The earliest case-based classification system was the PRISM telex classification system, developed by Cognitive Systems (Goodman, 1989). PRISM is used in several banks to route incoming international telex communications to appropriate recipients, a task relying on the accurate classification of telex to determine the appropriate routing. PRISM also demonstrated improvements in accuracy and speed over a previous rule-based implementation of the same type of system. It has about 1,000 preclassified telexes in its memory. When given a new text for classification, first, PRISM runs the text through a lexical pattern matcher to tokenize it. These tokens are then used for matching telexes in case memory. The retrieved telex is adapted using bank-specific information, so that it can be routed. PRISM is the first commercially deployed case-based system. Another application based on case-based classification is PROTOS (Bareiss, 1989) used in the domain of audiological disorders.

Case-Based Configuration

Configuration is a process of identifying and grouping parts. An example of a case-based configuration system is CLAVIER (Hennessy and Hinkle, 1992) for autoclave design, developed by Lockheed. Lockheed and other aerospace companies use composite materials to make parts for airplanes and satellites. These parts must be cured in an autoclave for long periods. The accuracy and consistency in configuring parts in the autoclave is very important, because the cost of the parts is very high. Human experts at Lockheed use pictures of layouts that worked in the past to help them work out new layouts. Therefore, this problem is very suitable for CBR. CLAVIER takes as input a list of parts needing curing and produces an appropriate layout for autoclave loading. Its case memory is made up of both successful and unsuccessful past layouts of parts in the autoclave. Cases are indexed by the parts they included. CLAVIER selects as the best case the one that includes the most parts of the new situation. CLAVIER performs adaptation by substituting some parts of the selected case with some other parts from other cases. It is also capable of learning from experience. This is one of the major advantages of the CBR approach. CLAVIER is currently in use at Lockheed's Sunnyvale Plant.

Case-Based Design

Design problems are specified as a set of requirements (i.e., goals and constraints) that must be met. Design is a process of generating a description of a method or a set of methods that satisfies all the requirements. Applying CBR to design involves recalling relevant past design cases from case memory and adapting those design cases to meet the requirements of a new problem. Although there are many similarities between design and planning, design differs from planning in that the design process involves topological, geometric, and physical properties and relations between them.

Several CBR systems have been built in the area of design. For example, CYCLOPS (Navinchandra, 1988) uses CBR for landscape design, and KRITIK (Goel and Chandrasekaran, 1989) and its successor, KRITIK2 (Stroulia, Shankar, Goel, and Penberthy, 1992), combine case-based with model-based reasoning for the design of small mechanical assemblies. CADET (Sycara and Navinchandra, 1989), a mechanical design system, uses an index elaboration or situation assessment technique as a means for finding and synthesizing whole cases or parts of cases. CADSYN (Maher and Zhang, 1993) integrates CBR with problem decomposition and constraint satisfaction to solve structural design problems.

Several case-based tools have also been developed to assist human designers. These systems assist designers by finding appropriate design cases for a given problem and by allowing designers to browse and view those relevant cases. For example, ARCHIE (Goel and Kolodner, 1991; Pearce, Goel, Kolodner, Zimring, Sentosa, and Billington, 1992) and its successor, ARCHIE-II (Domeshek and Kolodner, 1993), are tools for aiding designers during conceptual design in architecture. CASECAD (Maher and Balachandran, 1994) is a multimedia case-based assistant in the domain of structural design of buildings. ASKJEF (Barber et al., 1992) helps software engineers perform user interface design. PANDA (Roderman and Tsatlouis, 1993) is a case-based design assistant in the domain of fire engines. FABEL (Voβ et al., 1994) is a case-based assistant supporting building designers with CAD-like layout drawings by retrieving and interpreting semantic and geometric information.

Special characteristics of design that influence the use of CBR in design are:

- Most design problems in the real world are very large and complex.
- The representation of design cases requires various modes of representation, because their contents are made up of text, graphs, equations, and drawings.

- In design, often the mapping from a set of design requirements to a design solution in case memory cannot be predefined, and in some cases the initial specifications cannot be predefined.
- Designers use different types of knowledge in the design process. Therefore, the integration of different types of knowledge and reasoning methods becomes more important.
- In almost all design problems, finding a solution requires merging several parts of different old design solutions.
- The design process already makes use of computer programs, and a case-based reasoner should take into account other computer-based representations and processes.

A SIMPLE CBR PROGRAM

The previous sections of this chapter have discussed the component parts of a case-based reasoner, focusing on the issues associated with each. In the closing section of this chapter, we describe data structures and algorithms that can be used to develop a simple case-based reasoner as a whole. Building a case-based reasoner, even in its simplest form, involves a number of issues, such as case representation, case indexing and retrieval, ranking of cases, and adaptation. This section is meant to provide an example of how a case-based reasoner might be implemented, rather than to provide a definitive program.

Case Representation

Case representation is the process of determining the contents of cases and their organization. In its simplest form, a case is an entity described by a list of features (attribute-value pairs). A case can also be decomposed into a set of subcases, each of which can be described as a list of features. Cases in this example are each represented by a set of attribute-value pairs as follows:

```
<Case Label>
    <Attribute-1> :  <Value-1>
    <Attribute-2> :  <Value-2>
    <Attribute-3> :  <Value-3>
    .
    .
    .
    <Attribute-n> :  <Value-n>
```

A feature-based indexing is used in this example. A case can be retrieved in one of two ways: by the case label or by an attribute label. To retrieve a case by its case label, a list of case labels is stored as the value of a variable called *case-index*. To retrieve a case by attribute label, a list of attributes and associated case labels is stored as the value of a variable called *indexing-list*.

The procedure *add-case* adds a new case to case memory by creating an index to the case for each attribute. For each attribute(i)-value(i) pair in the new case, the indexing-list is searched to find the list of case labels associated with attribute(i). The new case label is then added if the attribute(i) exists in indexing-list; otherwise, the attribute(i) is added into indexing-list.

```
Add-case
begin
    add the case label into case-index;
    for each attribute(i)-value(i) pair in the case
        get the list of case labels associated with the attribute(i)
            in indexing-list;
    if the list of case label is empty
        then add attribute(i) into indexing-list;
            create a list containing the case label;
            associate this new list with attribute(i);
        else    add the case label into the list of case labels;
end
```

Case Retrieval

A case-based reasoner derives its power from its ability to retrieve relevant cases quickly and accurately from its memory. Case retrieval is the first process a case-based problem solver performs when given a new problem situation. Given the description of a new problem, identifying all perfectly or partially matching cases is the goal of the retrieval process. A new problem is described here as a list of attribute-value pairs representing the new problem situation.

```
<New Problem>
    <Attribute-1> :  <Value-1>
    <Attribute-2> :  <Value-2>
    <Attribute-3> :  <Value-3>
    .
    .
    .
    <Attribute-k> :  <Value-k>
```

Determining when a case should be considered for retrieval is the goal of indexing. Given a new problem in terms of attribute-value pairs, the case labels associated with the attributes in the new problem are recalled to compare to the new problem. For each attribute(j) in the new problem, if the values of attribute(j) in the case and the new problem match, the case is retrieved and stored in a variable called *retrieved-cases*.

The procedure *retrieve-case* retrieves cases that match a given list of attribute-value pairs in the new problem description.

```
Retrieve-case
begin
```

```
for each attribute(j)-value(j) pair in the new problem
    find the list of case labels associated with attribute(j)
        in indexing-list;
    if the list of case labels is not empty
        for each case(i) in the list of case labels
        get the value(i) of the attribute(j) in the case(i);
    if value(j) = value(i)
        then if case(i) is not in the retrieved-cases
            then add the case(i) into retrieved-cases;
end
```

Cases Ranking

A set of relevant cases is stored as the value of the variable "retrieved-cases" based on the new problem description. To select the most relevant case to use or adapt, the retrieved cases need to be ranked based on similarities of the cases and the new problem. The method for ranking cases used in this example is counting the numbers of matched attribute-value pairs in the retrieved cases and in the new problem.

The procedure *rank-cases* uses all cases that either partially or completely match a given list of attribute-value pair and ranks the cases according to the number of matches. For each case(i) in *retrieved-cases*, the attribute-value pairs are matched against the attribute-value pairs in the new problem. The matches for all retrieved cases are stored as the values of an array variable 'matches.' Cases are then ranked based on the numbers of matches. The case that has the largest number of matches is considered as the most relevant case.

```
Rank-cases
begin
    initialize matches(i) to 0 for all cases(i);
    for each case(i) in retrieved-cases
        for each attribute(j)-value(j) pair in the new problem
            find the value(i) of the attribute(j) in the case(i);
            if value(j) = value(i)
            then add one to the value of matches(i) of case(i);
    find the largest matches(k) in the matches;
    get case label in retrieved-cases corresponding to matches(k);
end
```

Case Adaptation

Adaptation is the process of fixing up the selected case to match the new problem. In its simplest form, case adaptation can be performed using substitution. In other words, each unmatched attribute in the selected case is given the value of the corresponding attribute in the new problem.

The procedure *adapt-case* performs case adaptation given a case and a list of desired attribute-value pairs. For each attribute(i)-value(i) pair in the new problem description, if attribute(i) is not found in the case, attribute(i)-value(i) is added to the case. If attribute(i) is found to have a non-desired value, then its value is replaced by value(i).

```
Adapt-case
begin
    for each attribute(i)-value(i) pair in the new problem
        if  attribute(i) is in the case description
            then get the value(j) of the attribute(i) in the case;
            if  not ( value(j) = value(i) )
                then replace value(j) by value(i);
        if  attribute(i) is not in the case description
            then  add attribute(i)-value(i) in to the case;
end
```

SUMMARY

Case-based reasoning is a computational model of problem solving that uses previous experience, as represented in a case memory, as a set of individual problem solving episodes. The process of CBR includes recalling a relevant case from case memory, and then adaptating this case for the solution of a new problem. The variations in CBR lie in the way case memory is organized, the procedures for recalling relevant cases, and the methods and knowledge available for adapting a case. CBR can be implemented as a simple search and retrieval process or as a complex exploration of previous experience and its reuse in new situations.

GLOSSARY OF TERMS

Analogy: a way of recognizing something that has not been encountered before by associating it with something that has.

Analogical reasoning: a computational process of learning new concepts from past experience.

Case: representation of a previous problem solving situation.

Case adaptation: a method for changing a case for a new situation.

Case-based reasoning: a problem solving paradigm that uses previous problem solving situations as the basis for solving a new problem.

Case base: a collection of previous problem solving episodes stored in a database.

Case evaluation: the process of checking a new case description for feasibility.

Case indexing: the identification of the attributes that a previous problem should have in order to be relevant to the new problem.

Case modification: the process of changing parts of a case description.

Case retrieval: the process of identifying which cases that have all or a subset of those attributes should be retrieved for further consideration.

Case recall: searching a case base for a relevant previous experience.

Case selection: the process of evaluating the retrieved cases so they may be ranked.

SUGGESTED READING

Kolodner, J. L. (1993). *Case-Based Reasoning.* San Mateo, CA: Morgan Kaufmann.

> This book addresses CBR as both a cognitive process and a methodology for building intelligent systems. The related issues to building a case-based reasoner are presented, in general, in terms of the reasoning methods and issues for implementing methods. The book provides conceptual guidelines for addressing the representation and indexing of cases, the retrieval of cases from the case library, and adaptation strategies and methods. Issues in building case-based systems are discussed, and several case-based reasoners that have been developed are introduced in terms of the reasoning tasks case-based reasoners support and the cognitive model they imply.

Riesbeck, C. K., and Schank, R. C. (1989). *Inside Case-Based Reasoning.* Hillsdale, NJ: Lawrence Erlbaum Associates.

> This book introduces the issues in dynamic memory and CBR, followed by extended descriptions of four major programming efforts conducted at Yale on CBR and understanding. These four projects are JUDGE, CHEF, COACH, and DAMP. Related issues to building each CBR project are discussed, including storing cases, retrieving and indexing cases, adapting closest cases, and learning. Each project is described with the micro-program version that is extracted directly from system implementation and executed in a standard Common Lisp.

Kolodner, J., and Mark, W. (Eds) (1992). Using history: Case-based reasoning [Special Issue]. *IEEE EXPERT: Intelligent Systems and Their Applications.* October.

> Two kinds of CBR are introduced in this issue: problem solvers that adapt old solutions to new problems, and interpretive reasoners that use cases to evaluate or justify new situations. This issue features three articles on CBR. The first article describes CASCADE, an interactive system that helps technical support engineers solve the problems of customers. CASCADE has a case library of failures of VMS device drivers, and it suggests solutions to new failures. Validated retrieval is presented as an important feature of CASCADE. The second article describes a case-based

aid system, ARCHIE, which is intended to help architects understand and solve conceptual design problems. The designer describes a problem to ARCHIE, which retrieves and presents cases to the designer. Each case teaches one or more lessons relevant to the issues at hand. The third article describes CLAVIER, which Lockheed is using to determine the placement of parts to be put into an autoclave. CLAVIER provides interactive support, using cases to propose load configurations and multiload plans. One of its key advantages is that it learns, becoming more competent as it acquires new cases.

2 Case-Based Design as a Process Model

Case-based reasoning as a process model of design is intuitively appealing because much of design knowledge comes through the experience of multiple, individual design situations. A major task in the development of computer support for design is the identification of the design knowledge to be included in the support tool. Although designers may have difficulty generalizing their heuristics or styles, they usually have no trouble telling stories about previous design situations. If this kind of reasoning can be captured in a computable model of design, the resulting design system may be capable of learning from design experience and maintaining a reasonable competency in design without major reprogramming. Developing such a model also improves our understanding of design and challenges some of the theoretical developments in CBR.

In order to effectively apply CBR to design, it helps to do a task analysis of design problem solving. Design process models begin to identify some of the computational models of design and the implications of implementing one of them. Such models can provide guidelines in the development and use of computer support tools. Three models considered in this chapter include a decomposition approach to design, a CBR approach, and a transformational approach. Focusing on the case-based design process model shows how the computational model introduced in Chapter 1 can be directly applied or where the difficulties lie in application.

Design, as ill-structured problem solving that has formal knowledge as well, presents challenges to the application of CBR. Using CBR requires the formalization of design experiences as a design case memory and the formalization of the reasoning processes of recall and adaptation. There are aspects of a design domain that have no formal representations, where the basics of CBR cannot be applied as a formalism. There are also aspects of a design domain that may already be formalized and these formalisms need to be integrated with the CBR model in order to have an effective design support tool. The idea of a hybrid case-based design system is defined and introduced in this chapter and is presented in more detail in later chapters.

Considering the implementations of CBR in design problem solving shows the variety of applications of the same computational model. CBR has been applied to the design of mechanical devices, the design of a meal, architectural and structural designs of buildings, and the design of computer programs. There are similarities in the use of CBR in these domains, and there are significant are significant differences. A brief review of a selection of implementations of CBR to design is included in this chapter. The purpose of this review is to introduce a variety of approaches to the application of CBR to design; the rest of the book focuses on a subset of these approaches.

DESIGN PROCESS MODELS

Design is characterized as an ill-structured problem in several aspects. First, the problem definition is incomplete. As design proceeds, the definition of design problems changes. The formulation of design problems is, therefore, dynamically refined. Design also appears to be ill-structured, in the sense that there is no straightforward process to be followed. The imprecision of pertinent design knowledge can be viewed as another aspect of the ill-structured nature of design. Design theories and principles are often insufficient to guide the design process. During designing, therefore, the formulation of the design problem is dynamically modified as design progresses; multiple types of design knowledge, such as design theories, heuristics, and past design experience, are combined to compensate for the insufficient domain knowledge.

The design process, although ill-structured, can be formalized at a high level of abstraction (Simon, 1973). The selection of a formalization depends on the intended role of the resulting model, as there are many ways to characterize, dissect, and order design processes (Dym, 1994). For the purpose of establishing the relevance of CBR to the broadly defined process of design, the design process is considered as comprising three phases: formulation, synthesis, and evaluation:

- *Design formulation* involves identifying the requirements and specifications of the design problem, understanding the problem, and producing an explicit statement of the design goals. This is sometimes referred to as the design brief or program, or more simply as the definition of the design problem.
- *Design synthesis* includes the identification of one or more design solutions consistent with the requirements defined during formulation and any additional requirements identified during synthesis.
- *Design evaluation* involves interpreting a partially or completely specified design description for conformance with expected performances; that is, this phase judges the validity of solutions relative to the goals and selects among alternatives. This phase of the design process often includes engineering analysis.

Although the phases may not be addressed in the order prescribed for the entire design process and are often carried out recursively and iteratively, there is an inherent order in which designers approach a design problem. Typically, a designer starts with a definition of the design problem, identifies one or more potential design descriptions, and then evaluates the design. Variation can occur in the revisions of the requirements and/or descriptions, and the iterations on the various phases. Therefore, certain feedback between the evaluation and the formulation phase complete the process model. Figure 2.1 illustrates the process, consisting of a progressive series of these three major phases.

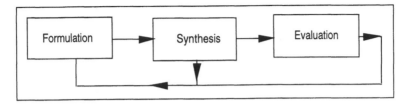

Figure 2.1. Three-phase design process model.

The identification of different phases in the design process is a beginning for the formalization and understanding of design. What is missing from such a description is how each phase is completed. A structured approach to design is helpful in identifying various design activities, but not in executing them. When a particular methodology does provide a procedure for executing a design activity, it imposes constraints on the representation and control of the design process. Rather than prescriptions for the execution of design activities, it may be more helpful to identify descriptive models that allow reasoning and creativity within a formalized representation of design knowledge and experience.

The focus for process models of design here is on the synthesis phase. Synthesis processes produce a design solution in the form of a structural description. During design synthesis, the form of the design solution is identified. Design synthesis develops a form, such that an object constructed according to this form would satisfy the requirements.

Design Synthesis

Design synthesis begins with a set of intended functions and design constraints that are generated from the formulation phase according to the client's needs or more general requirements, and then produces a set of alternative design structural solutions. Such tasks include the definitions of forms and the identification of design components for an object. In general, design synthesis constructs a design description by identifying the form of a design object and producing feasible structural design components of the object.

In the synthesis of design solutions, alternative structural configurations are generated and evaluated. Design synthesis is arguably the most difficult and least understood phase in the design process. The synthesis phase itself is a further form of formulation-synthesis-evaluation. From the perspective of the three-phase model, it is unnecessary for the design problem to be formulated completely before synthesis can begin. Complete formulation is then impossible in any but the simplest design task. Thus, in the course of design synthesis, the detailed formulation is involved when new problems occur during the generation of a design description, and when further design synthesis and evaluation of the design description will be performed. Therefore, design synthesis tasks must be concerned with a recursion from more general to more detailed.

Design synthesis is central to the design process because it plays a role of generating a design description. There is a question of how design synthesis is performed. In practice, this phase of the design process is not well supported by computer-based tools unless the design problem can be formulated in mathematical terms. For example, optimization techniques are used during synthesis when the design problem can be formulated as an objective function and its constraints. Although there appears to be no standard approach to synthesis suitable for all design problems, the recent use of knowledge-based systems for the synthesis of design descriptions has shown promise and forms the basis for the models described in this book.

Experienced designers resort to trial and error less frequently than novice designers when they synthesize designs, suggesting that the use of knowledge-based systems to represent "experience" may aid in synthesizing designs. The major issue, then, is the explicit representation of design experience in a knowledge base.

During design synthesis, a designer considers a design space that contains the knowledge that is used to develop the design solution. A human designer does not need to explicitly identify his design space, it is implicitly developed and expanded as he gains experience. A design program, however, does contain an explicit representation of the relevant design space. The nature of the knowledge in the design space must be explicit when we consider a knowledge-based approach to design synthesis.

Modeling Design Process

As a process, design can be a sequence of goal-directed actions that cumulatively generate a design description, or a number of alternative design descriptions, from a set of design specifications. In formulating a framework that facilitates design activity, a design process model is formed. In other words, design process models formalize problem solving activity in the generation of design descriptions. In the context of design, process models are useful vehicles for developing computer support.

Simon (1969) presented a general approach to modeling design even more specifically as a search process. The implication of search as a model for design processes is that design knowledge can be expressed as goals and operators. As a general approach to modeling design, search provides a formalism for expressing design knowledge; however, it does not directly address some of the intricacies and idiosyncrasies of design problems. Considering design as problem solving is a beginning to understanding and modeling design, but design problem solving has some additional characteristics that can be exploited by more explicit models.

Variations in both the goals and the state space descriptions as the design process proceeds, and the difficulty in predetermining the relevant operators, are some of the issues that are not readily addressed in using search for solving design problems. The goals of the problem may change during the problem solving process, which may indicate a different design space needs to be searched. One reason design has been difficult to implement as a search process is this change in definition of the problem during the problem solving process. One way of dealing with this difficulty is to identify models of the design synthesis process, assuming that formulation has occurred. Another way is to allow synthesis to proceed, even with a change of goals. The implication here is that using search as a model for the design process is too general; more specific models that employ search in various ways are needed to bridge the gap between a model of design and the eventual representation of design knowledge and experience.

Design process models describe the progression from design requirements to design solutions. Here, the major concern is with design processes, such as synthesis, in which the requirements do not include the variables that will be used to describe the solution, in other words, part of the design process is to determine the design variables, as well as the values of the variables.

Associated with a design process model is design knowledge, which supports the generation of design descriptions, and knowledge to perform certain design activity by manipulating a sequence of actions. A process model of design differs from a representation of design knowledge. A process model describes how the design proceeds. A representation of design knowledge describes the format of the knowledge used during the design process. It is possible, in some cases, to describe design knowledge representation without making an explicit reference to the process that uses the knowledge. It is also possible to refer to a process model without being explicit about the knowledge representation that drives the process. However, the two are closely coupled. The choice of a process model dictates, to some extent, the type of knowledge needed, just as the choice of a representation determines how it can be used.

Using a knowledge-based paradigm to model design processes makes design knowledge explicit. The design knowledge pertaining to a design domain is separated from the reasoning mechanism of the design model. The nature of design knowledge directly influences the reasoning methods used. Knowledge-based design process models are, therefore, distinguished by the representation of design knowledge. Furthermore, the formalism for representing design knowledge classifies design models. Three process models are presented here, where the design variables are identified and where reasoning mechanisms for finding feasible values for the variables are available. The process models presented assume that specific types of design knowledge are available. Each process model and its associated knowledge representation schemes are considered in terms of the AI techniques used and their implementations as knowledge-based design systems.

The three distinct models of design processes are:

1. Decomposition.
2. Case-based reasoning.
3. Transformation.

These models are distinct because they allow the design process to progress in very different ways and because they require different types of design knowledge.

Decomposition

Decomposition is an implementation of hierarchical refinement, in which the generation of a solution is a knowledge-based representation of general design methodology. The philosophy of this model is to break large, complex problems into small, less complex, manageable ones. Figure 2.2 shows a tree-like decomposition structure formed by decomposing a complex problem into subproblems and further primitive components. The design knowledge applied is encoded such that a general design goal can be decomposed into a set of loosely coupled subgoals or elements. A design solution is produced based on the recomposition of the solutions of design components whose solutions are compositions of more basic components.

In a design process model, design progresses by considering different levels of abstraction of the design problem. As each design subproblem is considered, decisions are made regarding the selection of a component or value for a variable or deciding whether the problem is to be decomposed into smaller problems. In developing a design model by decomposition in a particular domain, the substantial task is identifying the decomposable form of information. Many forms of information can be decomposed based on the concept of abstract refinement. Regardless of which domains and categories of design information are involved in refinement, the essential characteristic of the representation of such information is decomposable into constituent components. Maher (1990) proposed two approaches to the decomposition of a design problem in to subproblems:

1. To decompose a domain of design knowledge into structural systems.
2. To decompose a problem into the various functions that must be provided by a design solution.

Once a decomposition approach is used, recomposition becomes an issue. Recomposition can occur implicitly, in which case the solutions to the sub-problems are considered to be the solution to the entire problem. Recomposition usually introduces complications through the interaction of the subproblem solutions and the complex dependencies between constraints among subproblems. Therefore, putting the subproblems together must take into account the interactions. The typical way of representing such interactions is as constraints; then the issue of recomposition becomes one of constraint satisfaction.

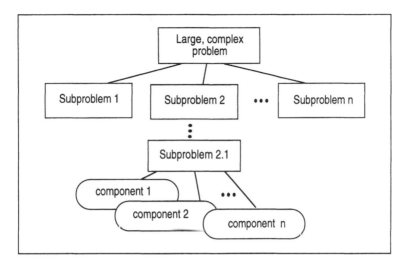

Figure 2.2. Decomposition model.

When we consider a knowledge-based approach to representing design knowledge, the decomposition model specifies the type of design knowledge needed. Knowledge-based systems for design by decomposition have been developed that identify specific languages for describing design knowledge. Examples of such languages include DSPL (Brown and Chandrasekaran, 1985), EDESYN (Maher, 1987), and VEXED (Steinberg, 1987). The issues associated with this model include the appropriateness of decomposing and of assuming that solutions to loosely coupled subproblems will combine to form a good design solution. The use of a decomposition model requires identifying decomposable systems and constraints for composing subsystems.

Case-Based Reasoning

Case-based reasoning is a form of analogical reasoning. The basic idea is to use specific design knowledge in terms of previous design episodes to generate a new design. The specific knowledge applied is usually represented as a repository of design cases. Rather than solving the problem from basic components based on general rational knowledge, a case-based design model recalls and adapts specific solutions to previous design problems to attain feasibility as a solution for a new design problem.

CBR provides a process model for applying prior experience to new problems. The CBR model is illustrated in Figure 2.3. There are several issues that must be addressed: organizing case memory and indexing cases, retrieving and selecting the most relevant case to the new problem, adapting past solutions to fit the new problem, and updating the case memory whenever a new case is generated.

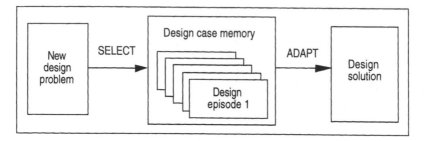

Figure 2.3. Case-based reasoning model.

In a design process model, design progresses by finding relevant previous design solutions to serve as a basis for the new design problem and then adapting the representation of a previous design problem to satisfy the requirements of the new design problem. CBR is becoming more attractive as a basis for knowledge-based design process models because it provides many advantages as a problem solver. First, CBR presents a shortcut for the generation of a new design solution, avoiding the time necessary to create a solution from scratch. In other words, CBR provides a way to reason holistically about previous solutions and, consequently, to preserve and exploit the internal consistency of previous solutions. By applying CBR to design, a previous design case suggests an entire solution to a new problem, and pieces that do not fit the new situation are adapted. Second, CBR alleviates the knowledge acquisition bottleneck because it directly employs previous design experience, rather than relying on generalizations of design experience. Developing generalized representations of design knowledge in a particular domain can be difficult and time-consuming.

There is a large and growing interest in the use of the CBR approach for building knowledge-based systems that aid in the process of design. Related work, including Sycara and Navinchandra (1989), Wang and Howard (1989), Maher and Zhang (1991), Goel and Chandrasekaran (1989), Hinrichs and Kolodner (1991), and Hua, Schmitt, and Faltings (1992), is aimed at employing design experience to solve certain classes of design problems using CBR. In using a CBR approach to design, some generalized knowledge is needed to model design process. For example, generalized knowledge is needed to adapt a previous solution to be a solution to a new problem. Sycara and Navinchandra used qualitative reasoning to adapt previous cases to be suitable as new solutions. Wang and Howard used a rule base, in addition to the case base. Maher and Zhang used decomposition knowledge to assist in the adaptation.

The issues associated with using this model for design include the identification of what is stored in a design episode in order to reason about its applicability in a different context, the meaning of a similar design, and the adaptation of the solution from the original context to the new context.

Transformation

Transformation is an approach to design where the design knowledge is expressed as a set of transformational rules in which the left-hand side (LHS) of the rule is replaced by the right-hand side (RHS) of the rule. Figure 2.4 shows a transformation model. The issues associated with using this model are the representation of the design description, the control in selecting an eligible transformational rule, and the termination of the application of rules.

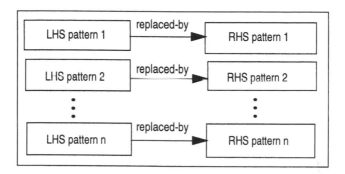

Figure 2.4. Transformation model.

The transformation model follows a theoretical approach to design in which the initial set of design requirements is transformed into a design description. Because grammars provide a formalism for the transformation model, the most common application of the transformation model of design is manifested as grammars. A general rule-based system shares many characteristics of a transformation model, the distinction being a subtle one.

The considerations in using a grammar to represent design synthesis knowledge include (a) the definition of the terminal and nonterminal symbols, and (b) the identification of productions. The definition of the terminal and nonterminal symbols is based on a formal representation of the design requirements and solution. The identification of production rules provides the domain knowledge, where the production rules represent design transformations associated with a specific design domain. The collection of production rules represents a specific design approach, for example, the design of rigid-frame structural systems can be captured in a set of production rules or in the formalization of a design style, such as prairie houses.

The application of shape grammars to architectural design has illustrated the ability of shape grammars to formally represent generative design knowledge and capture design style. The most notable applications include grammars that characterize the design of Frank Lloyd Wright prairie houses (Koning and Eizenberg, 1981), Palladian villa plans (Mitchell and Stiny, 1978), and Queen Anne-style houses (Flemming, 1987).

Summary

The three models we have described provide a classification of knowledge-based approaches to design and provide guidance in the development of representations of design knowledge and design processes. The decomposition model is characterized by its use of a generalized knowledge base of classes of design entities and the incremental generation of a design solution by refinement. The CBR model is characterized by its use of specific design situations and its holistic approach to generating a design by starting with a previous solution. The transformation model is characterized by its use of a generalized knowledge base of rules and its incremental generation of a design solution by transforming patterns. The characterization of the three models is shown in Table 2.1.

Model	Knowledge Representation	Design Generation
Decomposition	generalized classes	incremental
Case-based reasoning	specific designs	holistic
Transformation	generalized rules	incremental transformation

Table 2.1. Characterizing three design process models.

CASE-BASED DESIGN PROCESS MODEL

CBR provides a process model for applying past experience directly to new problems. CBR has been presented as a cognitive model for problem solving. This has led to guidelines for the development of memory organization, indexing, retrieval algorithms, and selection methods. These guidelines provide a general understanding of CBR, however, and do not reflect how CBR is implemented to perform practical design problem solving. In addition, CBR in design applications is a new research area. The design process itself poses some fundamental problems for CBR (e.g., the identification of what is in a design episode in order to reason about its applicability in a different design context and the adaptation of previous design situations from an original context to a new context).

In general, a case-based design system involves the representation of design episodes in a manageable structure and the generation of a new design using previous designs as a basis. A case-based design system thus poses representation-related issues (e.g., representation of a design case, indexing of design cases, etc.) and process-related issues, such as design case retrieval, design case adaptation, learning, and so on.

A case-based design system is characterized here by three fundamental issues:

- Design case representation.
- Relevant case recall.
- Design case adaptation.

Design Case Representation

A case-based design system must be able to represent past design experiences in a manageable structure. When specific design knowledge is stored as previous design episodes or cases, the content and knowledge structure of design cases, as well as the organizational structure of case memory, must be considered because subsequent retrieval of relevant design cases and their adaptation will rely heavily on the selected model of case representation. A certain amount of domain-specific rational knowledge is required to support the performance of design subgoals. This leads to the issue of the inclusion of rational knowledge for a design case either inside or outside the case.

In general, the issues related to design case representation include the following questions:

- What information is stored in design cases?
- What representation schemes are used to represent design cases?
- How is generalized design knowledge represented in case memory?
- How is design case memory organized?

The contents of design cases must be represented and indexed in appropriate forms so as to be retrieved efficiently. Design knowledge associated with a design case needs to be represented at several levels, ranging from a topological description of the components to linguistic specifications. As a typical representation scheme, a hierarchical structure represents episodic information at different levels of abstraction ranging from more general (e.g., system), to more specific, levels (e.g., component). Such a knowledge representation structure not only allows a case-based design reasoner to use small chunks of cases, but also allows abstractions across parts common to several kinds of cases. Representing design cases also should take into account storing a design case in its entirety or breaking a case into pieces.

There is also the issue of storing the design solution or the operators used to produce the design description. The advantage to storing the design solution is that many existing cases can be used immediately, augmenting the geometric description with the relevant functions, and so on. The disadvantage is that adapting the old solution to fit the new problem is difficult. The alternative, storing the operators, allows the adaptation to the new problem to be an execution of the old solution operators using a new problem statement.

Whether to include the rational knowledge and the governing constraints of a design case within the case or to represent this knowledge outside the case is still an open research question. If rational knowledge is kept within a design case representation, it should be able to anticipate any possible new design contexts to which the case can be adapted. However, the rational knowledge in design cases might be redundant in some design domains, such as structural design and mechanical design, where a certain amount of deep knowledge used for supporting decision making and evaluating the performance are applied to different design contexts. If rational knowledge relies on generalized design knowledge separated from specific design cases, it is hard for domain experts to conceive of all the new contexts and variations for a particular case. In addition, such a case-based design system must consider the relationships between case knowledge and other types of knowledge.

Design Case Recall

A case-based design system must be able to recall the most relevant design cases. *Design case recall* in a case-based design model consists of the retrieval of relevant cases and selection of the most relevant case. The retrieval and selection among cases entails the recognition of the relevance of each case to a new problem and of how close a case is to providing a solution to the new design problem.

The retrieval of design cases requires recognition of the potential relevance of each case to a current design situation. To do this, design cases must be organized into some manageable structure with appropriate indexing. Design cases are typically indexed by features, the presence or absence of which plays a primary role in determining the applicability of a design case to a current situation. Those features used to index design cases are designated as *labels*. The fundamental choice in using feature-based indices is how complex and abstract the labels will be. Labels can be concrete. For example, labels might use a number of surface features in design cases and the current design situation, such that the retrieval process is based on the matching of features. Alternately, labels can be abstract. For example, design cases are indexed according to certain deep semantic features pertaining to functionality. Retrieval under such an indexing approach is based on functional relevance. Based on the indexing of design cases, the retrieval process searches case memory to find the relevant design cases. The search method is dependent on the structure of the memory organization.

Case selection involves assessing not only how close the past cases are to the new problem, but also the relative importance of the relevant similarities and differences. The retrieval process searches through the cases according to the new problem definition and identifies the similarities between cases and the new problem. The selection process then compares the similar design cases to choose the most relevant ones. There are various techniques that are explored to model this selection process: For example, a weighted count of matching features can be applied. The result of case selection is a previous design that will serve as the basis for the new design solution.

Design Case Adaptation

A case-based design system must be able to recommend or perform actions required to adapt one or more design cases to fit the current design situation. Adaptation of design cases plays a problem solving role in the case-based design process model. Design case adaptation includes identifying the differences between the retrieved cases and the new problem and consistently modifying the previous designs. The benefit of using a case-based model for design is the efficiency, in terms of effort expended computationally, in producing a design description. Because previous designs cannot be reused without changes, reasoning about these changes needs domain knowledge. Hence, additional reasoning processes need to be defined, and certain domain knowledge is essential for design generation by case adaptation.

Because the reasoning methods are different from domain to domain, adapting design cases becomes complicated. Central to design case adaptation, however, is the way old cases are transferred to fit a new problem. Several transfer inferenceshave been developed that provide a background understanding of case adaptation. These inferences include structural adaptation (Carbonell, 1983) and derivational adaptation (Carbonell, 1986). These inferences, to a certain extent, appear to correspond to what are known as "weak" methods: abstract, domain-independent problem solving methods.

In design problem solving, a previous design is either proprietary or customized for a specific context. Previous designs cannot be reused without substantial changes. It is possible that the ideas or concepts in previous designs can be used again, but their application is different. Design case adaptation often forms the essence of design synthesis in a case-based design model, using a holistic approach to design by starting with a solution and adapting it to fit a new context. The issues raised by adaptation are:

- The representation of domain knowledge about the adaptation.
- The maintenance of consistent modification when some aspects are transformed.
- The verification of a feasible solution.

As a design process model, adaptation assumes that case selection provides a description of a specific design solution that is close to the acceptable final solution, and changes those aspects of the design solution that are inconsistent. First, a potential solution to a new problem is proposed as the solution using the selected case. This potential solution is adapted to change the differences in specifications to match the new context, which introduces some inconsistencies between the design specifications and the design description. This potential solution is then *verified*, the process of evaluating the new solution, and *modified*, the process of fixing an inconsistent design. The process of fixing an

invalid potential solution is based on using other reasoning methods. The
knowledge needed to fix an inconsistent solution is based on domain-specific
knowledge.

In applying CBR to design, the nature of the design process imposes needs
of generalized knowledge and underlying reasoning methods to augment or
support the CBR paradigm. Using underlying reasoning methods and/or domain-
specific knowledge in conjunction with a CBR paradigm, the idea of a hybrid
case-based design system emerges. The variety of representation forms for
generalized knowledge and underlying reasoning methods leads to different
implementations of CBR to design. To clarify the broad range of
implementations of case-based design, examples of applications of CBR to
design problems are presented in the form of hybrid systems.

HYBRID CASE-BASED DESIGN SYSTEMS

A hybrid case-based design system is a system that uses more than one
knowledge source (i.e. generalized knowledge in addition to case-specific
knowledge and/or more than one problem solving method). The generic structure
of a hybrid case-based design system is shown in Figure 2.5.

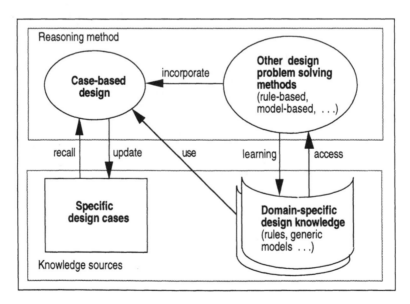

Figure 2.5. The hybrid structure for case-based design model.

The generalized domain knowledge can be represented in the form of rules,
models, logical causal relationships, design constraints, and so on, or encapsu-

lated within individual design cases. In a hybrid case-based design system, multiple reasoning methods, such as rule-based reasoning, qualitative reasoning and constraint satisfaction, are incorporated within a CBR paradigm to perform design problem solving.

A hybrid model for design, in which CBR is combined with generalized design knowledge, provides a flexible and comprehensive model of design. The process model integrates two representations of design experience: specific design situations and generalized design domain knowledge. Along with generalized domain knowledge, a case-based design process model consists of components of knowledge and main process, as illustrated in Figure 2.6.

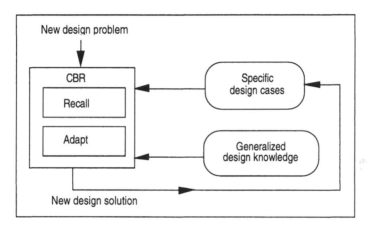

Figure 2.6. A hybrid process model for CBR in design.

The problem solving process is comprised of design case recall and design case adaptation. The underlying reasoning methodsare used to achieve the subgoals involved in design case adaptation, which is supported by the domain-specific knowledge. The representation of generalized design knowledge and underlying reasoning methods are often determined by the design tasks to be performed.

A hybrid case-based design system raises the issue of integrating different types of knowledge and reasoning methods within the framework of CBR. The types of available design knowledge and reasoning methods vary from context to context, thus leading to different ways to encode knowledge and apply this knowledge with CBR. In general, the issues raised in a hybrid case-based design process model include:

1. The distribution of design knowledge in case-based and generalized formalisms.
2. The incorporation of underlying reasoning methods to support the design process involved in design case adaptation.

3. The consistency of specific knowledge in design cases and domain knowledge in generalized formalisms.

How we address these issues for a hybrid case-based design model depends largely on the representation formalism of domain-specific knowledge and the underlying reasoning methods used, as well as the design task to be performed. The following section surveys recently developed case-based design models as hybrid case-based design systems.

APPLICATIONS OF CBR TO DESIGN

The issues relevant to the use of CBR to design are addressed in the remainder of the book through specific examples and applications. Many of the concepts presented here are advanced topics in CBR. They are presented briefly here, and, when appropriate, a more detailed treatment is given in later chapters.

Applications of CBR to design are presented in two categories, according to the representation of design cases. In general, cases can be representations of the actual design project or can be assumed to be an abstract design or plan generalized over several episodes. Using specific design situations corresponding to individual design projects as design cases is referred to as *episode-oriented case-based design*. Using generic design models as design cases is referred to as *model-oriented case-based design*. Several systems for each category are reviewed in the remainder of this section. All systems are presented as hybrid case-based design systems because they use several design methods in addition to the basic CBR methods.

Episode-Oriented Case-Based Design

The first category of hybrid case-based design is related to the separate representation of specific project-based knowledge and generalized design knowledge, in which the design case is treated as a single design situation without abstractions or generalized design knowledge. A design case includes a particular design problem and its solution and/or the reasoning steps taken to arrive at that solution. In addition to the engineering or formal design information associated with a design solution, an episode-oriented case memory may record information associated with the design context, including such items as the individuals involved in making the decisions, the idiosyncratic justifications of some decisions, the location in which the design solution was used, and so on.

In episode-oriented case-based design, solutions to new problems are derived using old solutions as a guide. Old solutions can provide almost correct solutions to new problems. The purpose of CBR is to find a relevant design project on which to base design decisions in the new design context. By assuming the old solution is almost correct for the new context, major revisions of the decisions are not made. During CBR, the old solution is slightly modified or refined for the new context. The modification and/or refinement of the solution assumes some representation of refinement or generative design knowledge.

Three episode-oriented case-based designs are described here: JULIA , DDIS, and CADRE. JULIA is an application in the domain of menu design. DDIS is an application in the domain of structural engineering design. The third application, CADRE, is in the domain of architectural design.

JULIA (Hinrichs, 1988; Hinrichs, 1991; Hinrichs and Kolodner, 1991) is a case-based design system developed by integrating CBR and constraint propagation. A common-sense task, meal planning, is chosen as an informal design application area. A specific design case in JULIA describes a particular menu in terms of objects of courses, dishes, and ingredients. Generalized design knowledge is represented as constraints.

As illustrated in Figure 2.7, a new meal menu is implemented by the incorporation of a case-based reasoner and a constraint propagator. The case-based reasoner retrieves similar cases and suggests values from those cases by constructing Truth Maintenance System (TMS) nodes that package the values, along with the reasons for and against them. The constraint propagator checks the suggested values and rules out those that violate constraints. A new menu is proposed based on the adaptation of previous meal cases, in which a constraint satisfaction cycle formulates constraints, evaluates the new menu, and refines the menu by propagating constraints.

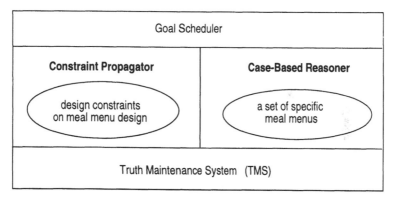

Figure 2.7. The problem solving architecture of JULIA.

The generation of a new menu uses a refinement paradigm that initially produces a consistent partial solution at a general level, then gradually reaches a complete detailed solution based on the maintenance of a consistent solution. In this approach to CBR, the case provides a general structure from a previous meal, the details of which are determined by considering the new meal context and the meal constraints through a constraint satisfaction process. The

Constraint Propagator and the Truth Maintenance System are the general methods that augment the case-based reasoner.

In Wang and Howard's (1991) integrated system (DDIS) for structural engineering design, case-based and rule-based reasoning are combined. A case stores information about a particular previous design, including the problem specification, final solution, design plans, and design history. Generalized design knowledge includes knowledge about performing a particular design task based on design codes, generalized procedural knowledge, and rule-based reasoning.

In this system, previous specific designs and generalized design knowledge work in a complementary fashion during a new design generation, as shown in Figure 2.8.

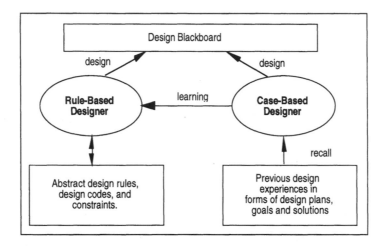

Figure 2.8. DDIS: Combining rule-based reasoning with CBR.

All the knowledge sources are treated the same, and compete for execution based on how well they match the needs/goals of the current design problems on the blackboard. A past design can be applied to a similar new design problem by replaying its design plans in the new design context. A conventional rule-based module applies design codes and analysis procedures to create the solutions of subgoals in the new design when case-based design actions are not available. Additionally, the model provides for the extraction of generalized knowledge from specific design cases through a learning process.

The two major reasoning components of DDIS are the rule-based designer and the case-based designer. The rule-based designer uses generalized knowledge taken from published design codes, constraints based on an understanding of the behavior of structural systems, constraints taken from design heuristics, and abstract, informal design rules. The case-based designer retrieves a similar design problem and executes its design plan to generate a design solution suitable for the new design context.

In CADRE, a case-based architectural design system (Hua et al., 1992), the representation of a case involves specific design knowledge about an architectural design episode, including building geometry, structural parameters, constraints, and environmental features. In addition, a previous design case includes generalized domain-dependent knowledge, such as transformation rules for possible topological discrepancies and grammars for syntax-directed translations. Therefore, both specific design cases and generalized design knowledge are recorded in design cases.

The retrieval of a design case is simplified by having few cases in case memory. The focus of this application is on adapting a previous design case for a new design context. Design case adaptation is achieved by combining a constraint satisfaction process and a rule-based reasoning process. Considering the context of the new architectural design in this project, constraint satisfaction deals with dimensional discrepancy by treating a specific design as a starting point; the rule-based reasoning is concerned with topological discrepancy in which relevant production rules and shape grammars are applied to guide the topological transformation.

Figure 2.9 illustrates design case adaptation where the combined reasoning approach is applied. After retrieval, a constraint satisfaction method is applied to solve the geometric conflict between the case and the new context. The rule-based reasoning method resolves the symbolic representation of the design topology. This process of constraint satisfaction followed by rule-based reasoning is applied iteratively, until the conflict is resolved.

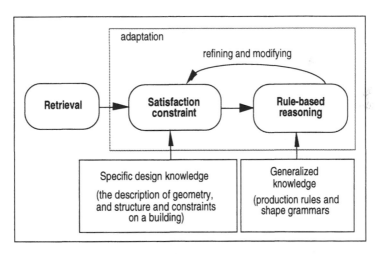

Figure 2.9. Dimensional and topological adaptation in CADRE.

Model-Oriented Case-Based Design

Another type of hybrid case-based design system extends the model-based reasoning with a CBR paradigm. In this approach, a case is viewed as a generic model description (i.e., a device model). As such, this category of hybrid case-based design systems is called *model-oriented*. This approach is described in the applications of KRITIK, CADET, and a prototype-based case-based design model.

KRITIK (Goel and Chandrasekaran, 1989) is a model-oriented case-based design method for the design of small mechanical assemblies. A causal representation of structure, function, and behavior about a device resides in a design model using a functional representation schema, whereas individual mechanical devices are represented as instances of relevant design models. Design knowledge used in the system is recorded in device models (or cases). A device model consists of its structure knowledge, functions that the structure can deliver, and a representation schema about function-behavior-structure. All device models are organized and indexed by their functions.

The generation of a new mechanism is largely based on the instantiations of generalized design models by a qualitative simulation. Given the function description of a new mechanism, relevant device models are retrieved first based on functional matching. The causal representation of the function, structure, and behavior of retrieved devices are then adapted to fit a new device mechanism design by qualitative simulation, during which primitive generic components of devices are identified to assist in refining the adapted design.

The design process of KRITIK is illustrated in Figure 2.10. The qualitative reasoning is applied to combine the functions of the retrieved device with the new device functions.

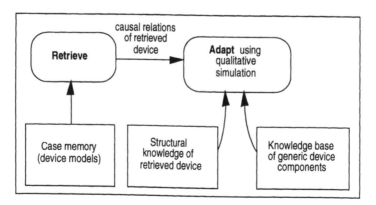

Figure 2.10. The design process in KRITIK.

Sycara and Navinchandra (1989) present a methodology for design synthesis (CADET) by combining model-based reasoning with CBR. A design case is represented as a graph-based behavior model about a particular device. The description of a case captures the relationship between physical form and qualitative function. In this approach, CBR is viewed as analogical reasoning for selecting and applying various design models, rather than reusing specific design episodes. The qualitative function captures the context in which the model can be reused.

A case-base reasoner searches design model memory to retrieve a relevant device description for the functional requirements in the new design context and transforms the structure of an existing device design to achieve a new functionality based on the underlying causal graphs and qualitative relationships in the previous design.

Design generation of a new device is illustrated in Figure 2.11. Past design cases (device models) with the same functions as the current design are retrieved. The new problem is then analysed, and the surface features of the new design are developed through a linguistic description. A case-based synthesis process produces a correct design by qualitative reasoning based on the relevant parts pulled from multiple design cases, during which the design produced is verified through qualitative simulation. Therefore, the design process in CADET is performed on the basis of integrating qualitative reasoning and case(model)-based reasoning.

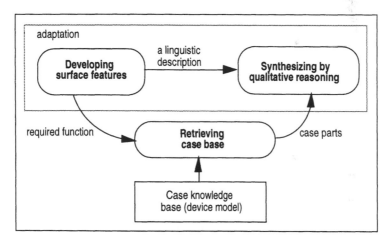

Figure 2.11. Case(model)-based reasoning and qualitative reasoning.

Rosenman, Gero, and Oxman (1991) proposed another approach to integrating model-based and CBR. A design case contains the problem description, the process used, and the set of instances that constitute the solution. These instances contain links to design prototypes that were used to derive the solution. In such an approach, general knowledge resides in the design prototype, and the design case is seen as providing detailed specific knowledge regarding a situation or an exception to the general "rule."

The relationships between design cases and design prototypes (Gero, 1990) is indicated in Figure 2.12. Previous design cases point to associated instances through which generalized design knowledge in the design prototypes assist in the generation of new design description.

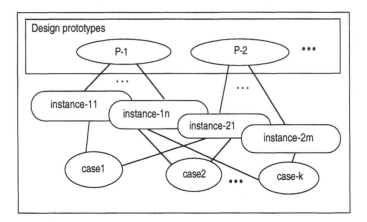

Figure 2.12. Design cases associated with design prototypes.

The design process, as illustrated in Figure 2.13, starts with the selection of a relevant design case based on the similarity of the descriptions of new and previous designs. The respective design prototypes and knowledge associated with the derivation of values of the retrieved case are accessed and re-run to provide a new instantiation through value modification. This integration of the design prototype and the design case formalisms uses the selection and retrieval concepts from CBR to assist in finding a relevant prototype. The generation of a new design solution uses the generalized knowledge in the prototype.

Discussion

The common characteristic of the case-based design applications we have described is the combination of reasoning methods within a framework of CBR. Along with the combination of reasoning methods is the use of various representations of design experience and generalized knowledge. Specific design cases and generalized design knowledge in the variety of formalisms either are embodied in a single representation schema (e.g., CADRE and Rosenman et al.) or are represented separately (e.g., JULIA and DDIS). Different reasoning methods are combined with CBR in a complementary (e.g., DDIS), or synergistic, fashion (e.g., JULIA, CADRE, and KRITIK). Table 2.2 summarizes the knowledge sources and reasoning methods in the case-based design systems we have described.

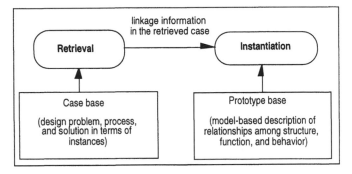

Figure 2.13. Combining both specific design cases and prototypes.

SYSTEM	DESIGN DOMAIN	DESIGN CASE	GENERALIZED KNOWLEDGE	OTHER REASONING METHODS
JULIA	meal design	individual meal description as attribute-value pairs	design constraints	constraint satisfaction and problem reduction
DDIS	structural design	design problem solution, plans, and history	design codes and procedural knowledge	rule-based reasoning
CADRE	architectural design	building geometry, structural parameters, and constraints	production rules on topological knowledge	constraint satisfaction and rule-based reasoning
KRITIK	mechanical design	causal representation of function-behavior-structure		qualitative reasoning
CADET	mechanical design	relation between physical form and qualitative function		qualitative reasoning
Roseman et al.	architectural design	design problem, solution, and history of process	relationships among structure, function, and behavior	instantiation

Table 2.2. Classification of case-based design systems.

SUMMARY

Design is a complex intellectual activity that has many formal representations. Here, the view of design is limited to one formal view: formulation, synthesis, and evaluation. Design synthesis, the focus for this chapter, is the stage of design during which alternative design solutions are generated. Three computational models of design synthesis are decomposition, CBR, and transformation; each is characterized by the representations of design knowledge used and by the problem solving approach to design generation. Applications of CBR in design is presented as a hybrid approach when more than one knowledge source and/or more than one problem solving method is used. The issues in applying CBR in design include: the representation of a design case, the use of generalized design knowledge, and the associated reasoning methods. Two categories of case-based design models are introduced as episode-oriented case-based design and model-oriented case-based design.

GLOSSARY OF TERMS

Case-based reasoning: solving a problem through the reuse of a previous problem solving episode.

Decomposition: the process of dividing a complex problem into simpler subproblems.

Design case adaptation: modifying a previous design solution for a new design problem.

Design case recall: identifying a previous design that is relevant to a new design problem.

Design process model: an abstraction of the design process that identifies the major subtasks.

Design synthesis: the generation of alternative design solutions.

Hybrid CBR models: the use of multiple knowledge representation paradigms and/or reasoning paradigms in a CBR framework.

Episode-oriented case-based design: using design cases representing individual design situations or design episodes corresponding to design features.

Model-oriented case-based design: using design cases as representations of generic models in particular design domains.

Transformation: modification of a problem description by putting it into another form.

SUGGESTED READING

Maher, M. L. (1990). Process models for design synthesis. *AI Magazine* **11**(4): 49–58.

> Three models of the process of design synthesis are presented in this paper: decomposition, CBR, and transformation. Each model provides a formalism for representing design knowledge and experience in distinct and complementary forms, which provides guidance in the development of knowledge-based systems for design. The purpose of identifying more than one design model is to find appropriate formalisms for representing design knowledge

Simon, H. A. (1969). *The Sciences of the Artificial.* Cambridge, MA: MIT Press.

> This book explains how a science of the artificial is possible and illustrates its nature. The science of the artificial is addressed from multiple fields in the book: economics, psychology, cognition, and planning and engineering design. Curriculum in design is drawn up in the science of the artificial. Some of the modern tools of design are surveyed from both theoretical and computational views, which provide guidelines for creating the artificial in design. Artificiality is also discussed when it concerns complex systems. It is argued in the book that hierarchy is one of the central structural schemes that the architect of complexity uses.

Pu, P. (Ed.) (1993). Case-based reasoning in design [Special issue]. *Artificial Intelligence for Engineering Design, Analysis and Manufacturing* **7**(2).

> This issue reviews some of the important issues concerning applying CBR techniques to the design domain. The contents, representation, and indexing of cases are addressed in the design context. The approaches for constructing design solutions based on the adaptation of design cases are presented. Through discussions of these issues, the current status of the case-based design field is described with surveys of existing case-based design systems.

3 Representing Design Cases

The representation of design cases is the essence of a case-based design system. The details of design case memory determine what the case memory can be used for, how cases can be retrieved, and whether there is enough information for case adaptation. When considering the representation of case memory, three major issues are raised:

1. The content of design cases.
2. The representation paradigms for case memory organization.
3. The presentation of design cases to the user.

Dealing with each of these issues assures that design case memory will serve the purpose for which it was intended. These issues also lead to other considerations. For example, when determining the content of case memory, issues related to the acquisition of design cases become relevant. Will the design cases be acquired automatically through the use of computer tools for design? This implies that the content is already defined by the tools currently being used by designers. Will the design cases be acquired through interviews with designers, or will designers enter their own design cases into case memory? These alternatives imply that the content of design cases is not yet determined and needs to be considered through a task analysis of the purpose of the case-based reasoning system.

When identifying the representation paradigms for case memory organization, the issues of flexibility and efficiency become relevant. An efficient representation leads to better performance when design case memory becomes very large. This implies that design cases can be retrieved in a short amount of time for the system to be interactive. Flexibility in storage and retrieval means that a given design case can be retrieved by different features, or that there are many pointers to every design case.

The presentation of design cases to the user is of ultimate importance if the case-based design system is to be an interactive tool. User interface technology now supports multimedia and multimodal interaction. When considering the representation of design cases, the use of multimedia provides design information that cannot be conveyed in traditional text-based interfaces.

In this chapter, these three issues are addressed. Standard approaches for defining the content, organization, and presentation of design cases are considered, as are options for more comprehensive systems.

CONTENT OF A DESIGN CASE

When considering the content of a design case, a fundamental question arises: What is a design case? A design case, as a simple definition, describes a previous design situation. The description then needs to be defined. A design case may be an abstract concept that was helpful in solving a previous design problem, such as a bundled tube as a structural design concept for a high-rise building. A design case could also be a sketch that conveys the use of space for the layout of a building. Although this question cannot be answered comprehensively to satisfy the developer of a case-based reasoning system for design, several guidelines can be identified that can further specify the implications of answering the question: What is a design case?

The contents of case memory determine what can be done with the case-based design system. The symbols/features in a design case provide the basis for indexing, retrieving, and adapting a previous design for a new design context. A typical approach to storing information in case memory is to use words as features. This raises the issues of which words to use, whether the words are strung together to form stories, whether the words are used as indices, or whether the words are the basis for attribute-value pairs. Furthermore, can the words be categorized to convey further meaning, such as function, intention, or performance? Describing a design using words is limiting in some design domains. An alternative is to describe a design using the drawings associated with the previous design. Then the drawings can be searched and reused. Because algorithms for searching through drawings for information are not well-developed, the drawings are typically indexed by file name or, alternatively, by words as features describing the drawings.

This section considers alternative approaches to defining the content of design cases. Two major considerations in defining the content of case memory are:

1. Is the content of the case already in a computer file?
2. Is the selected design case description currently made explicit at all?

Using drawings as the basis for case memory can be done directly when the drawings are already archived on the computer. The sole use of drawings as design cases has limitations for reasoning about retrieval and adaptation. Considering the nature of design problem solving leads to other approaches to the content of case memory, for example, storing the design requirements in addition to the design solution or categorizing the contents according to function-behavior-structure descriptions.

Design Cases as Design Drawings

Drawings are a unique and most effective form of communication in design. They also serve as a powerful medium to handle the complexity of design information. Drawings used during conceptual design express an alternative design solution through sketches of form, interaction, and intended behavior. More detailed drawings are used to communicate how the design can be constructed or manufactured. The graphical representation of design allows the designer to understand and evaluate the design easily and quickly, regardless of the complexity involved. The use of drawings is pervasive at all stages of the design process, even though the drawings themselves serve different purposes. Examples of drawings that communicate design solutions are shown in Figure 3.1. As a form of communication, drawings can convey geometric information to people more readily than words.

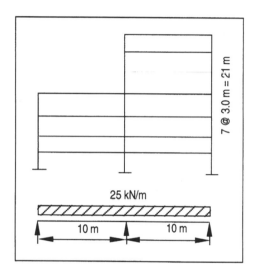

Figure 3.1. Drawings illustrating the conceptual design of a structural frame.

Storing drawings as cases in a case-based reasoning system requires that the drawings be stored on the computer or, more specifically, in a case base. Archiving design projects as CAD drawings that are generated on the computer is becoming standard practice. Using existing computer-based drawings for case-based reasoning could mean that less effort is needed to create and update case memory. The consideration in using drawings that already exist on the computer is the nature of storage, retrieval, and reuse of the drawings.

Computer-generated drawings in design projects are typically done using a CAD system. Figure 3.2 shows an example of a CAD drawing for a building. The information that the drawing communicates is available to those professionals who understand the symbols. In order to use this as the basis for indexing or retrieving design cases, these symbols need to be isolated and made explicit. Because CAD drawings are used to communicate the result of the design activity, therefore, indexing a previous case as a CAD drawing needs to include some aspect of the problem specification or should be based on expected results of the new design. Currently, CAD drawings are indexed by the name of the project they document and ultimately by the filenames used to store the CAD files on the computer. Alternatively, CAD drawings could be indexed through a content-based retrieval schema. Content-based retrieval would allow the drawings to be more useful in a case-based reasoning system. However, there are issues raised about whether the computer programs that implement content-based retrieval are actually part of case-based reasoning, or whether they exist as a separate database retrieval system.

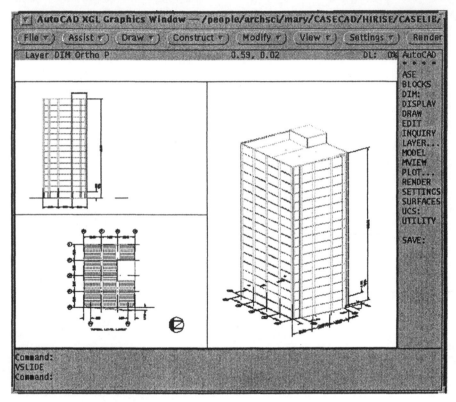

Figure 3.2. Example of a CAD drawing.

Drawings are already part of the experience of designers. The incorporation of this aspect of the designers' experience has advantages and disadvantages. The advantages of using drawings as the basis for the content of design case memory are:

- CAD drawings are already archived on the computer.
- Drawings convey geometric information to the users of the CBR system more readily than words.

- Drawings can be modified during design adaptation to produce new drawings.

However, there are problems with the sole use of drawings as the content of design case memory, including:

- Drawings are not automatically indexed, except by file name.
- CAD systems have no representation of the drawing created by the user other than its graphical manifestation on the screen and a syntactic model in a data structure.
- Computer programs for 'reasoning' about drawings are still being researched.
- Design drawings communicate the result of design activity and not necessarily the context of the design problem.

The value of drawings as the content of design cases depends on how well the drawings convey design information. In the domain of architectural design, it may be essential to include drawings when reasoning about the form and function of a building. In the domain of mechanical device design, drawings may not be needed until the design is defined and is being tested. When drawings are essential to convey design information to users, they should be part of case memory, augmented with indexing information about the context of the design.

Design Cases as Requirements and Solutions

In defining the content of a design case, consideration should be given to the way in which a case will be indexed for future retrieval and use. When solving a new design problem, the information available for recalling a previous case includes the requirements the new design should satisfy. If a design case contains only the design solution, there may not be anything in common with the new design requirements and the previous design solutions. In order to provide information about the design case that can match a new set of design requirements, the design case should include the requirements *and* solution of the previous design problem.

The design requirements vary from one design domain to another. In some domains, the requirements are stated in sentences describing the overall design context. In other domains, the requirements may be formulated as a set of features that the design solution must have, for example, its size, shape, and material. In most domains, the design requirements include a set of constraints that must be satisfied. These constraints may be made explicit in the formal requirements, or they may be implied through standard practice or preferred style. In determining design requirements for a design project, the following considerations are useful:

- Predetermined features (e.g., material).
- The design environment (e.g., loads).
- Explicit and implicit constraints (e.g., area < 30 m^2).

The design solution can be expressed as a set of design variables and their values. The use of variables to describe the design is a common approach in computer-based design. Variables are used to express the features of a design, where the values of the variables describe the result of design decisions. This model is used in computational approaches to design support, such as optimization, simulation, analysis, and knowledge-based design.

By combining the design requirements and the design solution within a case-based representation of design projects, the user is given more information for case retrieval and adaptation. The consideration of the content of the requirements and the solution is dependent on the design domain. Figure 3.3 shows the requirements and the solution of a beam design expressed as attribute-value pairs.

```
BEAM DESIGN

Requirements
  span: 10 m
  support: continuous over three equal spans of 10 m
  length: 30m
  material: reinforced-concrete
  dead-load: 12 kN/m
  live-load: 7 kN/m
  concrete-grade:  25
  steel-grade: 400
Solution
  depth: 625 mm
  width: 300 mm
  reinforcement details:
    negative                1712² mm   use 2No.30+2No.20
    positive, outer span  1416² mm   use 2No.30+2No.15
    positive, inner span    731² mm   use 4No.20
```

Figure 3.3. The requirements and the solution of a beam design.

The advantages of using requirements and solution as the basis for the content of design case memory are:

- Identifying the requirements and a solution of a design provides a guide for identifying the content of a case.
- Including the design requirements assures some commonality between the description of a new design problem and previous design cases.
- The design requirements can serve as indices to case memory.

The potential problems in using requirements and solutions as a guide for defining the content of a design case include:

- The requirements of one design problem may, in fact, be part of the solution of another design problem, so standardization of design case representation is difficult.

- The requirements of a design case are not comprehensively articulated, so determining the requirements as an explicit statement or set of features may not be possible.

Design Cases as Function-Behavior-Structure (FBS)

Design is typically an ill-structured problem in which the design requirements for one design problem may be part of the design solution of another problem. For example, when designing a beam, the designer may know the span of the beam before he designs it, or in another situation, the span may be a decision the designer makes as part of the design solution. The distinction between design requirements and design solutions may be inappropriate for some design domains. Another approach to characterizing the information in a design case is to classify the information as function, behavior, or structure.

The *function* of a design means different things to different designers. We use the word *function* to refer to the purpose of the design. The purpose of the design makes explicit what the design is to be used for: For example, the purpose of a beam is to carry a load over a distance; the purpose of a cup is to hold liquid. The function of an object is related to the perception of the object's use, rather than being inherently related to its structure.

The *behavior* of a design is a description of the response of the design to its use. Behavior describes how the design works: For example, the beam carries a load through bending stress; the cup holds liquid by providing an enclosed volume. Behavior provides a means of testing the performance of a design to determine whether it achieves the intended function.

The *structure* of a design is a description of the physical characteristics of the object. Structure defines geometry, material, color, and so on. Because the explicit definition of a design is an abstraction of the actual object, the structure attributes used to describe a specific design are typically related to its behavior, so the performance of the design can be tested, and to its construction or manufacture, so the design can be realized. Structure attributes that are not relevant to the design may not be specified in design case memory.

Including these three characteristics of a design case satisfies the need to include information that can provide indices for a new design problem, because a new design can be described in terms of its required function, behavior, and possibly some structural features. Figure 3.4 depicts a partial description of the FBS attributes of the structural system of a building.

The advantages of using function-behavior-structure as the basis for the content of design case memory are:

- Identifying the function, behavior, and structure of a design provides a guide for identifying the content of a case.
- Recalling design cases based on required function, behavior, or structure allows for flexibility.

- The attributes of a design case are classified according to the role they play in the design process.
- Any of the function, behavior, or structure attributes can serve as indices to case memory.

```
DESIGN CASE : structural system for a building
    FUNCTION ATTRIBUTES
        support-building-type
        support-grid-geometry
    BEHAVIOR ATTRIBUTES
        building-slenderness
        cost-of-construction
        lateral-displacement
    STRUCTURE ATTRIBUTES
        building-plan-shape
        number-of-stories
        material
        floor-system-type
        height-to-width-ratio
        floor-to-floor-height
```

Figure 3.4. FBS attributes of the structural system of a building.

The potential problems in using function-behavior-structure as a guide for defining the content of a design case include:

- There may be repetition in the function, behavior, and structure attributes and their values across many design cases.
- The function, behavior, and structure attributes of a design case are difficult to articulate.
- The representation of function, behavior and structure of a design can require a complex representation paradigm.

Summary

Determining the content of design case memory is an essential aspect of case-based reasoning in design that defines the potential use of the system. The considerations when defining the content of design cases include:

- What information is available in previous design projects?
- Is there enough information to retrieve a previous design for a new problem?
- Is the information best represented by words, numbers, drawings, or equations?

In this subsection, three approaches for determining the content of case memory are considered: design drawings; design requirements and solution; and design function, behavior, and structure. These three approaches provide guidelines for collecting information about design cases. The approaches need not be used in isolation from one other. A combination of all three is helpful in developing a design case base. A schematized layout of the potential contents of a design case is shown in Figure 3.5.

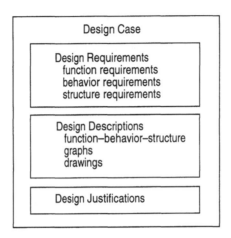

Figure 3.5. A schematized layout of the contents of a design case.

Design requirements are the design specifications of a design problem. They may be stated in terms of function, behavior and structure requirements. Requirements on function are general statements of the object's intended purpose. Requirements on behavior specify the expected performances of the object. Requirements on structure express the necessary physical properties of the object to be designed. Design descriptions are the statements of the design components that constitute the design solution, and can also be categorized as function, behavior, and structure. These descriptions may be described both symbolically and graphically. Design justifications make explicit the reasons for making the design decisions.

REPRESENTATION OF A DESIGN CASE

The representation of a design case is the form in which the case is stored in the computer as a part of a case base. The selection of a representation should include the following considerations:

1. Is the case base to be browsed by people, requiring that the representation be human readable?

2. Is the case base to provide the data needed for the case base reasoner to recall and adapt cases?

These considerations lead to decisions regarding the use of design case memory for aiding human designers as a resource of design examples or the use of design case memory as the basis for computer reasoning about a new design problem. This can be stated more simply as two extreme uses of design case memory: as a design aiding system and as a design automation system. Most applications will fall somewhere between the two extremes, but a consideration of these issues is essential when determining the representation of case memory.

The representation paradigms for representing the information in a design case include the many paradigms used in artificial intelligence, as well as data structures used in computer programming. Some examples of paradigms that have been used to organize design case memory are: sets of attribute-value pairs, text, object-oriented representations, graphs, and multimedia representations.

Attribute-Value Pairs

The use of attribute-value pairs to organize case memory is the most common form of representation. Each case is described by a set of features and each feature takes on a value. The features define the vocabulary for describing the previous designs, and the values identify the information specific to one design case. A generalization of this representation is:

---
case-1
    attribute-1: value-1;
    attribute-2: value-2;
    ...
    attribute-n: value-n.

The set of attributes is selected because they adequately describe a design case. Attributes can be viewed as indexing features into a design case or as the decision variables relevant to the original design situation. This notion of a design case as a set of attribute-value pairs also follows from the database management view of representing design data. The data is organized into tables of attributes, where each column in the table is a feature of the entity being recorded. The representation paradigm is generic, in the sense that it does not imply any specific forms of design knowledge. However, the representation paradigm does not provide any insight into the nature of the attributes and their values, or how to determine an appropriate set of attributes. Defining the attributes to be included in a design case defines the vocabulary with which previous and future designs are described.

An example of how this representation paradigm is used is illustrated by a design of a beam in Figure 3.6. In this example, the list of features determines how a beam design is described. As shown in the figure, a beam can be described by its span, length, material, and so on. A specific beam is described by the values for each of the attributes. Beam101 has a span of 10 m, which may distinguish it from another beam. The attributes shown in Figure 3.6 comprise the vocabulary for describing this particular beam and the vocabulary available for designing a new beam using this beam as the relevant case.

```
Case: beam 101
   span: 10 m
   support: continuous over three equal spans of 10 m
   length: 30m
   material: reinforced-concrete
   dead-load: 12 kN/m
   live-load: 7 kN/m
   concrete-grade:  25
   steel-grade: 400
   max-moment: 358.75 kNm
   width: 300 mm
   depth: 650 mm
   reinforcement: 1921  mm$^2$
   deflection: satisfactory
```

Figure 3.6. An attribute-value pair representation of a beam design.

Text

In some designs, the use of attribute-value pairs is too restrictive to represent the designers' intentions in a previous design. In such situations, it may be appropriate to represent a design case as a text description. The text description can convey anecdotal information about the design or describe the structure of the design in a more holistic way. The use of text to describe a design case is referred to as *design stories* in (Kolodner, 1993), based on the use of stories for memory organization (Schank, 1982). A design story can convey the design intentions and concepts that were important in a design situation. The story provides a flow of information rather than an unordered collection of attributes.

The use of text, or stories, to represent design cases is suitable when the stories are made available to the user of the design case memory. The use of text as a computational model of the previous design requires the identification of keywords, or indices, to the story for retrieval. The story does not necessarily provide a structure from which the case-based design system can reason about the relevance of the story to a new design problem or about how to adapt the story to fit the needs of the new design problem.

An example of a text representation to describe the beams in a building is shown in Figure 3.7. The description includes some of the words used as attributes in the previous example of attribute-value pairs as a representation of a beam design. However, a new set of words is used here that would not make sense in the attribute-value representation, such as *critical* and *shallow*. These words qualify the design description and provide additional information to the human designer, but are not easily incorporated in the computational model for case-based reasoning.

```
BUILDING-1
Beam Design Description:
    The structural system uses wide  and shallow beams because
    the floor-to-floor height is critical. The beam shells were designed
    with all positive beam reinforcement and were cast in place.
```

Figure 3.7. A text description of a beam design case in a building.

Object-Oriented Representations

Object-oriented representations are similar to sets of attribute-value pairs. An object-oriented representation formalizes the classes of designs, and each specific design is an instance of a class. In addition to describing design cases by their attributes, a case may also include procedural information and inherit information from other classes. This organization of the content of case memory has more information than the attribute-value pair representation, because it includes relationships among parts of cases and can include design methods with the description.

The object-oriented representation of design cases can be based on the notion of object-oriented programming and object-oriented databases (Hughes, 1991). The object representation is the fundamental unit of the language or database, where each object includes properties and methods. Each object definition represents a class of entities or an instance of a class object. This representation paradigm supports information sharing among objects through a mechanism called *inheritance*.

The benefit of using an object-oriented representation for design classes comes from the formalization of design cases as classes and instances. The development of classes of design cases provides templates for gathering design case data. The relationships among the object classes identifies an explicit hierarchy of case data. The disadvantages of an object-oriented representation of design case memory also lie in the formalization of design data—the paradigm assumes that all design cases can be described by one of the class templates in design case memory—and does not allow unusual design cases to be easily represented.

A simple class representation of the beam example is shown in Figure 3.8. The attributes that are used to describe a beam design are defined in this class template, where each beam design situation is recorded by giving values to the attributes span, length, width, and so on. The methods provide the procedural information used to check the performance, such as "check-stresses," or derive additional information, "propose-area," about the beam design. This example of an object-oriented representation of a beam class illustrates that the representation goes beyond the attribute-value pairs to include classes of design objects and methods associated with the design process.

```
Class: beam

    Attributes              Methods
       span                    calculate-stresses
       length                  check-stresses
       width                   check-deflection
       height                  propose-area
       material
       support
       MaxMoment
       deflection
```

Figure 3.8. A class description of the beam example.

Graph-Based Representations

A graph-based representation of a design case focuses on the relationships among the features of a previous design. In a graph-based representation of a design, the nodes in the graph represent distinct features and the arcs represent dependencies, or, more generally, associations among features. This representation structure is similar to semantic networks and has the advantage of case indexing on relationships as well as, or in place of, indexing on the labels used to describe the features.

Graph-based representations of design information have been used extensively in knowledge-based design. The representation of design knowledge as a dependency network has been used to generate new designs from generalized design knowledge (Duffy and MacCallum, 1989). Graphs representing associations between the attributes of a design system have been used as the basis for reasoning about creative design (Zhao, 1991). Graphs representing the relationships between behavior and structure have been used as the basis for design case retrieval (Sycara and Navinchandra, 1991).

The considerations in developing a graph-based representation of a design case include determining what information belongs on a node and what information is represented by a link. This provides a formalism in which design cases, and the way they are used in new design situations, are described. One of the major difficulties in using a graph-based representation is the complexity of finding a relevant design case for a new design problem, a graph-matching problem. Graph-matching algorithms can be np-complete (Qian and Gero, 1992).

A graph-based representation of a beam is shown in Figure 3.9. The attributes of the beam are represented as labels of the nodes in the graph. The links in the graph represent dependencies among the attributes. In the example, the attribute stress is dependent on the values of the span, load, material, and cross-section attributes. By representing a design case in this way, partial graphs can be identified and used as computational models during selection and adaptation. If the new design requirements do not include information about the deflection, the beam design case can still be identified, and through this identification, the need for checking the deflection performance is highlighted.

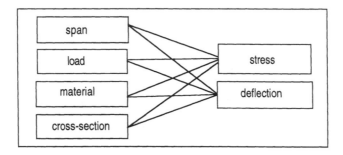

Figure 3.9. A graph-based representation of a beam.

Multimedia Representations

A multimedia representation of a design case combines many different representations as digital media. All representations (text, attribute-value pairs, drawings, video, sound, etc.) are combined into one database. The tools for representing multimedia include authoring tools, such as a hypertext tool, or, more recently, multimedia authoring tools that can include animation and video. An alternative to converting all representations to digital media for indexing and retrieval is to use a multimedia database management system, where the different media may be stored using the representation specific to the software that displays the information.

Multimedia representations of design cases have been used to develop stories associated with architectural designs (ARCHIE-II). Multimedia representations of design cases are currently focusing on the development of design-aiding systems by providing the designer with a rich set of media for understanding the design case. This is achieved by merging the user interface to design case memory with the memory itself. A potential problem with using a multimedia representation is that the case-based design system cannot reason about the graphic representations unless there are some features available to index the graphics.

Such case-based systems assume that the reasoning is done by the user and the system provides the information.

A simple example of a multimedia representation of a beam is shown in Figure 3.10. The example includes a brief text-based representation of the beam indicating that the beam participates in a larger system called a *rigid frame*, a set of attribute-value pairs that can be used to index the design cases, and two drawings that convey information about the load conditions on the beam and the resulting cross-sectional geometry. Using this representation paradigm, the designer can get a broad understanding of the design case by seeing both symbolic and graphic representations.

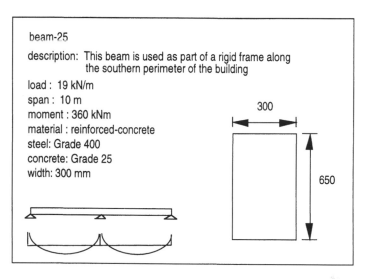

Figure 3.10. A multimedia representation of a beam.

Cases/Subcases Hierarchies

In some simple design domains, such as beam design, cases can be stored in their entirety in one place in memory. However, in many other design domains such as buildings and mechanical devices, the design cases are complex and composite objects. In such situations, each case is described as a set of components that are linked to their parent by "part-of" relations. Each component may itself be a structured object with its own components. Figure 3.11 illustrates the representation of a case as a case/subcases hierarchy. This form of representation makes it easier to handle complex design information. Furthermore, it provides access to parts of design cases to solve parts of new problems. Subcases contain pointers that can be used to reconstruct the entire case.

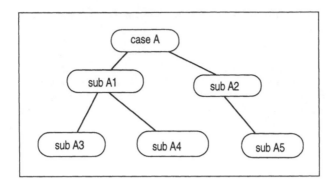

Figure 3.11. Case/subcases hierarchical representation.

DESIGN CASE MEMORY ORGANIZATION

Case memory is viewed as a special sort of database in which individual or multiple cases are treated as units for query. Case memory as a database must be organized into an appropriate structure in order for its retrieval process to find appropriate cases. The organization of case memory is concerned with the study of organizing cases into a structure in order to support an efficient retrieval of cases.

The organization of multiple design cases in case memory provides a means for accessing individual cases when searching for a relevant case. The issue of case memory organization is closely linked with case indexing schemes, retrieval strategies and the update of case memory. A good case memory organization might facilitate the efficiency and accuracy of retrieval. Retrieval of relevant cases is performed by a certain algorithm that searches the organizational structure of case memory for the right place where relevant cases may reside. Thus, the organizational structure provides platforms for how the retrieval process proceeds and how a new case is inserted in the case memory. Therefore, along with the discussion of organizational structures of case memory, the methods for building the structure are also taken into account.

CBR researchers have explored various ways to organize case memory. In general, each organizational structure attempts to partition the cases such that retrieval is both efficient and accurate. Each organizational structure of case memory is associated with a different algorithm for searching the case memory. The determination of an appropriate organizational structure depends largely on the number of cases in the case memory and on the indexing scheme. The organizational structures considered here for design case memory organization are flat structure, feature-based structure, and hierarchical structure. Along with each organizational structure, the approach to building the structure and updating case memory, and their advantages and disadvantages, are discussed.

Flat Structure

The simplest approach to design case memory organization is to store cases in a flat structure. A design case memory can be regarded as in a form of flat structure if design cases are put in a sequential data structure, such as a list. Computationally, this flat structure can be a simple list, an array, or a file. Moreover, in a flat structure, the name of each design case is stored in one flat data structure, with a pointer to the content of the case. A linear list is shown in Figure 3.12 as a type of flat structure that contains a sequence of names of cases.

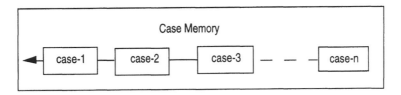

Figure 3.12. Organization of case memory as a linear list of cases.

Given a set of design cases, a flat structure of case memory can be computationally built using the following steps:

1. Get the names of all design cases.
2. Store these names as elements of a list, a file, or an array.

In this organization of cases, relevant cases can be found and retrieved directly by name. Each element of a flat structure is searched when one is looking for a specific case. Because every case is matched against a given new design problem, the retrieval process will not miss any matching cases. In a flat structure of case memory, the matching of each case and the given problem proceeds as the flat structure is searched. Updating case memory with a flat structure is also simple. To insert a new case, the name of the case is simply stored sequentially in the existing flat structure.

To illustrate the flat structure of case memory, suppose there are six structural design cases named str-c1, str-c2, str-c3, ..., str-c6. An array with six elements is selected as a data structure to organize these cases. A flat structure of this case memory is then formed: (str-c1 str-c2 str-c3 str-c4 str-c5 str-c6). In the course of searching this array, the content of a case is found by using the element as its pointer. In such a manner, the cases are matched against the new problem specifications in the order in which they were stored in the list.

As seen in the example, the retrieval of cases is performed by a serial search of each element in the flat structure. The retrieval would be inefficient and expensive as case memory gets large, because each case must be searched for each retrieval. Thus, the flat structure of case memory is appropriate if case memory is relatively small.

Feature-Based Structure of Cases

A flat structure of case memory, to some extent, uses the names of cases as indices. These indices serve as labels of cases and fail to fully describe design cases. One approach to improving this is to identify the key features of all design cases in the domain and store these features separately with pointers to the cases that have these features. This approach to case memory organization is characterized as *feature-based matching*.

In this approach, the design cases are indexed by chosen key features. Each key feature is an index to those cases including it in their representations. Before matching, one selects out only those cases that are pointed to by the key feature specified in the new design situation. Rather than attempting to match the new problem specifications with each case in the entire case memory, the retrieval process uses these key features to separate those cases that are worth paying attention to. Given a set of design cases, a feature-based case memory can be established according to these steps:

1. Identify key features used to discriminate cases based on the representations of design cases and/or domain.
2. Sort cases into subsets, where each subset is pointed by one key feature.
3. Store key features as elements of a structure (i.e., a list, an array, or a file).

During case retrieval, only those cases that include the feature, or features, of the new design problem need to be searched. Figure 3.13 illustrates the feature-based organization of design cases. In the retrieval of relevant cases, some of the key features, att-1, att-2, and att-3, are selected based on the new design problem specifications. That is, the selected key features specify the new design situation. Those cases that have the selected feature or features are then retrieved and matched against the new design situation. When a new case is stored in the feature-based case memory, the case is indexed by identifying the key feature that can specify the design situation of the new case.

The structural design cases in this example can be also organized in a feature-based structure. Suppose that the problem specifications in each structural design case are represented by the following set of design attributes: "str-material," "building-function," "stories," "loads," "core-location," "core-shape." Each case is then indexed by the attribute-value pair of the new problem specification. For example, str-c1 is retrieved when the feature "stories = 30" is part of the new problem specifications. The key features can be more general; for example, instead of selecting on the basis of the number of stories, the building can be indexed by a classification of type as "high-rise" or "medium-rise." The key features can also be indicated by a value range, for example, "number of stories less than 15," "number of stories between 16 to 25," and so on.

It is seen that key features are used to discriminate or differentiate cases. Determining key features is, thus, a crucial step in this approach. It is important to choose such key features so that they can capture the similarity of cases at appropriate levels. If the chosen key features are too specific, some potentially useful design cases might be omitted. On the other hand, key features that are too general would not cut down the number of retrieved cases significantly. A feature can be an individual attribute or a set of attributes. An attribute can be an attribute name or an attribute-value pair. In choosing key features, the features can be descriptive features directly from the representations of cases, or they can be derived features that capture partial similarities.

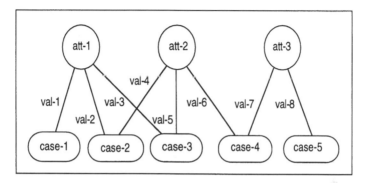

Figure 3.13. Feature-based indexing of design cases.

Using key features to index cases in the organization of case memory facilitates the retrieval of similar cases. This approach has been widely applied in many recent case-based design systems. The approach works under two conditions. One is when key features allow small numbers of cases to be retrieved. The other is when key features can sufficiently describe the similarities of cases to ensure that at least some of the potentially most useful cases are retrieved. The feature-based approach improves the efficiency of retrieval of relevant cases, to some extent, by using key features as indices of cases. However, using this approach for organizing design cases has some limitations: For example, to find the most relevant cases, a well-developed matching function is required. Feature-based indexing often forms a fixed organization of case memory that would not support a flexible retrieval.

Hierarchical Structure

To provide an organizational structure of case memory that reduces the number of cases searched into a subset of all cases, CBR researchers use hierarchical structures for representing the indexing features. As a typical organizational structure of cases, a hierarchical structure categorizes the design cases from more general features to more specific features. The benefit of using a hierarchical organization for indexing features of design cases is the efficient incremental retrieval of design cases.

In addition to the efficiency of retrieval, the hierarchical structure of case indices can be automatically derived, based on the use of various conceptual clustering methods. Each clustering method produces different clusters. Clustering methods generally identify the similarities over a set of instances and form categories based on those similarities. Hierarchies are formed when clusters are broken down into subclusters. Various clustering methods provide a means of clustering cases so that cases that share many features are grouped together. The hierarchical structure produced by a clustering method is an approach to organizing case memory that groups the features of design cases according to their utility in finding a matching case.

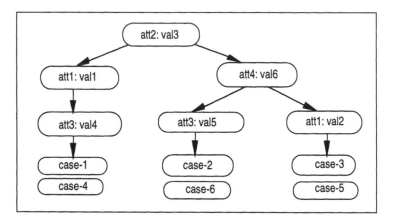

Figure 3.14. An indexing tree for accessing cases in case memory.

The result of clustering design cases is a hierarchy of features. As illustrated in Figure 3.14, each internal node of the hierarchy contains a feature or features shared by the design cases below. Leaf nodes contain design cases themselves. A path in the hierarchy leads to a set of relevant cases.

A hierarchy can be built by choosing a clustering method. A top node for the hierarchy is then created. Features shared by many cases are identified. These features provide a basis for partitioning cases. For each partition, a node is created; each is then attached as a successor to the top node. This process repeats itself by treating each new node as a top node, and cases in the partition of each new node are further partitioned. During the clustering, the feature or features in the internal node of the hierarchy are determined according to the chosen clustering method. For example, clustering can be based on the features shared by the largest number of cases, on individual features that divide the set into clusters of equal size, or on individual features that differentiate small groups of cases from the others.

The advantages of a hierarchical structure are that it supports an incremental retrieval of design cases and that the number of design cases actually considered is reduced to a subset of all cases in case memory. Features in the hierarchy form an indexing tree. During retrieval, these features are matched against a given new design situation from a higher level to a lower level. This implies that the hierarchy of nodes corresponds to the importance of features. Important features should be considered first, and clusters of cases that match best on those features are then considered further. If, however, unimportant features are high in the hierarchy, there is a chance that cases that share important features with the new situation will not be retrieved. Therefore, in building the hierarchy by clustering cases, the more important features are identified and used first as internal nodes. The determination of the relative importance of features becomes a key issue in organizing design case memory in a hierarchical structure. Domain knowledge is often needed to decide the importance of features.

Given a top node and a set of design cases, the basic steps for building a hierarchy of design cases include:

1. Find the shared features of design cases.
2. Select more important features among them based on domain knowledge.
3. Partition cases using the selected features. For each partition, create a node for each partition:
   - Regard the current node as a successor to the current top node.
   - If it contains more than one case, then apply the above steps to the cases in this partition by regarding the current node as a top node.
   - Otherwise, put this case into the node.

The major advantage of a hierarchical structure is that retrieval is more efficient than in a flat structure or a feature-based structure. Rather than having to attempt matches to all cases, it considers only a subset of cases. Given a new design situation, the search for relevant cases starts from the top of the hierarchy and progresses downward only when the features at a particular node are matched against the new design situation. The major disadvantage of a hierarchical structure is that a branch will be ignored when a particular feature does not match. The cases in this branch could be relevant, even though one of the higher features in the hierarchy do not match. With a hierarchical structure, updating case memory is more complex. Updating case memory involves finding the place in the hierarchy where the new design case fits best and installing it appropriately. The process for finding the right leaf node for a new case is similar to that for the retrieval of cases.

Using the relative importance of features to guide the building of a hierarchy for the six structural design cases is illustrated in Figure 3.15. Cases are first clustered according to the "building-function" as office or hotel, then according to the ranges of "stories," and then according to "core-location." The six cases reside in the leaf nodes.

In addition to specific design cases, a certain amount of generalized or compiled design knowledge may be part of a case-based design system. This leads to complexity in design case memory organization. The organizational structure of design case memory needs to consider the correspondence between the models used to represent generalized design knowledge and the specific design cases. The following section discusses the representation and organization of design cases in design case memory.

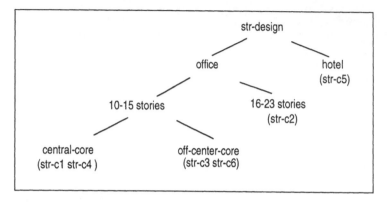

Figure 3.15. A hierarchy created based on the relative importance of features.

ROLE OF DESIGN MODELS IN DESIGN CASE MEMORY

A *design model* is an abstract representation of a generic entity or concept of a design domain. For example, in structural design, general knowledge about entities, such as beam, truss, frame, and column, can be treated as design models. Design models contain general knowledge about different kinds of cases, where design cases contain specific knowledge of a design episode. In other words, design models cover normative situations and design cases cover specific instances. Design models provide a basis for collecting and representing information about design cases in case memory. Furthermore, integratingdesign models and design cases in case memory provides a flexible memory organization, because design models provide many different abstractions that may be used as another set of indices into design cases. For example, one abstraction may be the function-behavior-structure model, another may be the dependency model.

Generalized knowledge in design models can be considered as different abstractions of domain knowledge, where each abstraction facilitates a perspective of the design problem. Design models have been developed in various design disciplines to enable more formal methods to determine performance. The design models considered in this section are:

- Function-behavior-structure (FBS) models.
- Dependency network models.

- Qualitative models.
- Dimensional models.

With respect to using a case-based reasoning approach to design, design models play an important role in determining what information may be stored in a case. In fact, design models can play many roles in case-based design:

- Organizing information within a design case effectively.
- Guiding clustering of design cases to form a hierarchy.
- Providing an organizational structure for indexing cases.
- Performing elaboration of a new design problem.
- Guiding case adaptation to meet new requirements.

Without a guide for developing a case-based reasoning system, the development and use of cases is an ad hoc exercise. Design models can provide a formalism for developing a case-based design system. This section presents a description and examples of the various design models and comments on the role these models play in case-based design.

The FBS Model

The FBS model of a given design entity explicitly represents its structure, intended functions, and behaviors. Using an attribute-value pair formalism for representing design knowledge, the attributes of a FBS model are grouped into three categories: functions, behaviors and structure. The function attributes are a set of attributes that represent the intended function features of a given design entity. The behavior attributes are a set of performances that allow the structure of an entity to achieve its functions. The structure attributes are the properties of a design entity that describe its physical existence. Design prototypes, proposed as a scheme for organizing and representing design knowledge, are examples of the function-behavior-structure model (Gero, 1990). The FBS model has been shown to be an effective medium for performing a design activity by reasoning at various levels of abstractions.

An attribute of a FBS model is described by its name, as well as a set of facets. Some examples of facets used to describe generalized attributes are type, default, units, range and dimension. Briefly, the semantics and use of these facets are as follows:

- *Type* is used to specify the type of an attribute value. For example, the value of the attribute beam span is of float type and that of the number of supports is of integer type.
- *Default* is used to specify the default value of an attribute. The default value of an attribute is used when there is no other means to determine the value of that attribute.
- *Units* is used to specify the measurements of an attribute value. For example, bending stress has the units Mpa. Some attributes, such as

number of stories and number of bays, have no units associated with them.

- *Range* is used to specify the value ranges for an attribute. For attributes that are of numerical type, the range is a simple numerical range; for attributes that are of discrete type, the range is a list of discrete values.
- *Dimension* is used to specify the dimension of an attribute. For example, the dimension of attributes that measure linear distance is [L] and of attributes that measure area is [L2].

A partial description of the FBS model of the beam is shown in Figure 3.16.

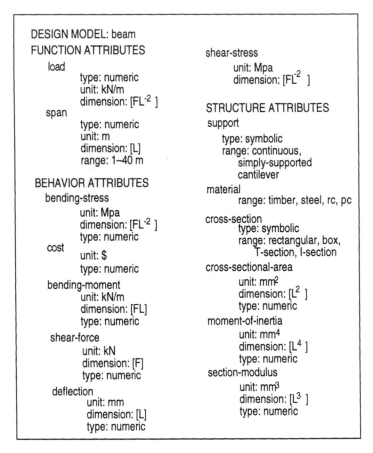

Figure 3.16. A partial description of the FBS model for a beam.

The function attributes of the beam include "load" and "span." This means that the intended function of a beam is to carry a load over a distance called span. The behavior attributes of a beam include "bending stress," "bending moment," "deflection," "cost," "shear force," and "shear stress;" these attributes are needed to evaluate the performance of a beam. The structure attributes of a beam include "material," "cross-section," "cross-sectional area," "moment of inertia," and "section modulus"; these attributes describe the physical characteristics of a beam so that it can be evaluated as a feasible beam.

The FBS model provides the basis for classifying the information within a design case as function, behavior or structure. Each design case is represented in terms of a multi-layered representation expressing the function, behavior, and structure of the design entity. Therefore, in describing a beam design case, function features, such as "resist load," and "provide span" will be given values; behavior features, such as "bending moment," "shear force," "deflection," and "cost," will be given values; and structure features, such as "material," will be given values. Figure 3.17 shows a beam design case representation based on the FBS model.

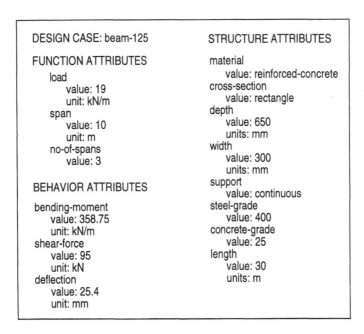

Figure 3.17. Design case representation on the basis of the FBS model.

Hierarchies are formed when a model is broken into submodels. Cases can be part of this hierarchy, where top nodes of a hierarchy represent design models and lower nodes represent design cases. This approach is similar to the object-oriented approach to organizing design cases as described previously, where design models are represented as individual classes of designs and design cases are associated with one or more design models using instance-of relationships. A hierarchical organization of case memory based on FBS models is illustrated in Figure 3.18.

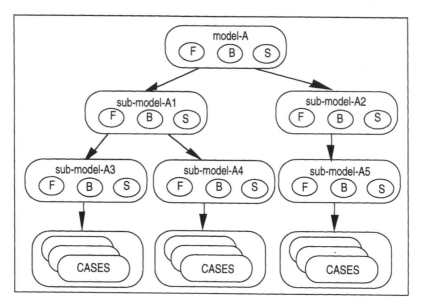

Figure 3.18. A hierarchical organization of case memory based on the FBS model.

Each design model in the hierarchy holds FBS features shared by the cases below it. One major advantage of this scheme is that the top nodes in the hierarchy provide a place to store generalized knowledge associated with various clusters of cases. It also aids in adaptation by providing a prescription of what needs to be satisfied in the design.

KRITIK (Goel and Chandrasekaran, 1989) is a case-based design system based on SBF models in the domain of the design of mechanical devices, such as heat exchangers. In KRITIK, cases provide methods for constructing solutions and FBS models provide knowledge needed for adaptation of retrieved cases. KRITIK justifies its solutions as a whole by constructing a causal model that explains how the solution works. KRITIK's SBF models express the causal dependencies between the device states, which enables the designer to trace the structural cause for the device's failure to achieve a desired function. KRITIK uses a specific FBS model called the behavioral component-substance (BCS) model, and a corresponding behavioral representation language for a class of physical devices. The BCS model of a given device explicitly represents its structure, intended functions, and internal causal behaviors. The structure of a device is viewed as a set of components (e.g., pipe, battery), and substances (e.g., water, electrical charge) and the relations between them. A function of a device is viewed as a transformation from one behavioral state to another. The functional differences between the new design and the retrieved case are used to access applicable modification plans. Modifications involve changes in relations, substitution of substances, parametric changes of components, and so on.

CASECAD (Maher and Balachandran, 1994b) is a case-based design shell that organizes design memory into FBS model memory and case memory. This system is described in more detail in Chapter 6. In CASECAD, model memory provides the general design knowledge and acts as a template for design cases in case memory. The models serve as indices to specific cases and as additional knowledge for elaborating the design specifications of new problems and for adapting selected design cases.

The Dependency Model

The dependency model provides and makes explicit the dependencies between the attributes and their values, and can be represented as a dependency network. Using dependency knowledge allows case memory to be searched for matching attributes or for matching dependencies. Once a design case is selected, a dependency model can provide the basis for completing the design description and checking that the dependencies are preserved in the new design. A dependency model of the beam is illustrated in Figure 3.19.

Let us consider a designer who specifies the following requirements for his or her design of a beam:

New beam requirements:
    load: 19 kN/m
    span: 10 m
    support: simply-supported

These requirements can be used to explore the case memory, to find relevant cases, and to lead to other cases that may not have been retrieved at first. This kind of case memory exploration is a valuable tool at the conceptual stage of design. In this example, load, span, and support are the features of the new design specifications. A partial dependency model of the beam shown in Figure 3.19 captures the dependency knowledge between various features of the beam. The model-based reasoner uses the dependency model to produce a new set of features that are dependent on the initial features. For instance, in our example, the following structure features are presented to the designer who then identifies the most critical ones:

Derived structure features:
    material
    section-lx
    section-area
    section-modulus

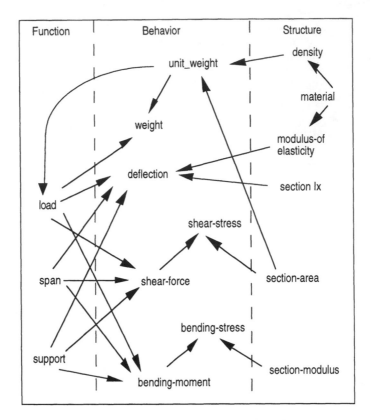

Figure 3.19. A dependency model of the beam.

The Dimensional Model

The dimensional model is an adjunct to the dependency model and can be derived from its dependency network by substituting for the names of the attributes their corresponding dimensions. Therefore, a dimensional model represents the dimensional relationships between the attributes. The dependency model shown in Figure 3.19 is shown as a dimensional model in Figure 3.20.

The dimensional abstraction provides the basis for comparing different design cases based on their conceptual similarities during case retrieval. It guides comparing two design cases from different disciplines. An example of this approach is the system CADET, which aids the designer in synthesizing hydro-mechanical devices (Sycara and Navinchandra, 1989, 1991). In CADET, the behavior of a device is described in terms of qualitative relations. For example, the following graph represents the qualitative relation between the flow rate and the input signal X, which is read as follows:

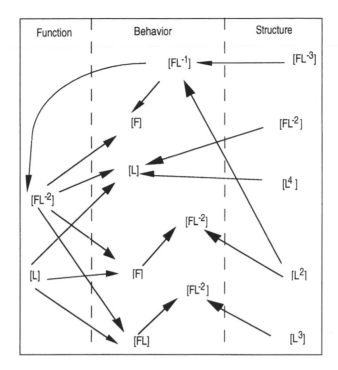

Figure 3.20. A dimensional model of the beam.

$$\begin{array}{c} + \\ X \dashrightarrow Q \end{array}$$

The flow rate Q increases monotonically with an increase any in the signal X. If parts of the behavioral specifications of the desired design match behavior indices of the cases in memory, then the cases can be directly retrieved. However, it is often not possible to find cases that match the desired behavioral specifications. CADET's approach to this problem is based on transforming an abstract description of the desired behavior of the device into a description that facilitates the similarity recognition and subsequent retrieval of design cases. Similarity recognition can be achieved by comparing dimensions of the nodes of the influence graph and the index influence graph. The goal of the retrieval process is to find devices or parts of devices in case memory whose influence graphs or subgraphs match the index influence graph.

Assume that we want to find a case that matches the influence graph given by:

$$\begin{array}{c} + \\ A \dashrightarrow B \end{array}$$

Assume that the system is unable to find cases that match this index. The next step is to elaborate the index in order to facilitate case retrieval. One possible elaboration is:

```
      +           +
A --------> X --------> B
```

where X is an unknown variable. The matching can be done by using these two influences in the elaboration. This approach allows retrieval of analogically related cases from other domains in order to synthesize design solutions that meet a given specification. The ability to use case memory in this way is facilitated when cases are stored as graphs—in this example, as behavior graphs.

The Qualitative Model

The qualitative model represents the qualitative influences between the design attributes. An *influence* is a qualitative relation between two attributes and can be positive or negative. A positive qualitative relation between two attributes indicates that a value increase in one attribute will result in a value increase in the other; a negative qualitative relation indicates that a value increase in one attribute will result in a value decrease in the other. Figure 3.21 shows a qualitative model of the beam.

The qualitative knowledge provides information on the effects of changing the value of a given attribute. It tells us what to change and how to change the type of knowledge, which are very important for case adaptation. For example, assume we want to design a beam section for a given span and given loading conditions. Assume that a selected section fails to satisfy the bending stress requirements. The next step is to find ways to reduce bending stress to a value that is acceptable. One possible elaboration is:

```
      −
X --------> bending-stress
```

where X is an unknown variable. The value of X is determined by searching the case base. The matching algorithm takes this qualitative relation and starts by looking for a match. From the qualitative model, the system determines that:

```
                  −
section-modulus --------> bending-stress
```

By increasing the value of section-modulus, the value of bending stress can be reduced. This shows how design models can be used during design case adaptation. The models provide generalized domain knowledge that can be applied when a selected design case does not match the new design specifications perfectly.

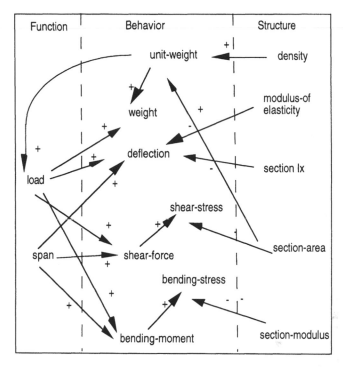

Figure 3.21. A qualitative model of the beam.

Summary

The use of design models in a case-based design system increases the complexity of the design support system. Design models tend to be complex representations and abstractions of specialized design knowledge. The advantage of including design models lies in the enhanced capabilities of the case-based reasoner to support and partially automate the recall and adaptation of design cases. An additional advantage in using design models in a case-based design system is that various design models have been developed to support specific design tasks, and the combination of model-based reasoning and case-based reasoning can draw on the advantages, and eliminate some of the disadvantages, of each.

PRESENTATION OF DESIGN CASE MEMORY

Design case memory is a resource for designers solving a new design problem. As a resource, design case memory is searched, browsed, and used as the basis for a new design. In all these activities, the designer is presented with design case information. The contents of case memory determine, to a large extent, what information is available to the designer. For example, a case memory that contains drawings will present drawings when case memory is being browsed. This presentation resembles browsing a set of CAD drawings, as illustrated in Figure 3.22. A case memory that contains attribute value-pairs will present to the designer sets of attributes and their values as words and numbers. This presentation resembles browsing data using a traditional relational database management system, as illustrated in Figure 3.23. One of the main purposes of the case presentation module is to communicate useful information to the designer effectively.

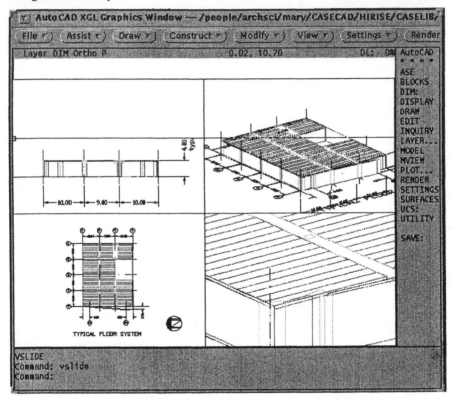

Figure 3.22. Browsing a set of CAD drawings.

The presentation of design cases defines the way the designer can interact with the case-based reasoner. In design problem solving, a combination of attribute-value pairs, paragraphs of explanation, and graphical images provide a more understandable presentation of a design. Understanding a design case only by reading the attributes and their descriptions can be difficult because of the large number of attributes. To help the designer understand design cases easily and quickly, a multimedia-based case representation combining graphical and audio representations with semantic descriptions can be used. In multimedia case-based systems, several modes of information, such as text, graphics, animation, and voice, are used to present relevant information to the designer.

Case-based design systems that have been developed using multimedia case representations include ASKJEF (Barber et al., 1992), a case-based assistant for user interface design; ARCHIE-II (Domeshek and Kolodner, 1993), a case-based aiding tool for architectural designers, and CASECAD (Maher and Balachandran, 1994), a case-based design assistant in the domain of structural design of buildings. This approach is very popular; no doubt there are many more multimedia case-based reasoning systems being developed every day.

CASE: 370Pitt	SUBCASE201
FUNCTION	FUNCTION
support-grid-geometry: rectangular maximum-span: 11 m support-building-type: office	transmit-dead-load: 3 kPa transmit-live-load: 3 kPa
BEHAVIOR	BEHAVIOR
cost-of-construction: 20 m number-of-stories: 17	fire-resistance: 2 hrs deflection: 18 mm
STRUCTURE	STRUCTURE
material: precast-concrete floor-to-floor-height: 4 m length-to-width-ratio: 1.84 height-to-width-ratio: 2.42 location-of-core: eccentric floor-to-ceiling-height: 3.5 m acad-file: 370Pitt/general.sld number-of-floors-above-grade: 17 number of floors-below-grade: 0	material: precast-concrete start-level: 1 end-level: 17 span-type: one-way maximum-span: 11 m typical-span: 9 m floor-depth: 250 mm span-to-depth-ratio: 44 maximum-aspect-ratio: 4.2 acad-file: 370Pitt/floorsystem.sld

Figure 3.23. Browsing attribute-value pairs.

A multimedia case-based system helps a designer understand a design problem by illustrating and explaining solutions to similar problems in multiple modes. Case information in such systems is represented in more than one modality, such as text, graphics, animation, and voice. Each design case points to several annotations. Design objects are represented symbolically with pointers to appropriate graphical images and animation and voice information. Once a relevant case is retrieved from memory, multimedia case memory organization provides direct access to other modes of information that point to the case.

Determining the role of the different media applications provides a basis for the presentation of designs. The structure of each case can be visualized by a CAD drawing. This is the typical use of CAD drawings: to convey the details of

the structure to the manufacturing or construction process. Some important
behaviors of cases can be visualized by 2-D abstract drawings. In structural
design, examples of such behaviors are moment variation, stress distribution,
and deflection pattern. The graphical illustrations of the design behavior of cases
inform the designer of the structural performance of the various design
components. The attribute-value pairs of the design case can convey discrete
design decisions and their assigned value. Browsing a multimedia case
representation is illustrated in Figure 3.24.

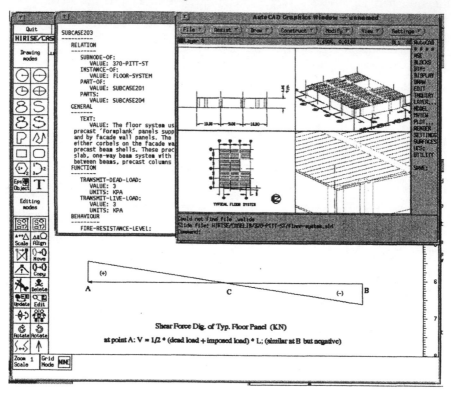

Figure 3.24. Browsing a multimedia representation of design cases.

SUMMARY

*In this chapter, we have presented central issues that need to be addressed in
selecting a schema for case memory organization. Three main interdependent
issues are: the content of design cases, the representation paradigms for case
memory organization, and the presentation of cases to the user. Case
representation methods include attribute-value pairs, text, graphs, object-oriented*

methods, and multimedia technology. Case memory organization schemes include a list of cases, a feature-based index, and an indexing tree. In some simple design domains, such as beam design, cases can be stored in their entirety in one place in memory. However, in many other design domains such as buildings and automobiles, the design cases are complex and composite objects. In complex design domains, design cases are decomposed into a set of subcases, and case memory is organized as a set of case/subcases hierarchies. Multimedia methodology for memory organization provides tremendous flexibility for presenting design cases in complex domains. Combinations of multiple modalities of presentation, such as animation with audio narration, maximizes the communication value of presentations.

GLOSSARY OF TERMS

Behavior: a set of attributes that represent measurable performances of the design entity.

Case-based reasoning: a reasoning process based on specific design experiences.

Cases/subcases hierarchies: trees in which components are linked to their parent by part-of relations. Each component may itself be a structured object with components.

Case memory: a special sort of database in which individual or multiple cases are treated as units for query.

Design description: the statement of the design components that constitute the design solution.

Design model: an abstract representation of a generic entity or concept of a design domain.

Design requirements: the design specifications of a design problem. They may be stated in terms of function, behavior, and structure requirements.

Function: attributes that represent the intended purpose of a design entity.

Graph-based representation: a representation of a design in which the nodes in the graph represent distinct features and the arcs represent dependencies among features.

Hierarchical structure: a structure that categorizes the design cases from more general features to more specific features.

Model-based reasoning: a reasoning process based on generalized domain knowledge.

Multimedia representation: a representation combining many different media, such as text, graphs, drawings, sound, and video, into one database.

Object-oriented representation: a representation that formalizes the classes of designs; each specific design is an instance of a class.

Representation of a design case: a representation that comprises the form in which the case is stored in the computer as a part of a case base.

Structure: attributes that are the physical properties of a design entity.

SUGGESTED READINGS

Gero, J. S. (1990). Design prototypes: A knowledge representation schema for design. *AI Magazine* **11**(4): 26-36.

> This article commences with an elaboration of models of design as a process. It then introduces and describes a knowledge representation schema for design called *design prototypes*. This schema supports the initiation and continuation of the act of designing. It is argued that the use of this representation effectively provides a translator between structure and function. Design prototypes are shown to provide a suitable framework to distinguish routine, innovative, and creative designs.

Rosenman, M. A., Gero, J. S., and Oxman, R. E. (1991). What's in a case. The use of case bases, knowledge bases and databases in design, in G. N. Schmitt (Ed.), *CADD Futures '91*. Zurich: ETH, pp. 263-277.

> This paper argues that both generalized knowledge, in the form of design prototypes, and specific knowledge, in the form of cases, are valid and important sources of design knowledge. A framework of an integration of two types of knowledge is presented. The contents and representation of design cases as important results of such an integration are addressed. The structure for representing design cases is explored, based on considerations of imposition by the design prototype formalism and the ability to access higher level abstractions where necessary.

Domeshek, E., and Kolodner, J. L. (1993). Using the points of large cases. *Artificial Intelligence for Engineering Design, Analysis and Manufacturing* **7**(2): 87-96.

> This paper addresses three issues: What sort of content should be captured in a design case? How should the content of a complex case be segmented into chunks for use? How should the resulting chunks be indexed for retrieval? A case-based aid for conceptual architects, ARCHIE-II, is presented, and the approaches to these three issues are described. The concept of story in case memory is introduced to support browsing a design case library.

4 Recalling Design Cases

Recalling design cases at the right time is critical to the application of case-based reasoning to design problems. A case-based reasoning approach to design uses a previous design situation as the starting point, or basis, for the generation of a new design solution. The appropriateness of the selected case determines how useful the case-based reasoning approach can be. As designers, we can recall a relevant previous design almost effortlessly. Sometimes we may struggle for a while to remember the relevant details, but we are easily reminded of previous designs. In order for computational support for this reminding to be useful, we need to consider an explicit way of recalling previous designs.

The concept of relevance is difficult to define in computational terms, but in this chapter some guidelines on how to establish criteria for relevance are presented. Conceptually, relevant design cases are those that have the potential to satisfy the requirements of the new design problem. In computational terms, this can have many interpretations: For example, a relevant case is one that has the largest number of requirements in common with the new design situation. Another interpretation is that the relevant case shares the most critical requirement with the new design situation, where *critical* is based on the context of the design problem, rather than on the efficiency with which the case can be found in a large case memory.

Case retrieval is usually carried out using the requirements of the new design as indices into the case memory. Therefore, an appropriate indexing scheme is important both to adding a new case to the case memory and to the retrieval of the case. In this chapter, the basic issues of indexing design cases are discussed and the efficiency and flexibility of an indexing scheme is stressed by presenting a scheme based on FBS relationships. Retrieval of a set of cases from case memory is an important step that separates the cases in case memory into two parts: cases for further consideration and cases that are not to be considered. In this chapter, several retrieval strategies are outlined in general terms. An iterative retrieval process is presented, in which the case selection process allows for the exploration of case memory, rather than a single-step search procedure. Some strategies for choosing the most relevant cases from partially matched cases are discussed.

For a particular design situation, the use of a previous design case as a starting point can have a significant effect on the quality of the final design. This chapter emphasizes that, in design, the case retrieval process should be modeled and performed as an exploratory process, because the specifications of a design problem are likely to change and expand as the design progresses. An indexing scheme that is capable of providing the flexibility needed in design is described. Two strategies for case retrieval that use case memory to explore the design space are presented, and the role of design models in supporting such case retrieval strategies is described.

INDEXING DESIGN CASES

The collection of design cases in case memory provides a potentially large space to be searched when one is looking for a relevant design case. If there are few design cases in case memory, this aspect of case-based reasoning is less important and need not be considered in much depth. If, however, there are many design cases in case memory, this aspect of case-based reasoning could become critical. In order to find a relevant design case in an appropriate amount of time, we need to discriminate among design cases. In general, cases need to be assigned labels that can designate situations in which cases are likely to be useful. We refer to these labels as *indices* to individual cases.

The content of design cases needs to be considered to determine an indexing vocabulary. The indexing vocabulary is often selected from the description of the design cases. Its members can be extracted directly from the contents of design cases or derived from the representation of design cases. To assign an indexing vocabulary to design cases, there must be some scheme to represent indices of design cases in the case memory. More specifically, an indexing scheme represents and organizes the design cases in such a way that the cases can be efficiently and flexibly searched. Figure 4.1 illustrates the indexing scheme as a representation derived from both the indexing vocabulary and the design cases.

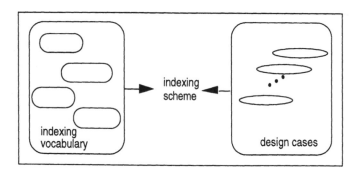

Figure 4.1. Deriving an indexing scheme from an indexing vocabulary and cases.

This section briefly discusses the issues in determining an indexing vocabulary. Two schemes for indexing design cases are presented: one conventional approach used in case-based reasoning and one derived specifically for indexing design cases.

Indexing Vocabulary

Kolodner (1993) defines an *indexing vocabulary* as a subset of the vocabulary used for full symbolic representation of cases. Many case-based reasoning systems determine relevance on the basis of features shared between the current situation and previous cases in case memory. In this manner, features are used as labels and are assigned to cases as descriptors. These features comprise the indexing vocabulary.

The selection of which parts of a case representation, or which of its features should act as its indices is a problem of defining the indexing vocabulary. In general, the indexing vocabulary is characterized as the selected features whose presence or absence plays a primary role in discriminating the applicability of a previous case to a current situation. The indexing vocabulary can be taken directly from the contents of cases (i.e., attributes used to represent cases): For example, in structural design, structural material can be used to index cases. The indexing vocabulary can go beyond the surface features of cases (i.e., causal relationships derived from the representation of design cases based on domain specific knowledge). Choosing indices on the basis of surface features extracted from case representation may be less useful than indexing by characteristics beyond the surface features. Such deep features are obtained through an interpretation or elaboration process, based on generalized models of the design domain. The use of surface features is easier to implement, because relatively less effort is needed to define design cases.

The indexing vocabulary identifies a set of features used to label cases. Identifying the indexing vocabulary for a design can be hard to do. How should a design be described so that it is usefully retrieved in a different design situation? Identifying some criteria for choosing the indexing vocabulary helps to structure the indexing vocabulary definition. Kolodner's (1993) four aspects of a good indexing vocabulary can be considered from a designer's perspective:

- *Prediction:* The index vocabulary must capture those aspects of cases that tend to predict solutions and outcomes of cases. Although design is not the same as prediction, an index vocabulary should include those aspects of the design that may be critical in determining the design solution. For example, in a high-rise building, the location of the service core is critical in determining the structural system type.
- *Specificity:* Index vocabulary must be specific enough to make all useful discriminations among items in memory. Indices should be concrete enough to be easily recognizable in future cases. When considering the index vocabulary for a design, the level of detail to be considered should be where two different designs can be

distinguished. For example, in designing a chair, the use of arm rests may distinguish between two different chairs with a similar function.

- *Generality.* Index vocabulary must also contain components general enough to capture relevant similarities among the items in memory. That is, indices should be abstract enough to ensure that cases can be useful in a variety of situations. In design cases, this may lead to the inclusion of functional information. Design cases may look very different, but their functionality may be the same: Two cars may look very different, but both serve as inexpensive subcompact cars.
- *Usefulness:* Recalling cases by index vocabulary should produce useful cases. This is more difficult to predetermine in design. Usefulness is only apparent to the user of the CBR system. However, we could conjecture that an index vocabulary is useful if it matches the vocabulary used by the designers who will use the system.

Developing an index vocabulary is, in essence, a process of identifying the possible descriptions of objects, concepts, and relationships in the design domain. Identifying an index vocabulary that can satisfy all the criteria is often thought of as a hard design problem in itself. One solution for such a design problem was suggested by Zacherl and Domeshek (1993). This approach involves an iterative process of analyzing the domain and task, proposing index components, and evaluating those components with respect to the criteria. For a design domain, this means considering the representation of previous designs as currently used by designers, adding an indexing vocabulary, and then revising the representation and the vocabulary until there is a compromise between the way designers talk about their designs and how they formally represent their designs. Ultimately, the indexing vocabulary should reflect the way designers refer to their designs.

Indexing Schemes

Using an indexing vocabulary to represent cases leads to the identification of an indexing scheme. Designing an indexing scheme is concerned with selecting some structure to organize the cases through the selected indexing vocabulary so that cases can be retrieved efficiently and accurately at the appropriate time. Therefore, an appropriate indexing scheme is important both to adding a new case to the case memory and to the retrieval of the case. The selection and retrieval of the relevant cases depends on how good the indexing scheme is. The indexing scheme is closely related to the case representation itself. There are various types of indexing schemes. Computationally, we classify indexing schemes here into two categories: *description schemes* and *relationship schemes*.

Descriptive Schemes. If designs are indexed only by a set of surface features, the indexing schemes for representing cases by assigning those features are considered as descriptive indexing schemes. This type of indexing scheme often adopts a fixed structure to represent cases. So, for example, we may decide that the indexing scheme for a beam would include the features "material," "span," "load," "support," and "cross-section." These features would be used as the indexing vocabulary for all beams in case memory. The organization of these features as pointers to specific cases defines an indexing scheme.

Computationally, two basic structures can be used to organize the descriptive features: a list and a tree. In a list organization of the indexing vocabulary, features are regarded as elements of a list. An element of the list can be represented by a single indexing feature or by a set of indexing features. Cases are assigned to elements of the list according to the description of cases. Each element indicates a set of cases that can be descriptively labeled by it. Figure 4.2 shows a simple list form of indexing scheme.

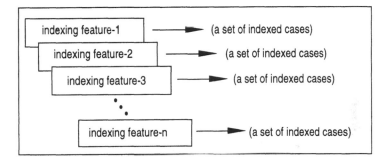

Figure 4.2. A list-based representation of the indexing vocabulary.

In a tree, features of the indexing vocabulary are distributed in the nodes of a hierarchical tree. The tree can be generated by clustering cases according to the indexing features. Cases are indexed in the tree from more general to more specific descriptors. The more the description of a case matches the indexing features, the more specifically it is indexed. As illustrated in Figure 4.3, case-4 is indexed by feature-1, whereas case-1 is indexed by a set of features, feature-1, feature-2, and feature-3. Case-1 is indexed more specifically than case-4. The tree representation of the indexing scheme is, to some extent, an efficient indexing scheme because only those cases at the leaf nodes of the tree might be considered for case retrieval.

Using a set of surface features from the description of cases is the simplest way to index cases. However, there are several problems with using pure descriptive schemes in indexing design cases. The first problem is that surface features can not fully anticipate the relevance of cases for the current problem. In other words, cases are indexed by a fixed set of features in pure descriptive schemes. In design, features that were salient at the time a case was experienced might not be important for judging the relevance for the current situation. Consequently, using a fixed indexing vocabulary may cause the retrieval of irrelevant design cases and the overlooking of relevant design cases. The second problem is that descriptive schemes cannot provide the flexibility needed in design. Specifications of design problems are likely to change and expand as design proceeds. Indexing schemes are required to provide flexibility so that indices of cases can be dynamically determined.

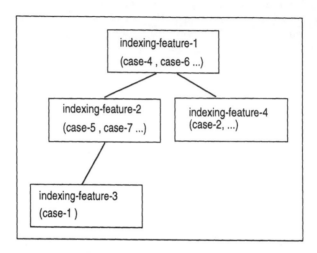

Figure 4.3. A tree representation of the indexing vocabulary.

Relationship Schemes. In many design situations, the relevance of a case to a new problem does not always depend on the surface features, but may hinge on abstract relationships between them. This is the basis of the relationship indexing schemes. Depending on the various relationships, the indexing schemes take on many different forms (e.g., a causal relationship scheme, a FBS scheme, or a qualitative model scheme). The essence of the relationship indexing scheme is the combination and composition of a representation of a domain model in the indexing representation. Figure 4.4 illustrates the relationship indexing scheme. The relationships can be represented as feature-based, object-based, or graph-based.

The objective of the relationship indexing scheme is to add several models or rational knowledge to facilitate the recognition of the relevance of cases. This type of indexing scheme requires the support of domain knowledge. Based on abstract similarity, relationship indexing schemes provide the potential for case-based reasoning in cross-domains. Based on the multiple indexing paths to the same cases, relationship indexing schemes provide flexibility in indexing design cases. For example, in the FBS relationship model, cases can be flexibly indexed by three aspects: function, behavior, and structure. We pursue this in more detail in the next section, due to its relevance to recalling design cases.

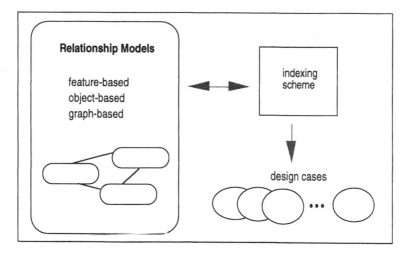

Figure 4.4. The relationship-based indexing scheme.

FBS Relationships as an Indexing Scheme

The structure and contents of design case memory play an important role in the development of an indexing scheme that supports efficient memory search during case retrieval. To better explain and demonstrate efficiency and flexibility of indexing design cases, we describe a relationship indexing scheme in this section that was developed on the basis of FBS models. In defining the contents of design cases, FBS models are developed as generalizations of all design cases. In this way, the design models become the indexing vocabulary and the design cases act as descriptions of specific episodes for one of the design models. For example, a FBS model of a beam includes a generalization of the function, behavior, and structure of the beam. A specific beam design would be an instance of the beam model, specifying the details of the function, behavior, and structure of one such beam.

In this indexing scheme, attributes of a design case are distinctively categorized based on the roles they play in different processes of design reasoning. Attributes of a design case are grouped into three categories: function, behavior, and structure. This approach to the content of case memory assumes that the requirements for a new design problem are specified as function, behavior, and structure requirements and, therefore, the indices into case memory are also categorized as function, behavior, and structure.

Case memory can be partitioned into two parts: design model memory and design case memory. Each subcase of a specific design case is linked to a generic design model by an instance-of relation, as shown in Figure 4.5. Each design case is described as a set of subcases that are linked to their parent by part-of relations. Each subcase may itself be a structured object with components. In this approach, efficiency can be achieved by partitioning case memory so that only a subset of cases is searched. The indexing scheme for case memory can improve the efficiency of the retrieval process when it partitions case memory before searching the contents of individual cases.

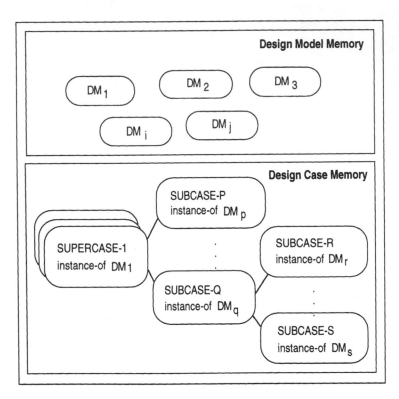

Figure 4.5. Case memory as design model memory and design case memory.

If design models are represented at different levels of abstraction, then specific cases may be a combination of several models forming a hierarchy. One characteristic of most design domains is that design cases are large and complex. Using design models as a guide for developing design case memory implies that a design case is more than a collection of attributes or descriptors; the design case is a hierarchy in itself. To provide flexibility in case retrieval, design cases are indexed at any level of abstraction.

A case memory based on FBS models can use a two-level indexing scheme for indexing design models and design cases: category and attribute indices. Category indices are intended to support searching a subset of a case or subcase.

Each category within a design case is indexed by an appropriate label, such as function, behavior, or structure. Figure 4.6 illustrates the first level of indices that are used to confine the search to a particular category during case retrieval.

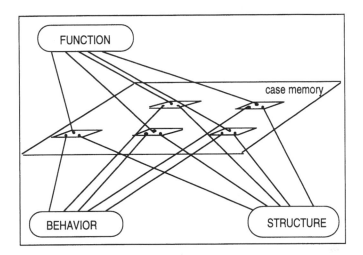

Figure 4.6. Partitioning the search space of case memory by FBS attributes.

Figure 4.7 illustrates the category indices by an example of the attributes in a beam design. This allows an efficient and flexible search of case memory. Efficiency is achieved because exhaustive search of the contents is not performed; only the category of interest is checked. Flexibility is achieved because there are many paths to the same case or subcase.

Attribute indices allow the cases to be ranked by the degree of match between the new design and the case being considered. This indexing mechanism allows for the retrieval of design cases based on specific function, behavior, or structure requirements. By focusing on one particular category of requirements, one may retrieve a different set of cases than one would when all categories are considered. This kind of flexibility plays an important role in assisting the designer in exploring all possible options. Moreover, the hierarchical organization of cases allows the retrieval and composition of parts of different cases in design synthesis.

In summary, the more efficient the indexing scheme, the more efficient the case retrieval process. Efficiency in case retrieval for design problems requires defining the criteria for eliminating cases from further consideration. In design, this may eliminate a potentially relevant case due to a bias in the way the new design was specified. As already seen, efficiency can be achieved by partitioning case memory so that only a subset of cases is searched.

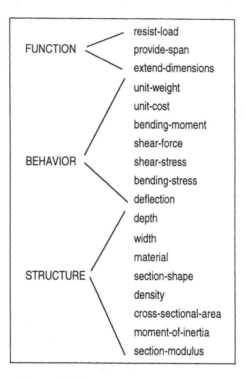

Figure 4.7. The category indices of a beam.

The indexing scheme in a case-based design system should provide flexible mechanisms for the retrieval of cases. Flexibility in indexing cases provides many paths to the same case and does not discriminate against a design case too early. Flexibility in indexing design cases can be achieved in the following ways:

- Any features or set of features in a case description can be used to search case memory.
- A feature-based, object-based, or graph-based indexing scheme can be used to search case memory.
- Indices to case memory can be determined dynamically.

RETRIEVING DESIGN CASES

In design, the major difficulty is that the design specifications are ill-formed and frequently change and expand as the design process continues. For a particular design situation, the most relevant case may not be the closest match to the initial specifications, but the one that satisfies all the critical requirements, including those expanded as the design progresses. Therefore, case retrieval strategies for design problem solving must make explicit the most relevant match, rather than the closest match. Given a set of initial specifications of a new design problem, the aim of the case retrieval process is to identify the most relevant design cases while allowing the design specifications to change and expand as the design process continues. In the rest of this section, based on the FBS indexing scheme described previously, we discuss two approaches to design case retrieval: model-based index elaborations and index revision through feature extraction.

Case Retrieval Strategies

Retrieving cases from case memory is essentially a search problem. A retrieval strategy embodies a method to search case memory and find relevant cases. Techniques for retrieval depend on the structure of case memory and index schemes. Index schemes make the retrieval process more selective and reduce the effect of the memory size. Different methods for structuring and manipulating case memory and for indexing schemes lead to different styles of retrieval processing. Three generic types of retrieval are briefly presented:

1. List-checking.
2. Concept refinement.
3. Associative recall.

The *list-checking* method uses a list of features for determining which cases to retrieve. Each element of the indexing list points to a set of relevant cases, as described in the previous section. Using the list-checking method, the cases indicated by the matched indexing element are retrieved as relevant cases. This retrieval strategy is based, in essence, on the feature match. List-checking as a retrieval strategy can be used for recalling cases and/or subcases. In other words, the indexing features can be associated with whole cases or parts of cases.

Concept refinement uses a tree indexing representation; search in concept refinement starts at the most general feature in the hierarchical representation of features, and progresses downward only when a match is possible. By *match*, we mean that the description of the new problem matches the indexing features in a particular node in the hierarchy. In this retrieval method, the more general or the shared features of various cases are selected first, eliminating large numbers of cases. Similar to list-checking, in using the concept refinement retrieval method, cases can be stored in their entirety or in pieces.

Associative recall considers the relationship-based indexing schemes, characterized by using generalized models of a particular domain. Individual cases are associated with domain models in terms of causal relations, FBS relationships, or qualitative models. Given a new problem, the retrieval of relevant cases under such an indexing scheme is undertaken based on the associations of design models and design cases. More specifically, cases are recalled through elaboration and explanation of the new problem specifications based on the relevant generalized models. Strategies used in relationship-based indexing schemes are referred to as *associative recall.* In associative recall, cases are recalled on the basis of the most relevant match, rather than the closest match. The relevance of retrieved cases to the current situation is determined on the basis of not just a surface feature match, but also a deep feature match based on domain knowledge. That is, domain knowledge is used in the identification of relevant cases in the associative recall methods.

Of these three retrieval methods, associative recall is more suitable to design case retrieval than the other two when design problem specifications are ill-formed and frequently change in the design process. In order to retrieve relevant cases to a given design problem, case retrieval depends on the explicit specification of the relevant set of requirements for the new problem. This should include the most critical features of the design problem. However, at the initial stages of a design, the designer may not be able to make all the critical features explicit. The utility of the specifications of a design problem depends on its relationship to the design cases already in case memory and the attributes used to describe the cases. Given a new design situation, the relevant cases should be ones that satisfy all the critical requirements, including those specifications that emerge in the design process.

To further define the associative recall method for recalling relevant design cases, two strategies for design case retrieval are presented in the remainder of this section: index elaboration and index revision.

Case Retrieval Through Index Elaborations

Index elaboration, as introduced in Kolodner (1984), is a process that transforms the given specifications of a new problem into a more appropriate set of specifications. The aim of the index elaboration process in design is to identify more discriminating and/or critical features that were not included in the initial specifications. Owens (1993) described a mechanism for integrating feature extraction and memory search and for explicitly reasoning about the costs and benefits of individual features. The focus in Owens' approach is the efficiency of the search. In retrieving design cases, there must be a consideration of efficiency of search, but also a focus on the identification of semantically relevant features. A two-phase iterative case retrieval process makes use of index elaborations or feature extractions through model-based reasoning and feature-based memory search.

In order to achieve index elaboration, the case retriever performs incremental retrieval. In the first phase, a set of appropriate design models are retrieved using the initial specifications of a new design problem. For example, in the structural design of a building, the purpose of the proposed building, the grid geometry, and the construction cost, are some examples of such initial specifications. The design models retrieved via the initial specifications are used to identify more discriminating and critical features of the new design problem. The FBS models provide the range and default values of various attributes that might indicate how critical or common the current specifications are. The selected design model provides additional specifications and/or identifies critical features of the new design problem. In the second phase, the elaborated specifications or the critical features are used to search case memory in order to identify the most relevant cases.

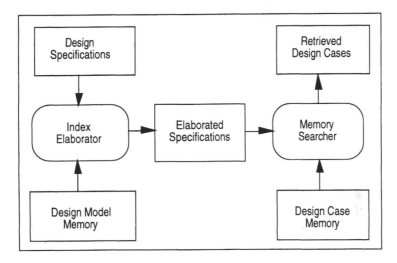

Figure 4.8. A case retrieval process using index elaboration.

The case retrieval process that uses an iterative approach combining model-based index elaborations and memory search is illustrated in Figure 4.8. The index elaborator uses the initial specification of the design problem, as given by the user, and the content of design model memory to generate an elaborated set of specifications. The initial specifications are matched with the indexing vocabulary of the design models, and a relevant model is selected based on the closest match. The relevant model provides additional specifications and generalized knowledge to critically assess the specifications for the new design problem. The elaborated specifications then form the input to the memory searcher, which uses these specifications to search design case memory. The elaborated specifications provide the basis for finding a case that is the closest match.

Case retrieval occurs at two levels in index elaboration. The first operates in the design model memory space, and the second in the design case memory space. The purpose of the two levels is to allow the user to explore the new problem specifications before considering a closest match in case memory. The important aspect of this strategy is the way in which the specifications are changed, in other words, the alternatives for index elaboration in design problem solving.

Index elaboration can occur in two ways:

- Additional features are added to the specifications of the new problem.
- Critical features are identified that characterize the new problem.

A design model can provide additional features by association: The initial specifications provide a partial description of a design problem and the design model adds to the description. For example, the specification of a building by its grid geometry and number of stories can lead to the retrieval of a design model for a medium- to high-rise building. This design model includes the location of the core. This feature is then added to the initial specifications of the new design problem. In this type of index elaboration, the number of indices used to describe the new problem gets larger as more relevant features emerge from the retrieved design model. This process of index expansion is illustrated in Figure 4.9.

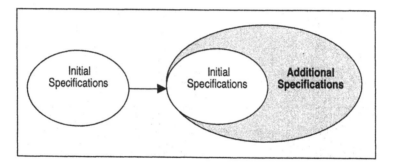

Figure 4.9. Index elaboration by expansion of indices.

A design model can identify critical features of a design problem by examining the values of the attributes in the initial specifications. For example, the new design problem may include the slenderness ratio of the building. In the retrieved design model, the slenderness ratio has a typical range of values. If the slenderness ratio of the new design is outside the range of values in the retrieved design model, this indicates that the slenderness ratio is a critical feature of the design. In this type of index elaboration, the number of indices used to characterize the new design problem gets smaller as the critical features emerge from the retrieved design model. This process of index reduction is illustrated in Figure 4.10.

To illustrate the index elaboration strategy for design case retrieval, consider that a designer specifies the following information about a new building.

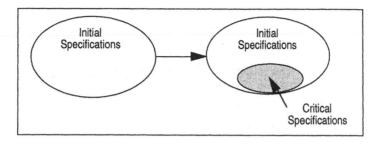

Figure 4.10. Index elaboration by identifying critical specifications.

New building specifications:

support-building-type:	office
grid-geometry:	rectangular
construction-cost:	<= $20 million
number-of-stories:	30
floor-to-floor-height:	3 m
width:	15 m

The case retrieval process begins with these features of the new design problem. Using these features as indices, the system retrieves a set of design models that have the same features as the new problem specifications. These specifications of the new building lead to the retrieval of the design model for a medium-rise office building whose features are listed below.

```
DESIGN MODEL: medium-rise-office
    FUNCTION
            support-building-type
            resist-wind-load
            grid-geometry
    BEHAVIOR
            building-slenderness
            overturning-moment
            lateral-displacement
            cost-of-construction
    STRUCTURE
            building-shape
            floor-to-floor-height
            material
            floor-system-type
            wind-system-type
            location-of-core
            number-of-stories
```

This design model includes features, such as the location of the core, the material, the height-to-width ratio, and the floor system type, that were not included in the initial specifications. These features are then added to the initial specifications of the new design problem where their values are known. Features whose values are not known form part of the design solution expected from the case-based reasoner, and are not added to the specifications. In this example, the building slenderness and the location of the core are known and are added to the set of specifications. The values of the overturning moment, lateral displacement, and material are not known, and therefore, are not added to the set of specifications. The expanded set of specifications is shown below.

Expanded new building specifications:

support-building-type:	office
grid-geometry:	rectangular
construction-cost:	<= $20 million
number-of-stories:	30
floor-to-floor-height:	3 m
width:	15 m
building-slenderness:	6
location-of-core:	center

In order to identify critical features, the value of the each specification is compared to the corresponding value range in the retrieved design model. Those values that fall outside the range are defined to be critical. The height-to-width ratio for a medium-rise office building has a typical range from 4.5 to 5.5. In this example, the height-to-width ratio is 6. This indicates that the ratio is a critical feature in identifying relevant cases. That is, it is no longer relevant if the case is an office building or not, it is important that the retrieved case have a height-to-width ratio near 6. The reduced set of specifications for case retrieval is shown below.

Critical new building specifications:

building-slenderness   6

This example has shown that the set of specifications for a new design problem given by the user may not be the set of indexing features used to search case memory. Using the index elaboration strategy, model memory is used to modify the set of specifications before defining them as indexing features. The modification of the specification, either to expand or to reduce the number of specifications, requires domain knowledge and may result in alternative sets of specifications. The domain knowledge can be made explicit in model memory and/or can be left to the user of the system.

Case Retrieval Through Index Revision

The second strategy for case retrieval that allows design exploration using case memory is *index revision*. In this approach, the case retrieval process begins with comparing a set of initial specifications with cases in case memory. Using the specifications as indexing features, the system may retrieve a set of design cases that partially or completely match on the basis of those features. The retrieved cases provide a set of alternative design spaces for the new design problem. Within each case is the possibility of identifying additional specifications and eliminating existing specifications as features for a second iteration of case retrieval. Using this retrieval strategy, the designer is influenced by the retrieved cases, and as a result of this influence, the designer changes the new design specifications.

The index revision process is illustrated in Figure 4.11. The initial design specifications are given to the memory searcher. The memory searcher uses the specifications as the indexing vocabulary for retrieving design cases from the design case memory. The retrieved design cases are then given to the index reviser, which may change some specifications, add others, and keep some specifications as they were initially.

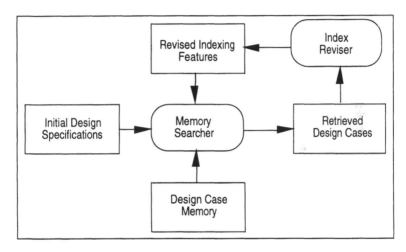

Figure 4.11. A case retrieval process using index revision.

A case memory that uses an FBS template allows index revision to use the categories of the specifications to identify alternative specifications. The initial case retrieval is based on the specifications within a single category (i.e., function, behavior, or structure). Using a FBS category as a basis for case retrieval can identify potentially relevant specifications from other categories in the retrieved case. The retrieval of a case based on the function category may provide structure attributes that are different from the structure attributes in the specifications of the new design problem. The structure attributes in the retrieved case can replace those in the new design specifications. For example, a new building may be specified by a grid geometry with a 30-meter span and material of reinforced concrete. The span defined by the grid is a specification in the function category and is selected as the category for the first case retrieval. The cases retrieved that match the span have a structure attribute "material" with a value of prestressed concrete. As a result of this retrieval, there is a change in the material specification from reinforced concrete to prestressed concrete. In the second iteration, the new specifications across all categories can be used to search case memory again.

Index revision is illustrated in Figure 4.12 as a shift in indices. The space of indices changes, but the change is not characterized as an increase or decrease in the indices, it is characterized as a change, where some indices may be dropped and others added. This approach to case retrieval allows exploration when the revised indices are used to search case memory again.

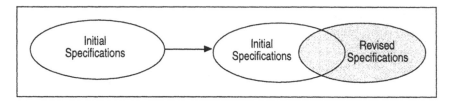

Figure 4.12. Index revision as a shift in specifications.

In summary, two retrieval strategies for retrieving design cases have been presented. The first strategy, index elaboration, is useful when case memory is partitioned into design model memory and design case memory. In this strategy, the design models help the designer identify relevant indices in case memory so that case retrieval returns a more relevant set of cases. The second strategy, index revision, is useful when case memory is made up entirely of design cases. This strategy enables the designer to be influenced by retrieved cases. Essentially, it is an iterative approach to case retrieval, where the design specifications are changed for the next iteration based on the cases retrieved.

DESIGN CASE SELECTION

The memory organization, indexing schemes, and retrieval strategies presented can retrieve a set of relevant cases for a given design problem, but they often provide too many cases. Consequently, an additional assessment is required to determine which case is the best case to use as the basis for a solution. The selection of the best case involves assessing not only how close retrieved cases are to the new problem, but also the relative importance of the relevant similarities and differences. The notion of the "best" case may be explained on the basis of the most similar match or the most useful match.

Researchers have pursued various metrics and ranking schemes for selecting the most applicable case to the problem in hand. Three approaches described here are:

1. Maximum number of matching features.
2. Weighted count of matching features.
3. Context-dependent matching.

The simplest approach is matching the maximum number of features, where a feature is either an attribute of a case or an attribute-value pair. The case that matches the most features in the problem is regarded as the best case in this approach. The most common approach is a weighted count of matching features. Each feature is associated with a specified weight that determines the importance of the feature. The weighted sum of shared features is used to identify the best case. The concept of a similarity metric is used in these two approaches, where the indexing features provide a similarity metric. Similarity metrics use a pattern as the basis for selection, where the case that is closest to the pattern is selected. A pattern may be a set of features, a graph, or even a set of constraints. The third approach for selection of the best case emphasizes the usefulness of retrieved cases to addressing the goal in the current design situation. In this approach, the best case is defined as the one that has the most potential to satisfy the requirements of the new problem. The selection of the best case is context-dependent.

Maximum Number of Matching Features

This strategy simply counts the number of matching features in each of the retrieved cases and the new problem that match. The case that has the highest number of matching features is considered the most applicable to the problem. A feature in the similarity metric can be a label of an attribute or it can be an attribute-value pair. The feature that is a label of an attribute is a comparison of the label as a string. The feature that is an attribute-value pair entails a comparison of both the attribute label and its associated value. When the value is a string, the comparison is, again, a string comparison. When the value is a number, the comparison includes some criterion for determining when a number is close enough to be considered a match. A general approach to this strategy is:

```
begin
  for each case
    count = 0;
    for each feature in similarity metric
      if feature is in case then count = count + 1;
    selected case is case with max count;
end
```

The selection of the best case in this approach is based on the similarity of surface features. The essence of this approach is the definition of features in the similarity metric that are important to match between a case and a new problem. This approach is useful when the features cannot be ranked according to their importance in finding a relevant case.

Weighted Count of Matching Features

All features used in the similarity metric are treated with the same importance in the first approach, however, this does not take into account the relative importance of features to achieve the goal in a case. A weighted feature scheme is an improved methodology for case selection that allows a designer to articulate his or her priorities about feature matchings. In using such a scheme, the designer assigns a weight to each feature that needs to be matched. The feature with the highest priority is assigned the highest weight.

This approach assesses the relevance of cases to the problem on the basis of the importance of each matching feature and the global evaluation of all matching features. First, the input features are matched with each of the retrieved cases. For each successful match, its weight is added to the score of the case being matched. In the final score, each retrieved case has a sum of all matching features' weights. The best case is determined based on a ranking of retrieved cases based on their scores. The case (or cases) with the highest score will be considered the most applicable. The score for each retrieved case is computed as follows:

$$score = \Sigma (w_i{}^* f_i)$$

where w_i is the weight of feature i
         f_i = 0 if feature i is not in the case, and
            = 1 if feature i is in the case.

Setting weights to features is crucial to the weighted count approach. There are three basic methods for assessing the relative importance of individual features: statistical, analytical, and heuristic. In some domains, statistical analysis of many cases can assign numerical weights to features. In other domains, there may be a causal analytical model of the problem solving task sufficient to infer the relative importance of features. Finally, in still other domains, it may be appropriate to assign weights to features based on heuristics.

The weighted count of matching features provides one way to select the best case, however, this does not take into account that the case itself may determine the importance of a feature. Weighting is often problematic because the weight of a feature is highly contextual and is not easily captured in a static model.

These two strategies, maximum number of matching features and weighted count of matching features, assume that the similarity metric can be articulated as a set of features that the selected case must have. If the similarity metric is a graph or a set of constraints, a different set of strategies for selecting a case is needed.

Context-Dependent Matching

The importance of a feature in measuring relevance is often derived in context, where retrieved cases themselves determine which of the features of the new problem are the most important ones for matching. Identifying the best case based on the usefulness of cases is another approach to design case selection. Given a set of retrieved cases that appear superficially similar to the new problem, this method attempts to figure out their usefulness based on domain-specific knowledge. The foundation of this approach is that the assessment of relevance is highly case- and context-dependent. The best case is the one that addresses the current problem in the best way. In this approach, domain-specific knowledge is applied to determine which of the retrieved cases is most applicable to the current problem.

Usefulness can be assessed in various ways. There are several methods proposed for doing this. For example, there are two preference heuristics methods (Kolodner, 1988): goal-directed preference and ease-of-adaptation preference. Goal-directed preference says that cases that can be used to address the current goal should be preferred over others. Ease-of-adaptation preference means that cases that require less work to adapt are preferred.

To avoid a static model for weighting features, Stanfill (1987) explored a method of dynamically changing weights of features. The relative importances of features are assessed by analyzing the new context and cases based on domain specific models so that the weights of features dynamically change in each individual context.

In summary, case selection requires a definition of the criteria for selection. If the criteria can be defined by the indexing vocabulary, then the maximum number of features or the weighted count of features provides the most objective methods for case selection. If, however, the indexing vocabulary only identifies potential when retrieving cases, the third strategy of context-dependent selection is appropriate. The method requires an analysis of the relationship between the retrieved cases and the new problem from perspectives other than the indexing vocabulary. This analysis requires either an explicit representation of domain knowledge or that the user have the expertise to select the appropriate case.

SUMMARY

Recalling design cases can be decomposed into indexing design cases, retrieving design cases, and selecting design cases. Because new design problems are ill-defined and often change as alternative solutions are considered, applying case-based reasoning in design imposes special requirements on indexing and retrieval strategies. In this chapter, the need for flexible retrieval of design cases is emphasized. Two iterative strategies for design case retrieval are index elaboration and index revision. The first strategy uses a two-phase case retrieval mechanism that combines model-based index elaborations and feature-based memory search. The second strategy uses index revision and iterative memory search. The case retrieval process begins by retrieving a set of design cases based on the initial design specifications and can lead to a shift in the specifications of the problem. The revised indices are then used in the subsequent memory search. This process continues until a relevant design case is selected.

GLOSSARY OF TERMS

Descriptive indexing scheme: indexing of design cases by a set of surface features.

Case memory: a computer representation of case-specific knowledge.

Case retrieval: a process that identifies relevant cases from case memory given a set of requirements of a new problem.

Case selection: a process that ranks and chooses one case as the basis for the new problem.

Context-dependent matching: a selection method where the best case is context-dependent and is defined as the one that has the most potential to satisfy the requirements of the new problem.

Critical feature: a feature that must be part of a retrieved case.

Index elaboration: a process that expands the set of initial specifications through searching model memory.

Index revision: the process of changing the initial specifications by searching case memory.

Matching feature: a feature that occurs in both the new problem specifications and a case.

Matching maximum number of features: a selection method where the case that matches the most features in the problem is regarded as the best case.

Model memory: a computer representation of generalized knowledge in the form of models.

Relationship indexing scheme: the indexing of design cases by abstract relationships, such as a causal relationship scheme, a FBS scheme, and a qualitative model scheme.

Weighted count of matching features: a selection method where the weighted sum of shared features is used to identify the best case.

SUGGESTED READING

Kolodner, J. L. (1984). *Retrieval and Organizational Strategies in Conceptual Memory: A Computer Model.* Hillsdale, NJ: Lawrence Erlbaum Associates.

This book presents a theory of organization and processing in long-term event memory. Memory organization, retrieval processing, and memory updating are addressed from the point of view of intelligent information retrieval, and from a psychological point of view. An implementation for the retrieval and organizational strategies, CYRUS, is presented, in which E-MOPs are used to organize both general information and individual episodes. The concept of elaboration is introduced to infer additional features of an event and transform already specified features into features used as indices.

Maher, M. L., and Balachandran, M. B. (1994a). Flexible retrieval strategies for case-based design, in J. S. Gero and F. Sudweeks (Eds), *Artificial Intelligence in Design '94*. Dordrecht: Kluwer Academic.

It is argued in this article, that the case retrieval process in design should not be modeled as search, but as exploration, because the specifications of a design problem are likely to change and expand as the design progresses. Two strategies for case retrieval are presented, which use case memory to explore the design space. The first strategy is based on index elaboration, which is a process that transforms the given specifications of a new problem into a more appropriate set of specifications. The second strategy uses index revision and iterative memory search. The role of design models is described in supporting such case retrieval strategies.

Kolodner, J. L. (1988). Retrieving events from a case memory: A parallel implementation, *Proceedings of the DARPA Workshop on Case-Based Reasoning*. San Mateo, CA: Morgan Kaufmann.

In this paper, research into memory organization and retrieval methods for a case-based reasoner, PARADYME, is presented. A hierarchical organization of knowledge and cases is explored for a conceptual memory. A concept refinement search is introduced as a retrieval method, which limits retrieval to only reasonable parts of the memory and allows memory probes to describe events by describing features of their substructures. A parallel retrieval algorithm is developed in PARADYME on the basis of concept refinement search.

5 Adapting Design Cases

Adapting design cases involves taking a selected design case, making changes to the case, and labeling the revised case as the new design solution. There are some major concerns in considering adapting design cases to generate new designs. For example, a design is either proprietary or it is customized for a specific context. Proprietary designs such as a Xerox® copier, cannot be used again without violating copyright laws. Customized designs such as buildings, cannot be used again because the exact context will not arise again. Consequently, previous designs cannot simply be re-used. The ideas or the concepts in previous designs can be used again, but their application is necessarily different. This implies that design case adaptation should provide a means of applying a design concept in a new situation or adapting a design description in such a way that the design is not simply "re-used." Unlike using case-based reasoning for diagnosing faults, where a similar situation can point to the same fault, using case-based reasoning in design requires considering the role the design case plays in generating a new design.

Case adaptation can be simply defined as making changes to a recalled case so that it can be used in the current situation. Recognizing what needs to change and how these changes are made are the major considerations. Adapting design cases is more than the surface considerations of making changes to the previous design, it is a design process in itself. Once a previous design has been recalled, the context of the new design is defined, but the solution is not. The adaptation of the previous design is, in effect, designing a new solution. For this reason, adapting design cases is presented more formally in this chapter than the related issues in applying case-based reasoning in design were addressed in previous chapters.

We present a formal method for adapting design cases that addresses the following issues:

- The need for and representation of generalized design knowledge used during adaptation.
- The maintenance of consistent modification when some aspects of a previous design are adapted.
- The verification of a feasible design solution.

Design knowledge is needed to adapt a previous design for a new context. This knowledge can be stored within the design case representation or can be represented in a generalized design knowledge base. Changing some aspects of a design case may introduce inconsistencies in the proposed solution. Knowledge for checking and maintaining consistency is needed for successful adaptation.

In this chapter, we give a brief introduction to generalized methods for case adaptation, each of which is considered in the context of design problem solving. A formal methodology for adapting design cases is presented that makes explicit the representation issues and transformations relevant to design case adaptation. The formal methodology for adapting design cases is explored further by the development of a specific application that makes assumptions about the organization and content of case memory, the available generalized design knowledge, and the use of specific reasoning methods. One strategy for the modification of a design during adaptation is to formulate a constraint satisfaction problem. This strategy is developed further, showing examples of how constraints lead to modifications of design decisions and verify potential design solutions.

A definition of routine versus non-routine design solutions is possible when a formal method is used to generate the design. After the formal method for adapting design cases is presented and further developed through examples, we revisit the method from the perspective of non-routine design. Non-routine design is employed when the available knowledge is insufficient to produce a feasible design (i.e., the constraint satisfaction process fails). The methodology for adapting design cases can then be expanded to include a search for a non-routine design. This revised method for adapting design cases for non-routine design solutions is presented at the end of this chapter.

METHODS OF CASE ADAPTATION

In general, the methods relevant for case adaptation vary for different tasks or problems to be solved. Adaptation can be as simple as substituting some components of a previous solution for others, or can be as complex as modifying the overall structure of an old solution. Several general methods for doing adaptation have been presented in Kolodner (1993). Three general categories of case adaptation are:

1. Substitution.
2. Transformation.
3. Derivational replay.

Substitution methods, as the name implies, rely on the substitution of values or components relevant to the new problem in the recalled case. Transformation methods employ rules or procedures for incrementally changing the recalled case into a new solution. Derivational replay assumes that the recalled case includes the method or procedure used to generate the solution in the case description and that this method is replayed for the specifications of the new problem. The use of the various methods for adaptation requires case and/or generalized knowledge in different forms. The form of knowledge used depends on how adaptation is done. The knowledge supporting adaptation can be commonsense knowledge, heuristics, or causal models specific to a task or domain.

When using CBR as a design process model, case adaptation is a process of generating a new design description. The complexity of design tasks and processes presents new challenges to the adaptation of design cases. General adaptation methods are insufficient to achieve design subgoals, due to the complexity of design solutions. For example, using methods based on the substitution of components or values of old solutions does not take into account the interaction among the newly substituted components and the existing components. In using general-purpose methods for design case adaptation, design problem solving is carried out by domain-independent approaches without taking into account the characteristics of design processes in a specific domain. Though these domain-independent methods are broadly applicable, application of problem solving methods and knowledge specific to a domain often produces better results with less effort.

Design case adaptation is a complicated problem solving process. In developing the method for carrying out the adaptation of design cases, it is necessary to consider domain-specific problem solving approaches along with the use of general purpose methods. Design case adaptation involves identifying the differences between new and old design contexts and modifying the previous design by taking those differences into account. The issues to be addressed in developing an adaptation method in a design context include the representation of domain knowledge for use in adaptation, the maintenance of consistent modification when some aspects are adapted, and the verification of a feasible design solution. Taking into account the multiplicity of possible design domains and the wide range of reasoning techniques available, a formalism for the generalized adaptation of design cases is presented in the next section.

GENERALIZED DESIGN CASE ADAPTATION

Design case adaptation can be described as effecting changes in the representation of a previous design episode so it is consistent with a new design context. Design case adaptation can be described symbolically in (1):

$$C' = \tau (C) \tag{1}$$

where C is the original design case,
       C' is a new design case, and
       τ is the adaptation operation.

To explicitly define design case adaptation, it is useful to clarify the contents of a design case. A design case formalism is described symbolically in (2):

$$C = \{C_p, C_d\} \tag{2}$$

where C_p is the design problem description, and
C_d is the design solution description.

The design case adaptation problem is then defined as follows:

Given
(i)   a new design problem C'_p
(ii)   a previous design description C_d, and a
corresponding design problem C_p in a design case C,
then produce a design solution C'_d by modifying C.

This generalized approach to design case adaptation highlights three aspects of the formalism: It delineates those parts of a design case that can be adapted, it describes what knowledge supports adaptation, and it explains what the adaptation operators are. This approach assumes:

- That case selection provides a description of a specific design solution that is "close" to an acceptable final solution.
- That generalized domain knowledge about causal relations or for decision making is available.
- That design is typically a satisfying problem; that is, a design solution is produced when all relevant constraints are satisfied.

Aspects of a Design Case That Can Be Adapted (C)

The first part of our formalism identifies those elements of a previous design that may need to be transformed. Generating a new design solution includes the identification of design form and the generation of the attributes of the components; that is, design descriptions consist of their constituent parts (components) and their arrangement or configuration (form or structure). For example, in the domain of structural design, the components could be slabs, beams, or columns, whereas the form or structure would be the relationship or arrangement of these elements into functional structural systems (e.g., rigid-frame).

A design description, therefore, represents the object's components and their relationships. This is shown symbolically in (3). In the adaptation of design cases, these two aspects can be modified in order to satisfy the new design specifications by changing the design descriptions of design cases.

$$C_d = \{C_{df}, C_{dc}\} \tag{3}$$

where C_{df} is the design form, and
C_{dc} is the design components.

The distinction between form and component may occur at multiple levels. For a highly decomposable problem, some components at one level of a design have their own internal structures (e.g., a 2D-lateral system is a component of the lateral load resisting system of a whole building, but it also has its own internal components such as beams, slabs, etc.). It is this representation of a decomposition that largely determines what might be adapted from an old design case to make it fit a new problem.

In addition to the components and forms of previous designs, it is often useful to be able to adapt the design problem itself. The design problem specifications in the previous design case can be adapted to match the new design specifications, or, alternatively, specifications in the new design problem may be changed. For example, if a problem cannot be solved because it is over-constrained, one solution to the problem is to reformulate the problem specifications in order to solve a simpler problem. In this sense, specifications in both the new and old design problem descriptions, C'_p and C_p (where C'_p and C_p are sets of specifications), can be adapted in the development of a new design solution.

Therefore, to construct the solution for a new problem by adaptation, the design form and components in a previous design case, as well as the specifications of the new problem and the previous design case, are identified as three adaptable aspects.

So, the adaptation described in (1) can be refined as:

$$C' = \tau(C_{df}, C_{dc}, C'_p, C_p) \tag{4}$$

where C_{df} is the design form or structure of a case,
C_{dc} is the design components of a case, and
C'_p and C_p are the design specifications in the new
problem and previous design case.

To adapt design cases, it is necessary to represent the "degrees of freedom" of adaptable features. Consequently, the potential for adapting these aspects of design cases depends critically on the representation of the adaptability of these aspects. Representing knowledge of adaptability is concerned with the dependency and range of variability of design features. For a given problem, a feature represents an independent variable if it can be directly manipulated, and a dependent variable if it cannot be. A feature is dependent if it is causally or functionally determined by other features. Such information is often provided by domain specific knowledge. For example, the bending moment of a beam is determined by some independent design features, such as beam-type (e.g., simple, continuous), load, and span. To change the values of the bending moment, it is necessary to review the associated independent features.

The range of variability of a feature indicates the degree of variation possible for that feature from instance to instance. This information can be categorized into two forms: a discrete set of potential values or a continuous range of numerical values. In adapting previous designs, the ranges of variability of features provide alternatives in decision making.

Knowledge That Supports Adaptation (K)

Previous designs cannot be reused without making some changes. Reasoning about those changes requires domain-specific knowledge to guide design decision making during adaptation. In addition, adaptation is a type of plausible reasoning, and the result of adaptation is often plausible but inconsistent. Adaptation in a design context necessarily uses knowledge to revise the adapted design and maintain the feasibility of the adapted design.

In general, knowledge about adaptation represents causal relations or reasons for decision making. This knowledge defines the capability of case-based design systems to generate design solutions. We reconsider (2) to include the knowledge for supporting adaptation, and generate (5):

$$C' = \tau\,(C, K) \tag{5}$$

During the adaptation of design cases, verification knowledge, K_v, is used to revise the case for consistency with the new problem and compare the adapted design against design criteria. Modification knowledge, K_m, guides the refinement of the adapted design by modifying unfeasible design decisions. The domain knowledge for design adaptation can be stated symbolically as in (6):

$$K = \{K_v, K_m\} \tag{6}$$

where K_v is verification knowledge, and
        K_m is modification knowledge.

The knowledge for adaptation can be represented through formalisms as generalized design knowledge, or embodied in individual design cases as part of the content of a design case. If the knowledge for adaptation is kept within each case, design cases may be very large, or there may be a representation of the same general knowledge in many cases. Generally, the nature of the design domain or set of problems helps determine the representation of adaptation knowledge.

Adaptation Operators (τ)

Adapting a previous design situation to be a solution to a new design problem is a problem solving process based on analogical reasoning. In theory, transformational analogy and derivational analogy (Carbonell, 1983, 1986) provide two basic inferences to adapt designs, but how to practically apply the ideas suggested in these methods varies with each design domain. Moreover, the complexity of design case adaptation has been underestimated, with a tendency for it to be modeled as the application of simple algorithms and heuristics. More commonly, multiple problem solving strategies are used in the adaptation of design cases to address the complexity.

When a complete causal domain theory or derivational trace of problem solving is available, derivational transformation is beneficial. However, without a complete derivational trace or causal model, a case-based design problem solver should exploit whatever domain knowledge is available to adapt a design.

An *adaptation operator* is defined here as a transformational process of changing previous design descriptions along with the necessary verification and modification of the adapted design into a new design description. A symbolic representation of the adaptation operator is shown in (7). An adaptation operation involves efficiently proposing plausible solutions, testing and verifying the validity of those solutions, and repairing invalid design parts as necessary.

$$\tau = \{\tau_p, \tau_v, \tau_m\} \tag{7}$$

where τ_p is a propose operation, and
τ_v is a verify operation, and
τ_m is a modify operation.

In the proposed operation, the design problem specifications of a previous case are compared with those of a new design problem. A plausible design for the new problem is proposed by structurally considering the previous design case as a potential solution, during which the discrepancies between the new design specifications and the previous design case are resolved. This phase of adaptation utilizes an empirical methodology to structurally or syntactically adapt the previous design case. Specifically, this adaptation operator is concerned with changing the design case to establish the consistency of old and new design contexts. We define this adaptation operation on the design problem specifications (C_p and C'_p) as a structural operation τ_s, where τ_s is a refinement of the more general operation, τ_p in (7). Domain independent substitution methods based on a set of general rules are often used to carry out the structural operator:

$$C's = \tau(C_p, C'_p) \tag{8}$$

where τ_s is an operation that makes C_p and C'_p consistent, and
C_s is a potential new design solution.

The construction of a potential design solution based on a consistent mapping from C_p to C'_p introduces inconsistencies within the adapted design case, so the solution must be checked for validity. To ensure consistency within the adapted design case, verification of the potential design (τ_v) and its possible modification (τ_m) are linked to form a single abstract operation. This operation characterizes the analytical aspects of adaptation, so it is referred to as an *analytical operation*, τ_a:

$$\tau_a = \{\tau_v, \tau_m\} \tag{9}$$

where τ_a is the analytical adaptation operator,
τ_v is the verify operator, and
τ_m is the modify operator.

The analytical operation uses domain-specific knowledge and specific reasoning models during the assessment of the potential design's feasibility and the modification of any invalid design elements. Given an adapted design, C'_s the analytical operation produces a feasible design C' by adapting C'_s, with the guidance of design domain knowledge K, including K_v and K_m, as shown in (10):

$$C' = \tau_a (C'_s, K_v, K_m) \tag{10}$$

The strategies for the evaluation and modification of a proposed design case are generally influenced by the representation of domain knowledge and reasoning processes. Techniques for analytical adaptation often rely on underlying problem solving processes (e.g., constraint satisfaction, qualitative reasoning, model-based reasoning, and heuristic reasoning).

In summary, design case adaptation can be generalized as consisting of three parts:

- The adaptable aspects of a design case: design form, C_{df}, design components, C_{dc}, and design specifications in the old and new problems, C_p, and C'_p.
- The domain knowledge needed for adaptation: verification knowledge, K_v, and modification knowledge, K_m.
- The nature of adaptation operators: structural operator, τ_s, and analytical operator, τ_a.

Discussion

Adapting design cases can be thought of as a process of generating a new design by modifying previous design descriptions along with the verification and maintenance of consistencies within the adapted design. The adaptation process is intrinsically a small problem solver (Hammond, 1989). Developing an adaptation method is, in fact, often related to the nature of the design problem at hand, in terms of design cases, design domain knowledge, and reasoning processes used, in order to find a solution to a problem. These three elements are indicated in Figure 5.1.

The use of domain knowledge and other problem solving methods in the adaptation of design cases raises the issue of the integration of different types of knowledge and reasoning methods within the framework of adaptation. The types of available design knowledge and reasoning methods vary from context to context. As a consequence of this, it is possible to characterize the adaptation generally, but each implementation differs.

In JULIA, a design case represents an individual meal description by attribute-value pairs. C_{df} and C_{dc} are expressed as courses and dishes or dishes and ingredients. The verification knowledge, K_v, is formulated as generalized constraints. During adaptation, the modification knowledge, K_m, is represented in a menu taxonomy. The structural operation, τ_s, is characterized as a replacement process in which a general skeleton of a new menu is generated by substituting the values from a previous meal's menu. Then, the analytical operation, τ_a, gradually refines and evaluates the potential meal through a constraint satisfaction cycle.

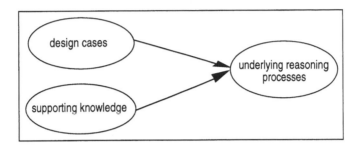

Figure 5.1. Design case adaptation is problem solving.

In CADRE, a design case is represented in multiple levels. Thus, design form and components, C_{df} and C_{dc}, are identified (e.g., building geometric description level and structural parameters level). An operator called *dimensional adaptation* performs a structural operation, τ_s. This operation changes the values of the numerical parameters that describe the geometry of a previous architectural design to form a potential design description to a new problem. Verification knowledge, K_v, is a set of design constraints, whereas modification knowledge, K_m, is a set of production rules and shape grammars that modify the topological description of the potential design. In this system, rule-based reasoning, as an analytical operation, τ_a, is used to maintain topological consistencies in adapting design cases.

KRITIK and CADET are two device design systems that represent the specific design case and domain knowledge, including verification knowledge, K_v, and modification knowledge, K_m, in an integrated formalism. Design form and design components, C_{df} and C_{dc}, are embodied as design devices and their component parts in the design cases. In both systems, qualitative reasoning is used to perform the analytical operation, τ_a, in the adaptation process. KRITIK uses a functional mapping between the new design contexts and the previous design case as the structural operation, τ_s. The knowledge for adaptation, including K_v and K_m, is integrated and represented in terms of relationships among the function, structure, and behavior of devices. In CADET, the structural operation, τ_s, is characterized as a mapping based on a linguistic description. A case-based synthesis process by adaptation produces a correct design by qualitative reasoning (τ_a) based on domain knowledge, K_v and K_m, which is presented as causal graphs and qualitative relationships.

The adaptation process in the applications we have presented, based on the terminology used in the generalized design case adaptation description, is shown in Table 5.1.

	C_{df} and C_{dc}	τ_s	τ_a	K_v	K_m
JULIA	courses, dishes, and ingredients	replacement	constraint satisfaction	generalized constraints	generalized taxonomy
CADRE	hierarchical description of building	dimensional adaptation	rule-based reasoning	constraints	production rules and shape grammars
KRITIK	devices and their components	functional mapping	qualitative reasoning	relationships among function, behavior, and structure	
CADET	devices and their components	linguistic description	qualitative reasoning	causal graphs and qualitative relationships	

Table 5.1. Different approaches to design case adaptation.

A SPECIFIC APPLICATION OF DESIGN CASE ADAPTATION

Generally, design case adaptation has been introduced in order to clarify the considerations for the entire process. The development of the computational process for design case adaptation depends on the nature of the design problem, including the consideration of the contents of design cases, the available domain-specific knowledge, and the reasoning processes appropriate to the design task. Therefore, the contents and representation of design cases and domain knowledge supporting adaptation, as well as the choice of underlying reasoning methods for adaptation operators, vary in different models of design adaptation. In order to demonstrate the use of the generalized design case adaptation presented previously, this section presents a specific application of design case adaptation for the structural design of buildings. Three issues are resolved: the contents and representation of design cases, the contents and representation of domain knowledge supporting adaptation, and the computational models of the adaptation operators.

The following representation decisions are made in the specific application:

1. A design case is represented in a hierarchy comprized of multiple subcases.
2. Verification knowledge is encoded as a set of elimination constraints.
3. Modification knowledge provides a space of design attributes and their potential values.
4. The adaptation operation comprises a substitution process based on a set of adaptation rules and a constraint satisfaction method.

Representation of Design Cases as a Hierarchy

A design case is comprised of specifications for a design problem and an associated design solution description. To support the adaptation process, a design case is stored declaratively in a hierarchical structure consisting of multiple subcases. The hierarchy of subcases can be produced based on the decomposition of the design task. Within each subcase, the design is described by attributes categorized as design specification or design solution. Each subcase represents a description of a solution for a specific subproblem. The subcases form a partonomic hierarchy, where the children of a node are part of the parent. An illustration of a generalized hierarchy for a design case is shown in Figure 5.2. Such an organizational structure for design cases allows the potential use of both specific design knowledge in each subcase and overall design knowledge in an entire case. Having each subcase correspond to a subtask makes it possible to combine multiple subcases from different design cases to generate a new design solution.

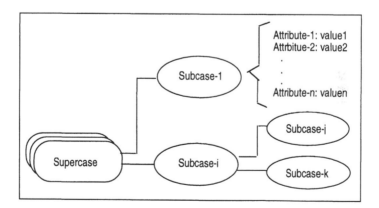

Figure 5.2. Generalized hierarchy for a design case.

An example of a design case in the structural design of buildings is shown in Figure 5.3. The overall context of the design problem (C_p) is described in the case part of the hierarchy, GEN-CASE, which represents design specifications, such as a general description of an 18-story concrete office building; geometric information, including length, width, and load information; and so on. The design description of the case (C_d) is represented as subcases in the hierarchy, such as LATERAL-X-SYS, GRAVITY-SYS, and 2D-LATERAL-X. Each subcase has a local definition of the design problem specifications, C_p, as well as a description of the design solution, C_d.

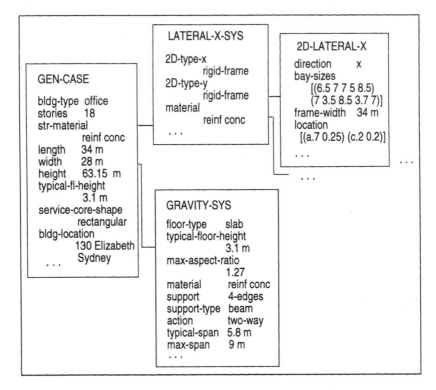

Figure 5.3. The hierarchical representation of a previous design case.

Having the design description organized as a hierarchy implies that the relationship between form and components occurs at multiple levels. In such a hierarchical representation, a lower subcase can be related to a component (C_{dc}) of a higher subcase, which can then be viewed as a design form (C_{df}). 2D-LATERAL-X is one of the design components (C_{dc}), whereas LATERAL-X-SYS is regarded as a design form (C_{df}) for the 2D-LATERAL-X subcase.

Representation of Design Knowledge for Adaptation

Design case adaptation is supported by verification knowledge, K_v, and modification knowledge, K_m. The design knowledge for adaptation used in this application is represented through generalized schemes, which are stored separately from the individual design cases. Verification knowledge, K_v, is represented as design constraints. Modification knowledge, K_m is grouped in multiple generalized design systems.

Design constraints are used to identify inconsistencies in the potential design solution. Because attribute-value pairs are used to describe the design case, each constraint is expressed as a set of attribute-value pairs that indicate an invalid design when they occur together. For example, in Figure 5.4, Constraint 1 specifies that slab is not used as the floor-type in a hotel or apartment building, or, when the floor-type is slab and the building-type is either hotel or apartment, then the design is invalid. Constraints 2, 3, and 4 indicate the conditions for when the flat-plate and flat-slab work as one-way or two-way floor systems.

```
Constraint-1
    (bldg-type) in (hotel apartment)
    (gravity/floor-type) = slab
Constraint-2
    (gravity/floor-type) = flat-plate
    (gravity/action)    = one-way
    (gravity/typical-span) <10 m
Constraint-3
    (gravity/floor-type) in (flat-plate slab)
    (gravity/typical-span) > 9 m
    (gravity/action) = two-way
Constraint4
    (gravity/support) in (4-edges cols-only)
    (gravity/max-aspect-ratio) > 1.5
    (gravity/action)  = two-way
```

Figure 5.4. Examples of design constraints.

Design systems knowledge is the representation of modification knowledge (K_m). Generalized (sub)systems are represented by their attributes, as well as the potential values for the attributes. Relationships among design systems create a hierarchy from more general to more specific; this hierarchy conforms to the design case hierarchy.

Figure 5.5 illustrates a hierarchical ontology for the structural design of buildings with each node representing a design system. An example of the generalized system description for the node gravity system is given in Figure 5.5. The potential values for the attributes are described as a set of values following the word selection, or as a continuous range of numerical values from which one value is computed using the procedure specified.

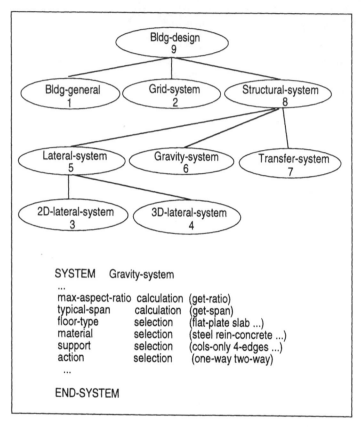

Figure 5.5. A hierarchy of structural systems and the description of the gravity system.

Representation of Adaptation Operators

In this specific application, the adaptation operators are modeled as a substitution operation and a constraint satisfaction method. Thus, τ_s is performed by a substituting process based on a set of heuristic adaptation rules, and τ_a is characterized by applying a constraint satisfaction process.

In the structural adaptation operator, problem specifications of the retrieved case and the new design problem, C_p and C'_p, are consistently mapped. A plausible design, C'_s, to the new problem is proposed by structurally considering the previous design description, C_d, as a potential design solution. To perform the structural adaptation, the previous design case becomes the initial potential design solution; then, a set of heuristic rules is applied to resolve the inconsistencies of attribute-value pairs between the new design problem and the previous design case.

The rules add new attribute-value pairs to the potential design solution or change the value of existing attributes. The rules are briefly stated as:

- If a new design specification is not in the previous design case, then add the new design specification to the potential design solution.
- If the value of a new design specification is different from the value of the same specification in previous design case, then change the value to match the new design specification.

Figure 5.6 shows the description for a problem of designing a gravity system for a 12-story hotel.

bldg-type	hotel
wind-load	20 psf
stories	12
length	36 m
width	23 m
height	29 m
typical-floor-height	3.4 m
...	

Figure 5.6. Part of the specified requirements for a hotel design.

Based on these rules, the case in Figure 5.3 is adapted and a potential design, C'_s, to the problem in Figure 5.6 is proposed in Figure 5.7, where "typical-floor-height" in the gravity system, for example, is adapted to a new value based on the new design problem specification, and "max-aspect-ratio" is associated indirectly with the problem specifications and is updated by evaluating its procedure. The attribute "wind-load" is added to the potential design solution, C'_s.

The analytical operation, τ_a, is concerned with the removal of inconsistencies within the proposed design description, C'_s, to the new problem. A constraint satisfaction approach is adopted to detect the inconsistent parts and search for acceptable substitutions for them. This is done by identifying violated constraints, selecting decisions related to violated constraints, and then searching for new values for these decisions.

In this model, the design decisions are viewed as design attributes and their values. When the adapted design generated in Figure 5.7 is tested against the constraints, K_V, in Figure 5.4, Constraints 1 and 4 are violated, and invalid design attribute-value pairs associated with the violated constraints are found in the adapted design solution. The attribute-value pairs in boldface are invalid design decisions. This information provides a basis for modification of the adapted design.

The values for the attributes "floor-type," "support," and "action" are defined by a set of possible values. These three attributes can therefore be adapted directly. Based on the domain of these three attributes in the modification knowledge in Figure 5.5, floor-type can be substituted by "flat-plate," support as "4-edges," and action as "one-way." Checking the constraints again shows that this potential design solution does not violate any constraints.

```
┌─────────────────────────────────────────────┐
│ Design context                              │
│                                             │
│         bldg-type            hotel          │
│         stories              12             │
│         length              36 m            │
│         width               23 m            │
│         height              19 m            │
│         wind-load           20 psf          │
│         typical-floor-height 3.4 m          │
│         str-material        reinf conc      │
│         ...                                 │
│                                             │
│ Gravity-system                              │
│         ...                                 │
│         typical-floor-height 3.4 m          │
│         max-aspect-ratio    1.56            │
│         typical-span        8 m             │
│         floor-type          slab            │
│         support             4-edge          │
│         action              two-way         │
│         material            reinf conc      │
│         ...                                 │
└─────────────────────────────────────────────┘
```

Figure 5.7. Example of an adapted design and its invalid attribute-value pairs.

We have illustrated design verification and modification in a relatively simple situation. When constraint violations become more complicated (e.g., the design decisions involved in the violated constraints come from multiple subcases of the adapted design), the dependencies and associations among the invalid attribute-value pairs make modification of the adapted design more complicated. The attribute-value pairs can be ordered and modified incrementally, rather than all in one cycle. The adaptation model presented can be characterized as a constraint satisfaction process that eliminates constraint violations in a potential solution. The details of the constraint satisfaction process can vary from implementation to implementation. Further consideration of design case adaptation as a constraint satisfaction problem is given in the next section. The computer implementation of the constraint satisfaction strategy described in this chapter is presented in Chapter 7.

ADAPTATION AS A CONSTRAINT SATISFACTION PROBLEM

Adaptation can be characterized as a heuristic search using a constraint satisfaction process. This adaptation by constraint satisfaction eliminates constraint violations in a potential solution by searching for acceptable substitutions for the design attributes.

The constraint satisfaction approach has been used in other case-based design systems for adaptation. Because constraint satisfaction problems (CSPs) are typically solved using heuristic search methods, the adaptation process based on a constraint satisfaction approach is characterized as searching for consistent assignments for all design features by using previous design descriptions and available design knowledge. However, search methods for feasible or legal substitutions vary in different adaptation methods.

The parametric adaptation stratgey (Sycara, Navinchandra, and Narasimhan, 1992) of CBR used in CADET can be formally characterized as a CSP in terms of set-theoretic operations. Cases are used to guide the search and to introduce partial solutions that can help reduce the search effort. The set-theoretic operations are domain-independent, and are concerned with dropping or relaxing constraints and resolving an impasse. This research work develops a theoretical approach to adaptation using the idea of constraint satisfaction.

Hua and Faltings implemented an adaptation model using constraint satisfaction for architectural spatial design in CADRE (Faltings, Hua, Schmitt, and Shih, 1991; Hua et al., 1992). The application deals with the problem of an integrated task of a building design from different perspectives (e.g., civil engineer, architect, user). The combination of dimensional and topological adaptations performs a constraint satisfaction process, producing a new spatial design. Constraints maintain the integrity of the building geometry. The adaptation is handled by algebraically solving the adaptation constraints violated in the new environment to find a legal combination for the parameters' values. The dimensional reduction approach generates solutions that simultaneously satisfy a set of different violated constraints with shared parameters.

In JULIA (Hinrichs and Kolodner, 1991), constraints play a major role in the generalized domain knowledge about meal planning. The generation of a new menu follows a problem reduction paradigm that initially produces a consistent partial solution at a general level, then gradually reaches a complete detailed solution based on the maintenance of consistency through constraint satisfaction. In the development of a new menu, the design decisions are treated as CSPs, in which potential variable assignments are generated and evaluated as part of the decision making process. In this model, the constraint satisfaction is performed throughout the generation of a new design.

In CADSYN (Maher and Zhang, 1993), constraints are represented separately from the case-based representation of specific design knowledge. The domains of variables are provided by generalized decomposition knowledge, which represents problem solving strategies. The constraint satisfaction process starts with a complete and inconsistent assignment for all variables and incrementally repairs constraint violations to reach a consistent solution. The determination of which invalid decision is to be modified first becomes a major issue and is based on the problem solving sequence in the decomposition approach.

Characterizing CSP in Adaptation

A variety of constraint satisfaction methods have been explored for computer science purposes. They are independent of specific domains and rarely reflect the nature of the domain knowledge available, other than to use heuristics to guide the search. Also, most computer science methods assume that the domain of the variables is a discrete set of values and/or that the constraints define the boundaries of the search space. While many of the ideas used in classic CSP solving are relevant to our design case adaptation, their implementation as algorithms is not directly applicable. In order to present our constraint satisfaction strategies, it is worthwhile to elaborate on a characterization of CSP in our adaptation model. The CSP problem in our adaptation framework can be characterized in terms of three aspects:

1. The domain of the design attributes.
2. The nature of the design constraints.
3. Attributes participating in multiple design constraints.

First, design attributes fall into two kinds of domains: One is a discrete domain; the other is a continuous domain. The domain of an attribute provides alternative values for that attribute. In our case, domains of attributes are represented in the design systems of the decomposition knowledge. Some design attributes are represented by the selection from a set of discrete values, whereas others are represented by the evaluation of functional procedures. The attributes with discrete domains are independent attributes, because their values can be selected independently of other attributes. The attributes with continuous domains are dependent, because the procedures for determining the value require other attributes.

The second feature of CSP is concerned with the nature of design constraints; that is, the presence of design constraints implies dependencies among constraining attributes. Some design constraints specify the restrictions on the values of independent attributes. The violation of such a constraint can be repaired by directly changing the values of any independent attributes involved. Some other constraints specify the relationships that must hold among dependent attributes. Repairing the violation of such a constraint proceeds in two steps: first, determining associated independent attributes with those dependent attributes involved in the constraint; and second, searching for valid values for the independent attributes in order to change the values of the dependent attributes.

Another characteristic of CSP is that design attributes in the different subcases are associated with multiple constraints. A hierarchical representation of a design case implies that attributes are grouped according to the subcase with which they belong. Each subcase has a corresponding system in the generalized decomposition knowledge. Design knowledge represented in terms of a hierarchy of systems leads to two types of associations among attributes in a constraint. One is within a system, the other is across systems. During the modification of a potential design, the changes of values of attributes can fix some constraint violations, but they can also cause the violation of other constraints. For example, in Figure 5.8, some design variables in node-5 (system) appear in the three constraints, C1, C2, and C4. It is possible that by repairing the violation of C1, the modification of the value of an attribute in node-5 could cause constraints C2 or C4 to be violated.

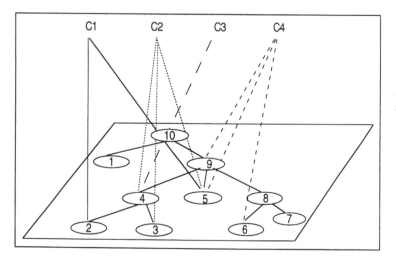

Figure 5.8. Association among constraints and attributes in systems.

Constraint Satisfaction Strategies for Design Case Adaptation

Considering these features, a design-specific constraint satisfaction approach is needed. Design case adaptation takes an initially inconsistent assignment for the design attributes and incrementally repairs constraint violations through a heuristic search process until a consistent assignment is achieved. In general, the adaptation operation by constraint satisfaction generates a feasible design by modifying the invalid systems in the inconsistent potential design. Invalid systems of the potential design are found by testing constraints and are modified by using generalized design systems adapted by constraint satisfaction. The determination of which invalid system is to be modified first then becomes a central task.

Given that the form and components of a design description in a design case are the adaptable aspects of the design case, it is they that are to be modified during CSP solving. When more than one system of a potential design are found to be invalid and need to be modified, the form-component relationships between these systems provide the guidance for selecting the invalid systems for modification. In other words, invalid systems of the potential design are modified according to certain heuristics. The heuristics specify that systems related to design components are given higher modification privileges because changing the detailed descriptions of component systems has no impact on form systems.

The heuristics for the selection of an invalid system are developed by considering the associations among invalid systems and violated constraints. The selection heuristics are embodied in a set of rules. Each rule attempts to select out a set of systems. When a heuristic rule does this, that set is sent to the next rule for pruning. When no subset of systems is selected using some rule, however, the entire set it was selected from is selected. In this way, the heuristic rules act as selectors, rather than restrictors. The heuristic rules used to select an invalid system for modification are:

> *Rule 1. Select the system which violates the most constraints.* This rule is based on the principle of repairing the most violated constraints in one cycle of the CSP. That is, if a system is involved in many violated constraints, appropriate modification of this system can satisfy all of these constraints.
>
> *Rule 2. Select the system if it is the only adaptable system associated with a violated constraint.* An adaptable system is one that is not part of the problem specifications. If only one of a constraint's attributes is in an adaptable system, then this system must be modified, regardless of other constraint violations.
>
> *Rule 3. Select the system at the lowest level of the decomposition hierarchy when two or more systems violate the same constraint.* The rule is based on the principle of changing component systems before form systems, thereby causing less change to the entire solution.

Rule 4. Select the system appearing earlier in the sequence of problem solving. This rule avoids unnecessary modification work and is based on the sequence in which the subsystems were designed.

Design case adaptation using constraint satisfaction consists of six main steps, as shown in Figure 5.9:

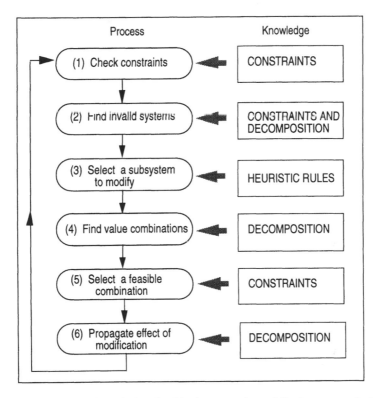

Figure 5.9. The basic tasks involved in the constraint satisfaction process in the adaptation.

1. Checking and looking for constraint violations in the potential solution.
2. Finding design subsystems involved in the violated constraints.
3. Selecting one system to modify.
4. Generating all feasible combinations of values for the selected system.
5. Selecting a combination of values as a new description of the selected system.
6. Propagating the effect of modifications by recomputing the associated procedures.

The process iterates by identifying new constraint violations until all constraints are satisfied. The six basic tasks in the constraint satisfaction process are further described below.

Checking Constraints. The potential design that is produced based on the structural adaptation of the retrieved (sub)case provides an initial assignment for design attributes. The routine adaptation process then commences by comparing this assignment to the design constraints in the generalized knowledge. This process identifies the violated constraints and the attributes associated with the constraints. If no constraints are violated, the current assignment for design attributes is regarded as a feasible design solution, and adaptation is completed.

Finding Invalid Systems. In order to repair constraint violations that have been detected, all adaptable systems related to those violations are listed. The attributes in a violated constraint are characterized as independent, having discrete domains from which new values of attributes can be selected, or dependent, having continuous domains. All systems corresponding to the independent design attributes in violated constraints are taken as invalid systems. For dependent attributes in violated constraints, the invalid systems are identified by the independent attributes associated with the dependent attributes. The systems corresponding to associated independent attributes with these dependent attributes are treated as invalid systems.

Selecting an Invalid System. After all invalid systems involved in constraint violations are identified, one system is selected for modification. The set of heuristic rules is used to select an invalid system.

Finding Value Combinations. A value for an attribute can be determined from a discrete set of values, or it can be computed using a procedure. The possible value combinations for the selected system are generated by assigning possible discrete attributes, then recomputing dependent attributes based on the value combinations of discrete attributes. All candidate value assignments are checked for local consistency. The constraints related to this system are regarded as local constraints. The result is a set of value combinations without local constraint violations. These value combinations are candidate descriptions of the selected system.

Selecting a Feasible Combination. Given a set of value combinations, one of them is identified as the new description of the selected invalid system. The determination of which value combination is used as a new system description is based on satisfaction of global constraints. The value combination that violates the least global constraints is regarded as a new design description.

Propagating the Effect of Modification. Repairing a constraint violation leads to a new value combination of a selected invalid system. Because multiple systems are associated through constraints and dependent attributes, appropriate modification needs to be made concurrently on other systems associated with the selected system. This process propagates the effect of modification on the selected system to those relevant dependent attributes. To do so, all relevant attributes with continuous domains in the potential design description are updated by evaluating their corresponding procedures.

CREATIVE DESIGN AS NON-ROUTINE ADAPTATION

The result of the adaptation of a design case can be classified as routine design or creative design. Routine design is featured as well-defined problem solving where both the solutions and the strategies for deriving the solutions are known a priori (Buhl, 1985; Brown and Chandrasekaran, 1985; Coyne, Rosenman, Radford, Balachandran, and Gero, 1990). The knowledge for routine adaptation in our model is well defined. Generalized design systems provide search spaces for the modification of invalid systems. A heuristic constraint satisfaction search process is presented as the strategy for routine adaptation by which constraint violations are incrementally repaired. During this process, invalid systems are modified by the substitutions of the values of design attributes in the systems. This adaptation can be thought of as a routine adaptation, in the sense that the design solution is found by searching predefined design spaces represented as generalized design systems.

Design problems are formulated as a set of specifications. A design problem is under-constrained when the given problem specifications under-specify the problem. There are many possible solutions for an under-constrained problem. In our model of adaptation by constraint satisfaction, if the solution for a problem can be generated by adapting the design descriptions of design cases, this problem is under-constrained.

Sometimes problem specifications over-constrain the design problem. In an over-constrained problem, no solution is possible if all constraints are satisfied. An over-constrained problem is identified as an impasse in the process of adaptation. When adaptation by constraint satisfaction fails to find a solution by changing the design description of a case, the problem is over-constrained. The solution to an over-constrained problem implies a non-routine adaptation.

The overall task of design case adaptation, consequently, is divided into two levels, routine adaptation and non-routine adaptation, which, respectively, deal with under-constrained and over-constrained problems. Given an inconsistent assignment of design attributes adapted from a previous design, constraint satisfaction strategies find a design solution to an under-constrained problem by modifying unfeasible design decisions. Whenever an impasse occurs in adaptation by constraint satisfaction, the design problem is treated as an over-constrained one and is converted to an under-constrained problem. Considered in this way, the solution space for a routine adaptation is a subspace of the solution space for non-routine adaptation, as illustrated in Figure 5.10.

In routine adaptation, new values of attributes for invalid systems are generated during the modification of a potential design. Sometimes, routine adaptation also changes the design form of the potential design by producing new subcases based on generalized design systems knowledge. Routine adaptation, therefore, can be described as modification of design component systems and design form systems in the potential design to meet new design requirements.

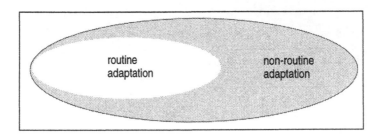

Figure 5.10 Routine and non-routine adaptation.

When the routine adaptation strategies are unable to produce the solution for a given design problem in adaptation by constraint satisfaction, the problem is considered over-constrained in our adaptation model. Solving an over-constrained problem in adaptation by constraint satisfaction is viewed as non-routine adaptation. An over-constrained problem is recognized as an impasse in the constraint satisfaction process. This section discusses the methods for recognizing an impasse, the strategies for non-routine adaptation, and the types of over-constrained problems defined by impasses in adaptation by constraint satisfaction.

Recognizing an Impasse

An impasse means that the process goes on, but is not able to find a consistent assignment of attributes through simply modifying form and component systems in the potential design description. To recognize an impasse, all violated constraints and relevant attribute-value pairs are stored for each modification iteration. On the whole, an impasse occurs when the information about the current modification state matches previously recorded information. There are three possible circumstances in which impasses can occur:

1. The same violated constraints appear in a previous repairing iteration.
2. All values for independent variables have been tried.
3. All adaptable variables are from design problem specifications, not from design form or components systems.

When the same set of constraints remain unsatisfied after several modification iterations, this impasse implies that the alternative values of the design attributes involved in these constraints are not capable of satisfying these constraints concurrently.

The second form of impasse is present when a specific constraint violation cannot be satisfied. Such a situation arises if all values of independent attributes involved in a constraint violation have been tried, and the constraint is still not satisfied. Furthermore, this situation is caused by the lack of more alternative values for independent attributes.

Another form of impasse is when the design problem itself is over-constrained. This situation happens when it is found that the attributes that must be changed in order to repair constraint violations are from the design problem specifications.

Strategies for Non-Routine Adaptation

One principle for non-routine adaptation is converting an impasse situation to a situation where a design solution can be found by using strategies of routine adaptation. Releasing an impasse and applying the strategies of routine adaptation are treated together during the non-routine adaptation. Once an impasse is recognized, it must be broken in some way, the potential design is then adapted based on the strategies of routine adaptation during which a new impasse may be recognized. This process continues until a feasible design description is achieved. The strategies for non-routine adaptation, therefore, are mainly concerned with the detection and breaking of an impasse.

It is worthwhile understanding how and why an impasse occurs in order to further explore non-routine adaptation. Based on the three impasse circumstances described, an over-constrained design problem may be caused by three general events. These are:

1. An inappropriate problem statement.
2. The same state reached again in constraint satisfaction.
3. Incomplete domain knowledge.

Accordingly, the following techniques for non-routine adaptation can be pursued:

- Revise the problem statement.
- Relax one of the contradictory constraints.
- Add new values to the domains of attributes.
- Add new attributes.

Revise Problem Statement. When the specifications of a design problem are inconsistent, adaptation by constraint satisfaction treats the problem as an over-constrained problem. To solve this problem in non-routine adaptation, the specifications of the problem can be reconsidered to make the specifications consistent with one another. Non-routine adaptation can then generate a solution to the reformulated problem by using routine adaptation processes.

The specifications of a given problem can be reconsidered using the violated constraints as a guide. For example, assume the problem is stated as a concrete building design with 50 levels. The current problem specifications violate the constraint that design material cannot be concrete when the number of levels of a building is more then 40. To resolve this impasse, this problem could be refined as a steel building with 50 levels.

Relax One Constraint. When several constraints cannot be satisfied concurrently by modifying the potential design, non-routine adaptation relaxes one constraint from those constraints. In other words, the verification knowledge is changed in non-routine adaptation.

For example, three constraints are employed to check whether the core has uplift and cannot be satisfied at the same time by a potential design in the adaptation by constraint satisfaction. One of the given constraints could be removed in order to satisfy the remaining constraints.

Expand the Domains of Attributes. One of the major reasons for impasses is the incompleteness of domain knowledge. A solution to an impasse in non-routine adaptation could be the expansion of the domains of attributes. In the process of adaptation, if none of alternative values for an attribute satisfies some constraints, new values can be added to the domain of the attribute to satisfy the violated constraints.

For example, in the lateral system, the domain of attribute "2D-lateral-type" has two alternative values, rigid-frame and braced-frame. During adaptation, neither of these two values could satisfy the new design specifications and design constraints. The domain of "2D-lateral-type" can be extended by adding "truss-based-frame" in order to expand the design space.

Add New Attributes. Adding new attributes to the domain knowledge, another technique of non-routine adaptation, also addresses the incompleteness of domain knowledge. In this technique, new design attributes are added to design systems in the decomposition knowledge. In this case, non-routine adaptation occurs in the sense that the design space defined by domain knowledge is changed.

For example, the gravity design is represented in the current domain knowledge by attributes "floor-type," "typical-span," "material," "support," and so on. When none of the value combinations for the gravity system based on the current system definition can meet the problem specifications, a new attribute, "subsidiary-support," can be added to the current gravity system definition. A design solution may now be produced based on the new gravity system definition.

Characterizing an Impasse

In non-routine adaptation, an impasse is represented as a set of constraints and a set of involved systems. Based on the associations among constraints and involved systems, an impasse can be characterized as one of three basic groups:

- Partially shared.
- Interwoven.
- Isolated.

To simplify the description, it is assumed that all violated constraints have two systems involved. In representing an impasse, a constraint is indicated by a circle with two symbols; a shadowed area indicates a common system among several violated constraints.

If all violated constraints have a common system, the impasse is a partially shared situation. An impasse with a common system is illustrated in Figure 5.11, where S_4 is a common system.

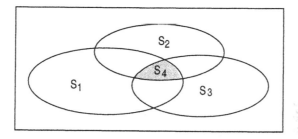

Figure 5.11 A partially shared impasse.

If two constraints share different systems of another constraint in a chain, it is an interwoven situation. In the situation shown in Figure 5.12, systems S_2 and S_3 are shared by two constraints in a chain.

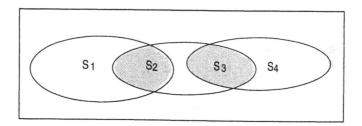

Figure 5.12. An interwoven impasse with two shared systems.

In contrast, if two or more constraints exist independently in an impasse, it is an isolated situation (e.g., as illustrated in Figure 5.13).

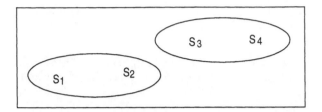

Figure 5.13. An isolated impasse with no common systems.

These three circumstances are the basic types of impasses. An impasse might be more complex than these basic types. Based on the basic types of impasses, a complicated impasse can be decomposed into several sets of basic types. For example, in Figure 5.14, a complex impasse is decomposed into two basic types of impasses: one is partially shared, the other is interwoven.

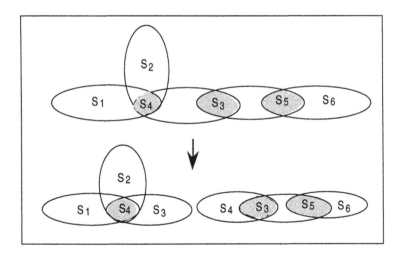

Figure 5.14. Decomposing a complex impasse into basic types.

Based on the representation of an impasse, sets of basic types of impasses can be identified. The four techniques presented can then be applied to the impasse according to its basic groups.

An effective way to solve a partially shared type of impasse is to focus on the common system. When the shared system is related to the design description (e.g., design form or design components) of a potential design, one may add new attributes and extend the domains of attributes. When the shared system is a design problem system, one may redefine the problem specifications.

To solve an interwoven type of impasse, relaxing the shared constraint could be the most efficient strategy. Of course, resolving the common systems is an alternative resort for breaking the impasse.

To solve the isolated type of impasse, all techniques mentioned can be adopted. Each constraint involved in an isolated impasse can be either relaxed or satisfied by one of following three techniques: reformulating the design problem, if the problem system is a participant in the constraint; extending the domains of existing attributes of the systems involved in the constraints; or exploring new variables in the systems involved in the constraint.

5.5.4 Non-Routine Adaptation Processes

Non-routine adaptation resolves the impasses occurring in adaptation by constraint satisfaction. Strategies for non-routine adaptation involve resolving an impasse and applying routine constraint satisfaction. Four techniques have been presented as means of breaking an impasse. Sometimes, more than one technique is applicable to an impasse. In such a situation, the determination of which technique is to be used is based on a specified order:

- Refining the problem specifications.
- Relaxing constraints.
- Extending the domains of variables.
- Exploring new variables.

Once an impasse occurs during the adaptation by constraint satisfaction, the processes of non-routine adaptation can be generalized by the following steps, where Step 3 and Step 5 are concerned with the processes of routine adaptation:

Step 1. Identify the basic groups of constraints in the impasse.
Step 2. Choose an appropriate technique for resolving the impasse.
Step 3. Test design constraints: If all constraints are satisfied, the adaptation is terminated.
Step 4. Detect the occurrence of new impasses. If a new impasse is recognized, then go to step-1.
Step 5. Find invalid systems and modifying the potential design, then go to Step 3.

In the non-routine adaptation processes, a feasible design solution to an over constrained problem is produced in the phase of use of routine adaptation. Figure 5.15 gives an overall constraint satisfaction based adaptation that includes non-routine and routine adaptations. As illustrated, non-routine adaptation is developed by dealing with impasses and performing the routine adaptation. The core of CSP solving in the adaptation is the routine adaptation.

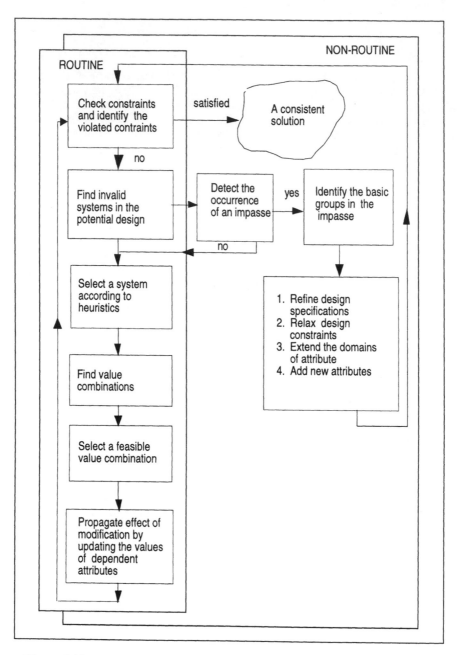

Figure 5.15. Adaptation by constraint satisfaction including routine and non-routine adaptations.

SUMMARY

Adaptation of design cases is the task of adapting previous designs to meet new design requirements. A generalization of design case adaptation has been presented in terms of three issues: identification of the adaptable aspects of design cases; representation of domain knowledge; and explanation of the adaptation operation. A specific approach to adapting design cases has been described, which employs a generalized representation of design knowledge in the forms of design systems and design constraints, using constraint satisfaction to modify the previous design. Creative design as non-routine adaptation is presented through the description of types of impasses and strategies to resolve them.

GLOSSARY OF TERMS

Adaptation: modification of a previous solution for a new problem.

Analytical adaptation: modification of a case by deriving new values for attributes that are consistent with the new problem.

CSP (Constraint Satisfaction Problem): the characterisation of a problem as a set of constraints on variables and the domains of the variables.

Impasse: a situation in which the problem cannot be solved using the given set of constraints and variable domains.

Nonroutine adaptation: a sitatuion in which a new design problem requires additional knowledge, or relaxation of constraints and/or specifications to find a valid solution.

Propose-verify-modify: an iterative process for adapting a case by generating a potential solution, testing the potential solution, and modifying those aspects of the potential solution that violate constraints.

Routine adaptation: a situation in which a new design solution can be found using the given knowledge base and problem specifications.

Structural adaptation: modification of a case by changing the attributes and values to match the new problem.

SUGGESTED READING

Zhang, D. M. (1994). *A Hybrid Approach to Case-Based Design.* Ph.D. Thesis, University of Sydney, Australia, Department of Architectural and Design Science.

This thesis addresses the issues of case adaptation in the context of design. An adaptation model using an ontology of generalized design systems and design constraints is developed. A relevant design case is adapted structurally by the manipulation of its design components and design form to generate a potential solution to a new problem. A feasible design solution is found through repeated cycles of revision and evaluation of the potential solution. A design-specific constraint satisfaction approach is developed to achieve the design subgoals in the adaptation process. Adaptation of design cases is discussed in both routine and non-routine perspectives in light of constraint satisfaction, which gives support to the concept of the case-based design approach being the foundation of creative design.

Hinrichs, T. R., and Kolodner, J. L. (1991). The role of adaptation in case-based design, *Proceedings of the DARPA Workshop on Case-Based Reasoning.* San Mateo, CA: Morgan Kaufmann, pp. 121–132.

This article presents a model of design that can solve ill-defined problems using a method of plausible design adaptation. Adaptation is described as a process of heuristic debugging on the basis of constraint satisfaction. Adaptation transformations are used to adapt the components and structure of a design and constraints on the design problem. A computer program, JULIA, as an implementation of the presented adaptation model in meal design, is described, which designs the presentation and menu of a meal to satisfy multiple interacting constraints.

Hua, K., Schmitt, G., and Faltings, B. (1992). Adaptation of spatial design cases, in J. S. Gero (Ed.), *Artificial Intelligence in Design '92.* Dordrecht: Kluwer Academic, pp. 559–575.

This paper presents a method of case adaptation for building design that uses an interleaved processes of dimensional and topological adaptation. The dimensional adaptation modifies dimensions while maintaining the presence of the components and their connections by a dimensionality reduction process. The topological adaptation changes the components and their connections while maintaining basic functions based on a set of problem-specific transformation rules. The representations of building design cases and generalized design knowledge used in adaptation are also described. A prototype using such an adaptation procedure is shown for the adaptation of building structures to new environments.

6

CASECAD: A Multimedia Case-Based Reasoning System for Design

This chapter presents a multimedia case-based reasoning system called CASECAD in terms of its architecture, implementation, and user interaction. Memory organization, case representation schemes, indexing and retrieval strategies, and the implementation of the various modules of the system are described in detail. Examples from the domain of building structural systems are used to illustrate various implementation details. The Lisp code from CASECAD is documented in Appendix A, and the structural design cases used in CASE-CAD are presented in Appendix B.

CASECAD is a domain-independent design assistant system based on an integration of case-based reasoning (CBR) and computer-aided design (CAD) techniques. CASECAD provides a flexible and effective approach for acquiring and retrieving episodic design knowledge. CASECAD employs a memory organization scheme that partitions memory into model-based memory and case memory. Model-based memory provides an organizational schema for case memory, as well as generalized knowledge about the design domain. Case memory is a multimedia representation of design episodes using an object-oriented representation of design indices, CAD drawings, and graphical illustrations of behaviors of design cases.

CASECAD incorporates a multimedia design case library browser, which is a useful tool for designers, because they can view and compare relevant past design cases in both symbolic and graphical modes. Case retrieval can be carried out using the strategies of index elaboration and index revision, as described in Chapter 4. Once a set of suitable cases is retrieved from the case library, the designer can navigate the retrieved cases in the multimedia environment in order to select the most applicable case for the current situation. The designer can then modify the text and graphic descriptions of the selected case for the new design context if needed. This is possible using text editors for the object-oriented representation, a CAD system for the CAD drawings, and a drawing program for the graphic representation of behaviors. The current version of CASECAD is considered a design-aiding system, as opposed to an autonomous design system.

A number of design support issues have been considered in the development of the CASECAD system:

- The system should store design cases in multiple media, such as text and graphics, because designers often use different forms of representation to record design information.

- The system should support the conceptual design stage, as opposed to detailed design, because this is the part of the design process that is not well supported by procedural and algorithmic models.
- The system should support designers in making their decisions by providing them with suggestions. Suggestions from past design cases often help designers elaborate design problems, propose and refine solutions, critique and modify proposed designs, and justify their choices.
- The system should offer designers multiple types of knowledge. Access to both design cases and design models is useful because designers often use multiple types of knowledge during designing.
- The system should present relevant information to the designer in both a useful and an effective manner. In design problem solving, a combination of attribute-value pairs, text-based explanations, and graphical images provides a more understandable presentation.

THE CASECAD SYSTEM

CASECAD is an integrated multimedia case-based system for design applications. It addresses several important issues in case-based design that were discussed in the previous chapters. CASECAD combines traditional computer-aided design techniques with the evolving field of case-based reasoning. It is a domain-independent designer's assistant that can incrementally acquire design knowledge from past experience in the domain of the user. A significant feature of CASECAD is the ability to store and utilize design cases in both textual and graphical modes. The main modules of the CASECAD system are a case memory, a casebase manager, a case-based reasoner, a CAD package, and a graphical user interface. The CASECAD system has been developed and implemented on SUN workstations under the Xwindow environment.

The current version of CASECAD is focused on three issues: case content and segmentation, case indexing and organization, and case retrieval and selection. The following features were considered important for addressing these issues:

- Storing information about a design that makes it distinct from all other design cases in the system.
- Facilitating the creating, modifying, viewing, and browsing of the case memory as desired by the designer.
- Providing flexibility in indexing and retrieving cases.
- Providing methods for assisting the user in selecting the most applicable case(s) from a set of partially matching cases.
- Integrating CBR with graphics-based design environments, such as CAD.

Currently, CASECAD implements the following features:

- Allows case memory to be organized in terms of both specific design cases and design models, represented in both graphics and text media.
- Allows design specifications to be given as function, behavior, and structure attribute-value pairs.
- Allows the user to provide only partial initial specifications and assists the user with adding or changing these specifications during the retrieval process.
- Identifies and suggests parts of old design cases as possible solutions to subproblems of a new design problem.
- Allows the user to modify, browse, and display any part of case memory in both textual and graphical modes.

System Architecture

The system's architecture is centered around a case-based reasoning system. A schematic layout and control flow of the CASECAD system is shown in Figure 6.1. CASECAD consists of five modules: a graphical user interface (GUI), a case-base manager (CBM), a case-based designer (CBD), a CAD package (CAD), and a case memory module (CMM).

The Graphical User Interface (GUI) allows the designer access to the case-base manager, the case-based designer, the CAD package, and, indirectly, the case memory. The GUI provides a window-based interface to each module of the system. The user chooses a module by selecting a button that initiates an event in CASECAD. The user of CASECAD can be the case-base developer, adding models or cases to case memory, or a designer, browsing and retrieving cases and/or models from case memory.

The Case Memory Module (CMM) contains the knowledge to perform a case-based design. It is basically made up of two components: model memory and case memory. Model-based memory provides an organizational schema for case memory, as well as generalized knowledge about the design domain. Case memory is a multimedia representation of design episodes using an object-oriented representation of design indices, CAD drawings, and graphical illustrations of behaviors of design cases. The graphically represented examples are indexed symbolically so that they can be retrieved given a problem specification in symbolic form.

The CAD package provides the capability to supplement textual data about design cases with graphical data. The CAD package consists of two CAD programs: AutoCAD (Autodesk, 1992) and XFIG. AutoCAD is a general purpose CAD modeling system. The graphical descriptions of design cases are created as 3-D models and stored as .sld files. XFIG is a general purpose 2-D drawing system. The graphical descriptions of behaviors of subcases are created as 2-D drawings and stored as .fig files.

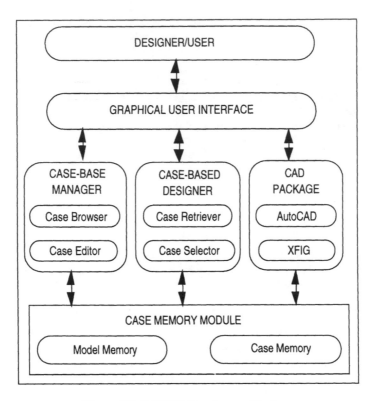

Figure 6.1. CASECAD system architecture.

The Case-Base Manager (CBM) provides facilities for creating, browsing, modifying, displaying, and saving information associated with model memory and case memory. A mouse-based editing facility allows text and/or graphics to be modified conveniently. The CBM allows a user to modify an existing case and store the modified case as a new case. This supports user-based case adaptation.

The Case-Based Designer (CBD) is made up of two modules: the Case Retriever and the Case Selector. The task of the Case Retriever is to retrieve relevant cases given a set of requirements of the current problem in terms of function, behavior, and structure. The Case Retriever identifies cases that match partially or perfectly, using one or more categories of specifications. Once a set of relevant cases is retrieved from the database of design cases, the designer can browse those retrieved cases in order to select the most applicable case for the current situation. The Case Selector ranks the retrieved cases and presents the ranking to the user.

User Interaction

User interaction is illustrated in Figure 6.2.

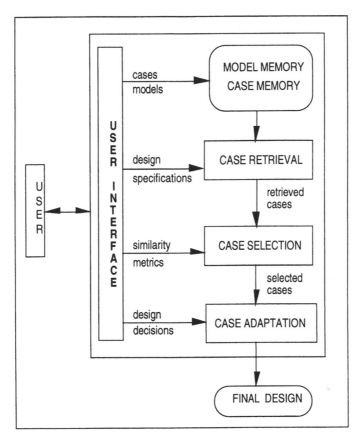

Figure 6.2. User interaction in CASECAD.

Interaction occurs at two levels in CASECAD: user as case manager and user as case reasoner. The user as case manager interacts with the system to add design cases to case memory and to modify or add design models in model memory. As a case reasoner, the user interacts with the system for assistance with a new design problem. This type of user is referred to as a *designer*. The designer describes his or her problem in terms of its goals, constraints, and specifications. The designer then queries the system for relevant past design case(s). The case-based reasoning module of the system retrieves the design cases most relevant to the given problem. Once a set of design cases has been retrieved by the system, the designer can browse those cases in both textual and graphical modes. The case retriever typically will find more than one case or subcase. The designer provides a measure of similarity in order to rank the retrieved cases. The designer then modifies the text and graphical descriptions of the selected case for the new design context.

Figure 6.3 illustrates the CASECAD interface. The figure shows the graphical user interface as buttons and menus giving the user access to the case manager, case reasoner, and CAD system. The figure is taken as a snapshot of the screen while the user is browsing the case base of building designs. The case is displayed in both symbolic and graphical descriptions. The symbolic description provides information about the function, structure, and behavior of the building. The CAD drawing provides a 3-D view of the structural system of the building, where structural components are modeled as line elements, and the CAD drawing also provides selected 2-D drawings of the structural system. A selected behavior of the structural system is illustrated using a 2-D drawing of the deflection of the building.

System Implementation

CASECAD has been developed and implemented on SUN4/SPARC workstations under the UNIX operating system. The Graphical User Interface (GUI) is based on SUN Open Windows and is implemented using the XView toolkit. The underlying programming environment of CASECAD is UNIX, Xview, C, and Lisp. C is used for programming the GUI because it can directly call the XView toolkit. The GUI is implemented as an event-driven interface. Lisp, the Unix dialect of IBUKI Common Lisp, is used for programming the case-based designer. All retrieval and case display routines are written in Lisp because it supports list and frame-based reasoning. The case memory and class memory are implemented as frames.

The Case Memory Module (CMM) is organized as two types of information: symbolic (or text-based files) and graphical (or drawing files). The text-based information is created and edited using Lisp functions. The symbolic representation is implemented using a frame-based representation in Common Lisp. This representation system is built using FRAMEKIT (Nyberg, 1988). FRAMEKIT is a general-purpose frame-based knowledge representation system, written in Common Lisp, that provides basic mechanisms of frames, inheritance, demons, relations, and views. The graphics files are created and edited via the CAD package.

The CAD package (CAD) is implemented using AutoCAD (Autodesk, 1992) and XFIG programs. These CAD programs can be invoked independently of the CMM from the main icon panel. The graphical representation of design cases is saved as .sld and .fig files. When the user displays the graphical representation of the cases, the program used to create the drawings is invoked as a separate window. The user interacts with the drawing program directly to view the graphical representation and to make changes to reflect the use of the case in a new design context. The two different CAD packages were selected because they provide different utilities for documenting the design. AutoCAD provides 3D modelling and utilities for producing dimensions, layers, etc. XFIG provides utilities for 2D drawings that are not necessarily formal design documents. The decision to invoke the CAD packages directly from CASECAD was based on the requirement that the user to perform case adaptation by editing the case description. This assumes that the user knows how to use these particular CAD packages. However, it also means that CASECAD can be used to browse, retrieve, and adapt design cases.

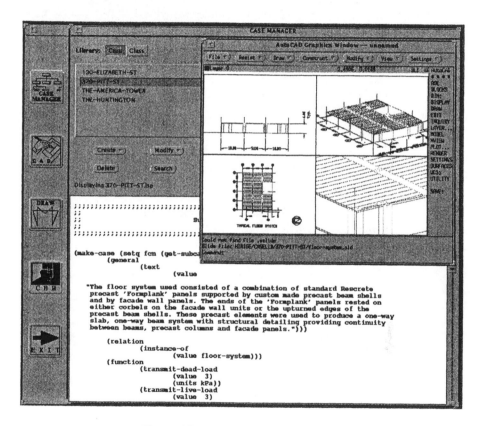

Figure 6.3. CASECAD system interface.

The Case-Based Designer (CBD), the module that provides the user with the case-based reasoning functions, is implemented in Common Lisp. The capabilities of the CBD include:

1. Loading and representing design specifications.

    2. Loading and representing design cases and design models as frames.
    3. Searching and retrieving design models and cases.
    4. Ranking and presenting retrieved cases.

The CBD is responsible for executing and loading files for the external programs. The communication between the CBD module and the CAD programs is based on the concept of UNIX pipe communications and is implemented in Common Lisp.

    The Case-Base Manager (CBM) is implemented in C as a stand-alone module. It provides facilities for creating, modifying, displaying, printing, and browsing information in the case memory. The Case-Base Manager provides utilities for the user to store and manage design models and design cases in case memory. The C program accepts an event from the user, determines what Lisp function needs to be executed, and sends a message to the Case-Based Designer. When a user wants to browse a file in case memory, the CBM displays a file in a window for the user to view and/or edit.

CASE MEMORY ORGANIZATION

The content and organization of case memory is fundamental for the development of case-based design systems, because it defines both the design space and the indices for locating specific design states in the space. Case memory should be organized in such a manner that case retrieval can be done as flexibly and efficiently as possible. In CASECAD, memory is organized using a schema that is similar to MOPs (Memory Organization Packages) (Schank, 1982), and is partitioned into two modules: model-based memory and case memory. MOP-based memory techniques involve standard AI notions, such as frames, abstraction, and inheritance. Model-based memory provides an organizational schema for case memory, as well as generalized knowledge about the design domain, whereas design cases contain specific knowledge of the design domain.

    Generally speaking, design models cover normative situations and design cases cover specific instances. A design model represents a range of design solutions and contains relevant design knowledge from which a number of different abstractions can be derived. Integrating design models and design cases in case memory provides a rich source of knowledge for performing case-based design. Generalized knowledge contained in design models can play a variety of roles in case-based design:

    • Organizing information within a design case effectively.
    • Selecting appropriate indices and clustering for design cases.
    • Performing elaboration of a new design problem.
    • Guiding case adaptation to meet new requirements.

    Hierarchies are formed when a model is broken into submodels. This approach is similar to the object-oriented approach to organizing design cases, as described in Chapter 3, where design models are represented as individual classes of designs and design cases are associated with one or more design models using instance-of relationships. One major advantage of this approach is that the top nodes in hierarchies provide a place to store generalized knowledge associated with clusters of cases.

Because design in many domains is composed of subproblems, it is feasible that design solutions to subproblems can come from completely different design cases. The organization of design case memory based on decomposition allows for the generation of new designs using pieces of different cases. Design models serve both as a basis for decomposing design cases into subcases and for determining relevant or critical features to describe new design problems. Design models also provide for flexible indexing of case memory, because they have many different abstractions.

Representation of Design Models in CASECAD

A design model is a schema for organizing design knowledge. Design models within a domain can be organized into a hierarchy. The hierarchy represents part-subpart relationships. The hierarchical organization of design models provides templates for the organization of a design case. Figure 6.4 shows a hierarchical organization of the design models representing a structural system of a building. The structural system of a building can be based on models for different types of grid systems, alternatives and parameters for framing systems, simple or complex floor systems, and models to represent the core structure. This is not the only way to decompose the structural system into models, but represents a functional decomposition, where each submodel serves a primary structural design function.

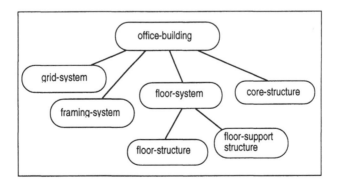

Figure 6.4. Design model and submodels of a structural system for a building.

To support flexibility in both indexing and retrieving design cases, CASECAD uses a design model that represents function (F), behavior (B), and structure (S) properties distinctly. This design model is derived from the design prototypes schema proposed by Gero (1990), where each attribute of a prototype is categorized based on the role it plays in reasoning about a design feature. Brief definitions of these categories are given in Figure 6.5.

FUNCTION ATTRIBUTES - The functions of a prototype
describe the purposes that can be fulfilled by using the
prototype. A rigid-frame for example might have
provide-span, resist-gravity-load and resist-lateral-load
as its functional attributes.

BEHAVIOR ATTRIBUTES - The behaviors of a prototype
are the expected performances of an instance of the prototype
in a particular context. All attributes describing internal forces,
internal stresses, and deformations of a structural entity are
behavior attributes.

STRUCTURE ATTRIBUTES - The structure of a prototype
defines the physical properties of an instance of the prototype
in terms of structural attributes and structural elements.
Attributes describing geometry and material properties of a
structural entity are structure attributes.

Figure 6.5. Categories of attributes in CASECAD.

Attributes characterize the design instance through their labels and values. In the design model, additional information about an attribute can be represented as attributes of attributes, or the facets of an attribute. In CASECAD, the facets of an attribute include type, default, units, range, and dimension. The semantics and use of these facets are briefly described in Figure 6.6.

In developing case-based design systems, a number of different types of design models have been used to capture design knowledge. Examples include the decomposition model (Maher and Zhang, 1993), the functional model (Goel and Chandrasekaran, 1989), the function-behavior-structure model (Stroulia et al., 1992), the graph-based behavioral model (Sycara and Navinchandra, 1989), and the design prototype-based model (Wang and Gero, 1991). Design knowledge representation using FBS models has been shown to be an effective basis for performing a design activity by reasoning at various levels of abstraction (Chandrasekaran, 1990; Rosenman et al., 1991).

Frames (Minsky, 1975) and object-oriented databases (Hughes, 1991) provide representation paradigms suitable for representing a hierarchy of design cases. In CASECAD, the frame-based formalism is used for representing and organizing both design models and design cases. Some of the most useful features of the frame-based formalism that support the representation of both specific and generic design knowledge include inheritance, demons, defaults, and relations. The definition of a design model for a floor system is shown in Figure 6.7. The frame-based representation of the model of a floor system includes a relational attribute, part-of, that relates the floor system to the building model. The remaining attributes of the model have facets that indicate the category of the attribute as well as the type, range, and so on.

TYPE – is used to specify the type of the value of an attribute. For example, the value of the attribute "beam-span" is of numeric type and that of "material" is of symbolic type.

DEFAULT – is used to specify the default value of an attribute. The default value of an attribute is used when there is no other means to determine the value of that attribute.

RANGE – is used to specify the value ranges for an attribute. For attributes that are of numerical type, the range is a simple numerical range; for attributes that are of discrete type, the range is a list of discrete values.

UNITS – is used to specify how the attribute value is measured. For example, "bending-stress" has the units Mpa. Some attributes, such as "number-of-stories" and "number-of -bays," have no units associated with them.

DIMENSION – is used to specify the dimension of an attribute. For example, the dimension of attributes that measure "linear-distance" is [L] and of attributes that measure "area" is [L^2].

Figure 6.6. Facets of attributes in CASECAD.

Representation of Design Cases in CASECAD

The major knowledge source for a case-based design system is its case memory module, which represents previous design solutions individually. In order to store a design case, one must identify the salient features that describe it. In CASECAD, design cases are described by a vocabulary and hierarchical organization derived from the definition of the design models. A similar approach for representing design cases based on primitive generic components has also been described by Alberts (1992). A design case is organized into a partonomic hierarchy in which each node is described by the most discriminating function, behavior, and structure attributes.

CASECAD was implemented using a case base developed from a collection of medium- to high-rise buildings in Sydney. The design data for the building cases were collected through the cooperation of the engineers in Acer Wargon Chapman Associates. The engineers provided the CAD drawings and access to the analysis results. The drawings provided information about the design solution, but very little about the functional decomposition of the structural systems, and nothing about the original design specification. The analysis results provided some insight into the functional aggregation of structural components, but did not make this information explicit. Interviews with the engineers clarified the assumptions made about the intended function of the structural system and subsystems.

```
(make-model floor-system '(
    (relation
        (part-of
            (value building)))
    (function
        (transmit-dead-load
            (type numeric)
            (dimension (F)))
        (transmit-live-load
            (type numeric)
            (dimension (F))))
    (behavior
        (deflection
            (type numeric)
            (dimension (L))))
    (structure
        (start-level
            (type integer))
        (span-type
            (type symbolic))
        ... ))
```

Figure 6.7. A partial floor system model in a frame representation.

The case base currently contains about 20 partial building cases. The buildings are primarily medium-rise office or hotel buildings, each with a core structure used to resist wind load. The buildings are distinguishable by their geometric constraints, represented by the grid system, and the use of structural components to complement the core structure, represented through a different set of subcases for each building. Each case in the case memory is a single building design. A subcase is a structural component of the building, for example, a rigid frame or a floor system component.

The cases and subcases are related to the design models stored in model memory. Figure 6.8 shows the relationship between design models and design cases in CASECAD.

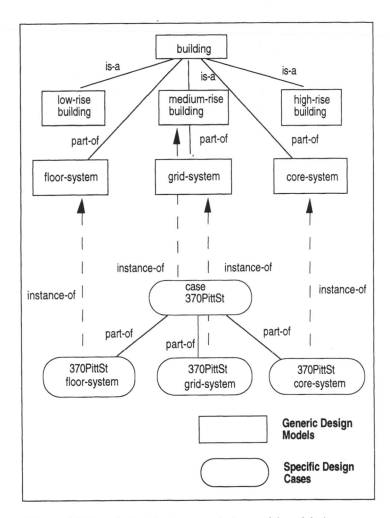

Figure 6.8. The relationships between design models and design cases.

Case memory can be viewed as a set of inheritance hierarchies, with generic design models being on the highest level and specific design cases being on the lowest level. Each design case is described as a set of subcases that are linked to their parent by part-of relations. Each subcase may itself be a structured object with components, in turn. This makes it easier to access parts of old design cases to solve parts of new problems. Subcases contain pointers that can be used to reconstruct the entire case.

The content of a design case/subcase is made up of attribute-value pairs, including symbolic and graphic attributes. The labels and facets of the symbolic attributes are derived from the relevant design model, and the values are specific to the design project. The graphic attributes assume a value that points to a file in which the graphic representation is stored. Figure 6.9 shows the frame-based representation of a subcase representing the floor system of the building at 370 Pitt Street.

```
(make-case 'subcase1001 '(
(general
   (description
      (value
   "The floor system is a combination of standard Rescrete precast
   'Formplank' panels supported by custom-made precast beam shells
   and by facade wall panels. The ends of the 'Formplank' panels rested
   on either corbels on the facade wall units or the upturned edges of
   the precast beam shells. These precast elements were used to produce
   a one-way slab, one-way beam system with structural detailing
   providing continuity between beams, precast columns, and facade
   panels")))
(relation
   (part-of
      (value 370-PITT-ST))
   (instance-of
      (value floor-system)))
(function
   (transmit-dead-load
      (value 3) (units kPa))
   ... ))
(behavior
   (deflection
      (value 18) (units  mm))
   (xfig-file
      (value "floor-system.fig")))
(structure
   (material
      (value precast-concrete))
   (acad-file
      (value "floor-system.sld")))
   ... ))
```

Figure 6.9. A frame-based representation of a subcase.

The case representation includes a text-based description, relational attributes that link the subcase to the root of the case hierarchy, and attributes categorized as function, behavior, or structure. The facets of an attribute in a case representation include the "value" facet, indicating the value of the attribute.

Graphical representations are traditionally used by designers to store and communicate information about their designs. They serve not only to communicate design ideas effectively, but also to manage the complexity of design information. In the CASECAD system, graphical data is included to provide a visualization of the design case. The structure of each subcase is visualized as a CAD model. Some important behaviors of subcases are visualized by 2-D abstract drawings. Examples of behaviors that are of particular interest to structural designers include stress distribution, deflection pattern, and bending moment variation.

We use two graphics packages for the graphical data representation: AutoCAD (Autodesk, 1992) and XFIG. AutoCAD is a general-purpose CAD modeling system, and XFIG is a general-purpose 2-D drawing system. The frame-based representation of the case/subcase stores the name of the graphic files as the value of the attributes "xfig-file" and "acad-file." Each of these attributes is categorized as a behavior or structure attribute.

Figures 6.10 and 6.11 illustrate the graphical representations of the behavior and structure of a subcase. The behavior diagram in Figure 6.10 shows the bending moment diagram of a typical floor panel, where the bending moment is positive across the length of the panel, and the shear force diagram, where the shear force varies linearly from one support to the next. Figure 6.11 shows a CAD drawing of the floor system of the building, indicating the grid numbers, dimensions, and the orientation of the panels.

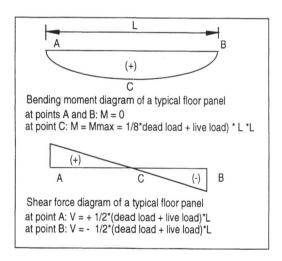

Figure 6.10. Graphical representation of behavior.

In summary, a design case contains the following information:

- A hierarchy of subcases representing a structural decomposition of the design case. Each subcase in the hierarchy is linked to the subcases above and below it in the case hierarchy. The subcase is also linked to the relevant model in model memory.

- A text-based summary of each subcase identifying the critical aspects of the design.
- The function-behavior-structure attributes and their values. These attributes comprise the primary indices to the subcase.
- A CAD model illustrating the structural description of the subcase as a documented CAD drawing.
- A 2-D graphical illustration of selected behaviors of subcases.

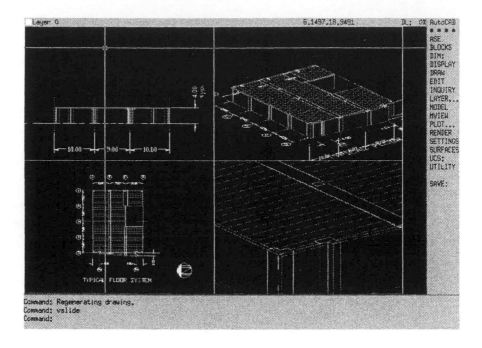

Figure 6.11. Graphical representation of structure.

Organization of Design Cases in CASECAD

The design cases in CASECAD are organized as lists of case names, where a case name refers to the name of the frame representing the case or subcase. There are four lists of case names to provide direct access to a case or subcase based on a specific type of index. The four types of indices are: name of the root node, name of function indices, name of behavior indices, and name of structure indices. A list of case names comprising the root nodes of all case hierarchies is maintained to provide direct access to the entire case description. A list of cases/subcases for each function attribute is maintained for direct access to a case with a specific function. Similarly, a list of case names for each behavior and structure attribute is maintained. This organization of cases and subcase is referred to as *feature-based indexing* in Chapter 3. The indexing scheme in CASECAD is illustrated in Figure 6.12.

```
FUNCTION INDICES

support-building-type: case 101, case103
support-live-load: case1206, case 1307
...

BEHAVIOR INDICES

deflection: case1555, case1543
shear-stress: case 1555, case1435
...

STRUCTURE INDICES

building-shape: case 101, case103
number-of-stories: case101, case103
floor-system-type: case1102,
case1203
```

Figure 6.12. Indexing scheme in CASECAD.

A flexible indexing system provides multiple access paths to case memory. A new design problem is specified as a set of requirements that the new design must satisfy. The requirements may include the functional specifications, including the purpose or use of the structure; the behavioral specifications, including performance requirements on deflection, stress, and so on; and the structural specifications, including predetermined geometry or material constraints. CASECAD employs a two-level indexing scheme. The first level of indices are category indices. These are intended to support selection of a particular category of memory to perform the search procedure. Each node of a design case is indexed by three labels: function, behavior, and structure. The second level of indices are attribute indices. These indices include the function, behavior, and structure attributes of all cases in case memory. One of the key aspects of this indexing approach is that it allows a case to be indexed by focusing on the function of the case, the behavior of the case, or the structure of the case. By focusing on one type of requirement, a different set of cases may be retrieved than if all requirements are used.

Each case in CASECAD is organized as a separate hierarchy of subcases, as illustrated in Figure 6.13. Cases are represented in frames, where each frame has a name. The root of each case is a distinct frame, retrieved through the feature-based indexing scheme. Each subcase is also a distinct frame, retrieved through the feature-based indexing scheme or through the link to the other nodes in the case hierarchy.

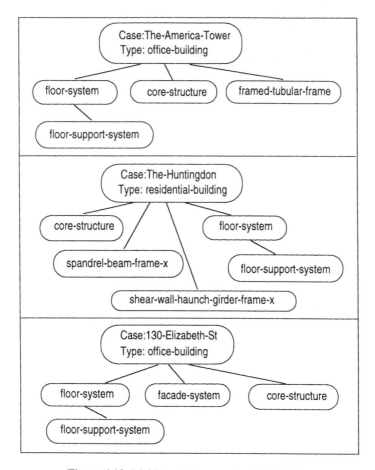

Figure 6.13. Multiple design cases in CASECAD.

RETRIEVING DESIGN CASES

The retrieval process begins when the designer specifies a design problem. The problem description is referred to as the "specifications" in CASECAD. The specifications are categorized as function, behavior, and structure, and are stated by attribute name and value. An example of specifications for a new problem in

CASECAD is given in Figure 6.14. The frame-based representation of the specifications is shown in Figure 6.15.

```
NEW DESIGN PROBLEM SPECIFICATIONS

FUNCTION REQUIREMENTS
support-building-type: office
support-grid-geometry: rectangular
maximum-span: 9 m

BEHAVIOR REQUIREMENTS
cost-of-construction: <= 20 $millions

STRUCTURE REQUIREMENTS
material: reinforced concrete
```

Figure 6.14 Specifications for a new design problem

```
(make-frame
  specifications
    (function
      (support-building-type
        (common (= office)))))
      (support-grid-geometry
        (common (= rectangular)))
      (maximum-span
        (common (= 9 m)))
    (behavior
      (cost-of-construction
        (common (<= 20 $millions))))
    (structure
      (material
        (common (= reinforced-concrete))))
```

Figure 6.15. The frame representation of the specifications.

CASECAD uses the problem specifications to search for relevant design models or design cases from case memory. When searching case memory, the case retriever finds all cases and/or models that match the given specifications perfectly or partially. The user uses the retrieved cases and models to modify the problem specifications. The iterative process of retrieving cases is referred to as *index elaboration* and *index revision* in Chapter 4.

Finding a case that has the most requirements in common may not be the best case to use for adaptation. The specifications can be used to explore case memory, to find relevant cases, and to lead to other cases that may not seem relevant at first. This kind of case memory exploration is a valuable tool for designers at the conceptual design stage. CASECAD provides the options of case retrieval using one of the categories of specifications, all categories of specifications, or one attribute only.

Case retrieval is carried out in two steps. First, a category of attributes of the cases/subcases is retrieved, followed by an attribute-value matching process. The system only retrieves cases that have at least one match with the specifications. The system ranks the retrieved cases by their similarity to the problem specification. The similarity of a case to the problem is measured by the number of matching attributes in their specifications. Figure 6.16 shows the cases retrieved using the function attributes of the specifications.

```
SPECIFICATIONS

FUNCTION
    support-grid-geometry : (= rectangular)
    maximum-span: (= 9 m)
    support-building-type: (=  office)

BEHAVIOR
    cost-of-construction: (<= 20 $millions)

STRUCTURE
    material:  (= reinforced-concrete)

CASE RETRIEVAL USING FUNCTION SPECIFICATIONS
    subcase-node          case-name              number-of-matchings

    SUBCASE401        THE-HUNTINGTON                    3
    SUBCASE301        THE-AMERICA-TOWER                 3
    SUBCASE101        130-ELIZABETH-ST                  3
    SUBCASE402        THE-HUNTINGTON                    2
    SUBCASE302        THE-AMERICA-TOWER                 2
    SUBCASE201        370-PITT-ST                       2
    SUBCASE103        130-ELIZABETH-ST                  2
    SUBCASE202        370-PITT-ST                       1
```

Figure 6.16. The cases retrieved using the function attributes.

One advantage of the case retrieval in CASECAD is that the search for matching cases can be done using different categories of specifications independently. During the retrieval shown in Figure 6.16, the search was confined to one particular category of case attributes, thus minimizing the search time. If the same set of specifications was used to focus the search on the behavior attributes of the specifications, a different set of cases would be retrieved. This highlights the effect of focusing on one category of the specifications and shows there is no single best case for a particular design situation.

Once a set of cases is retrieved by the system, the designer may add more requirements of the problem in order to explore the case memory. The user can browse the retrieved cases in order to select the most applicable or "best" case for the current problem. The case retriever provides a list of cases or subcases after searching the case memory. The user can then display the contents of any of the retrieved cases, select one to adapt, or modify the specifications and initiate case retrieval again. Figure 6.17 shows how the user can view the retrieved cases in the multimedia environment.

IMPLICATIONS OF THE CASECAD SYSTEM

Case-based design is a task that combines generalized and specific knowledge of the design domain. In the development of the CASECAD system, effort has been expended in identifying, organizing, representing, and making use of these distinct types of knowledge. An adequate knowledge representation has been achieved by the combined use of design models and design cases. In this way, the designer can be provided with multiple forms of knowledge. Access to both models and cases might be especially useful for designers, such as architects, because they use multiple types of knowledge when designing buildings.

In practice, designers use drawings, text, and formulas extensively to record their design information. The prototypical system presented in this chapter has shown the practicability of handling such multimedia information within an integrated environment. The importance of combining knowledge-based techniques and conventional CAD techniques in case presentation has been realized.

The CASECAD system was not developed as an autonomous design system, but it has been developed as an aid to professional designers who want to employ case-based reasoning techniques in their design tasks. The current version of the CASECAD system is designed to be used at the conceptual design assistant stage, because this is not well supported by procedural or algorithmic models.

A key feature of the system is the integration of CBR technology with existing computer-aided design systems. This shows the practicability of this approach in real design practice. Flexible indexing strategies are very important, because they allow designers to explore their design options flexibly and efficiently. In CASECAD, function, behavior, and structure attributes have been used to index design cases. Even without the consideration of a case-based reasoner, CASECAD provides an implementation for indexing and retrieving CAD drawings.

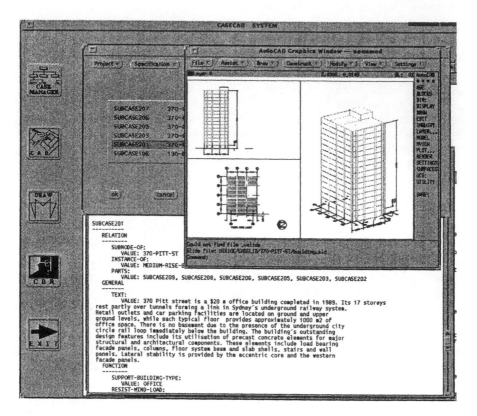

Figure 6.17. The retrieved cases in the multimedia environment.

The process of design case acquisition continues to challenge case-based design systems developers. In our experience, we found that it is not easy to find well-documented cases of structural systems design of buildings. Drawings and pictures are readily available, but their analyses are not easy to find. Even the design goals and constraints are unclear. It is a difficult and tedious process to interpret drawings and identify justifications for the designers' decisions. We have found that interviewing human designers is helpful in obtaining crucial design information that is not available from drawings.

SUMMARY

This chapter has described a multimedia case-based reasoning system, CASECAD, in terms of its purpose, architecture, implementation, and performance. The implementation of CASECAD identifies solutions to several representation issues that are fundamental to the use of CBR in design: identifying the contents, representation, and presentation of design case memory; identifying schemes for case indexing and organization; defining procedures for case retrieval and case selection; and integrating CBR with external programs, such as CAD systems.

GLOSSARY OF TERMS

CAD (Computer Aided Design): refers to a class of computer programs that assist in the graphical documentation of a design.

Case-based designer: a design system that uses a case-based reasoning approach to design problem solving.

Case-base manager: a program that provides facilities for creating, browsing, modifying, displaying, and storing information in case memory.

Case memory: a computer representation of case-specific knowledge.

Case retriever: a process that retrieves relevant cases from case memory, given a set of requirements of a new problem.

Model memory: a computer representation of generalized knowledge in the form of models.

Multimedia: combining various media, such as graphics, text, video, and sound in a single presentation or database.

Object-oriented databases: a database methodology based on the notions of type, data abstraction, inheritance, and persistence.

SUGGESTED READING

Maher, M. L., and Balachandran, M. B. (1994a). Flexible retrieval strategies for case-based design, in J. S. Gero and F. Sudweeks (Eds), *Artificial Intelligence in Design '94*. Dordrecht: Kluwer Academic.

> This paper provides the theoretical basis for the development of the CASECAD system. In this article, the ideas behind the case retrieval strategies used by the CASECAD system are presented. These methodologies are based on the fact that, in design, the case retrieval process should allow designers to explore the design space easily and flexibly. Two different strategies, index elaboration and index revision, are described and illustrated through examples. The role of domain models in supporting such case retrieval strategies are described.

Domeshek, E. A., and Kolodner, J. L. (1992). A case-based design aid for architecture, in J. S. Gero (Ed.) *Artificial Intelligence in Design '92*. Dordrecht: Kluwer Academic.

This paper presents a case-based design aiding system called ARCHIE-II, developed in the domain of architectural design. The focus of ARCHIE-II is similar to that of CASECAD (i.e., assisting designers during the conceptual design phase). The main issues addressed in this paper are representing large cases by breaking them into pieces, indexing and organizing cases, and browsing design cases, using multiple modes. Like CASECAD, ARCHIE-II uses multiple types of indices to make them available at appropriate times in the design process.

Maher, M. L., and Balachandran, B. (1994a). A multimedia approach to case-based structural design, *ASCE Journal of Computing in Civil Engineering* **8**(3): 359-377.

One of the key features of the CASECAD system is the use of multiple modalities for representing design cases. This article describes a multimedia approach to case representation and case presentation in the domain of structural design. It discusses issues involved in the integration of multimedia computer systems, database management systems, and case-based reasoning. The schema used by the CASECAD system for multimedia case representation is described in detail and illustrated by structural design examples.

7

CADSYN:
A Hybrid Approach to
Case-Based Design

A hybrid approach to case-based design implies that more than one reasoning paradigm and/or more than one knowledge representation paradigm are used within a framework of case-based reasoning. This chapter presents the design and implementation of a computer system to embody and demonstrate a case-based design model that incorporates a constraint satisfaction approach to case adaptation, making use of case-specific and generalized design knowledge. The system is named CADSYN, Case-based reasoning And Decomposition for SYNthesis, and is applied in the domain of the structural design of buildings.

CADSYN is a domain-independent case-based reasoner that retrieves and adapts design cases using a combination of case memory and generalized design knowledge in the form of system definitions and constraints. CADSYN integrates the mechanisms of case retrieval and design synthesis through the elaboration of design specifications by systems decomposition, and through case adaptation by constraint satisfaction. The elaboration of design specifications and the constraint satisfaction process both use a systems decomposition knowledge base, where design models are represented as components that can be recomposed into hierarchical design solutions. CADSYN does not emphasize user interaction and graphic-based representations. The concepts of case adaptation, as implemented in CADSYN, are introduced in Chapter 5.

The major issues considered in the development of CADSYN are:
- The representation of generalized knowledge to support design case retrieval and adaptation.
- The content and organization of case memory for case adaptation.
- A hybrid model for case-based reasoning that incorporates multiple knowledge sources and multiple reasoning paradigms.
- The retrieval and adaptation of case information at any level of abstraction.
- Heuristics needed for a constraint satisfaction approach to conceptual design.

THE CADSYN SYSTEM

CADSYN is a hybrid case-based design system that combines case-based reasoning with design by decomposition and constraint satisfaction. CADSYN uses two major types of design knowledge: episodic design cases and generalized design knowledge. CADSYN represents an implementation of case-based design from case retrieval through case adaptation and updating case memory. A significant feature of CADSYN is the generic approach to design case adaptation and the representation of the design knowledge that supports adaptation.

CADSYN implements the following features:

- A case memory as a hierarchy of subcases comprising attribute-value pairs.
- A generalized decomposition design knowledge base.
- A generalized representation of design constraints.
- A case retrieval process that includes design by decomposition when a suitable case is not available.
- A case adaptation process based on constraint satisfaction.
- A case combining process for combining solutions to subproblems.
- A case update process that incorporates an adapted case into case memory.

System Architecture

The architecture of CADSYN is illustrated in Figure 7.1. There are three knowledge base modules included in the architecture: case memory, general design knowledge base, and design context. Case memory is a repository of specific previous design situations and indexing information that serve as a starting point for a new problem. The general knowledge base contains the knowledge required to decompose and expand the new design problem specifications. It is comprised of a hierarchy of design (sub)systems, constraints, and procedural functions. The design context is a representation of the new design problem and its current solution.

Five process modules are included in the architecture of CADSYN. The retrieval mechanism is used to identify a relevant design (sub)case based on the retrieval of a set of cases from case memory and the selection of a relevant design case. If a relevant (sub)case is found, the adaptor is applied; otherwise, the problem is decomposed into subproblems. The case adaptor is responsible for the adaptation of a selected case. The decomposer serves as a mechanism for searching through the generalized decomposition knowledge to expand the design problem specifications and possibly generate a feasible solution to a given subproblem. It is developed based on the EDESYN shell (Maher, 1987). The combiner consistently composes subsolutions from the adaptor and decomposer. The updater stores the new design description into case memory for future use.

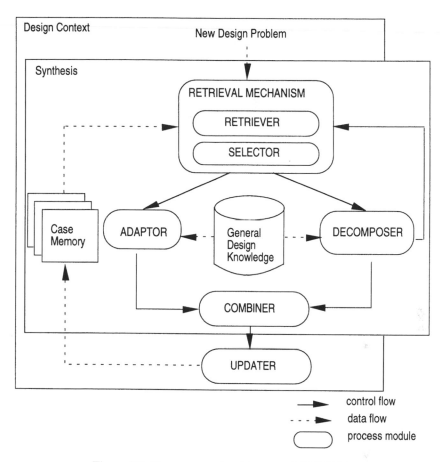

Figure 7.1. The conceptual architecture of CADSYN.

System Implementation

CADSYN makes use of available knowledge representation languages and knowledge-based tools. The implementation of CADSYN includes an existing decomposition mechanism, EDESYN, which provides a basis for the generalized design knowledge representation structure. More specifically, the representation language for decomposition and design constraints used in EDESYN are adopted in the implementation of CADSYN, thus to a certain extent, saving development efforts.

To develop a case memory, a set of previous design situations must be available. We, therefore, met with engineering consultants to access their building projects and extract the design data from design drawings, design reports, and interviews with design experts. Each design case represents structural design knowledge specific to a particular building, in which the problem specifications and design solution description of a building are encoded in the form of attribute-value pairs.

The system is developed on SUN stations under a UNIX operating system and uses IBUKI Common Lisp and FRAMEKIT (Nyberg, 1988), a frame-based representation language that provides the basic mechanisms of frames, inheritance, demons, and views.

Structural Design in CADSYN

To use CADSYN to generate a design solution, the preliminary structural design of buildings is chosen as the application design domain. Structural design, as a specific design domain, can be viewed as a sequence of three major stages: preliminary design, analysis, and detailed design. The scope of the structural design knowledge in CADSYN is aimed to produce a potential design description for the preliminary stage, where heuristics, rather than detailed analytical knowledge, are used to identify relevant design alternatives.

In CADSYN, a preliminary structural design is represented by a hierarchical set of structural systems, which, in turn, are represented by relevant attributes and their values. The attributes represent the design requirements, the expected performances, and the structural description. The structural systems are selected from the case base in accordance with the knowledge about general structural systems in the knowledge base.

The representation of the building, as the context for the structural design problem, includes the architectural specification and the preliminary structural design. The architectural specification includes the geometric, topological, and functional attributes of a building, and environmental elements, such as load information. The preliminary structural design produced by CADSYN is represented by various structural systems, such as the lateral resistance system, the gravity resistance system, and so on. This solution presents a conceptual structural design, and assumes a more detailed analysis and a more detailed design will be done to refine the solution. The structural design in CADSYN, as illustrated in Figure 7.2, can be understood as taking design problem specifications as input and producing a design structural description as output.

DESIGN CONTEXT

The design context in CADSYN is a repository for all the information specific to the current design problem being solved. The design context consists of the following information:

- An input design problem description in terms of attribute-value pairs of specifications.

- Solutions to the subproblems generated by CADSYN.
- A complete design solution to a given input problem.

The representation of each of these components of the design context is described in the following sections.

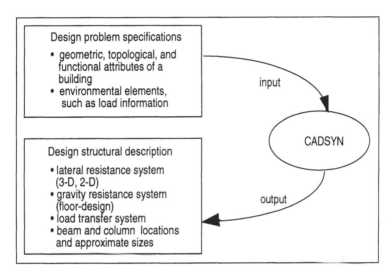

Figure 7.2. CADSYN applied to preliminary structural design.

Design Problem Specifications

A design problem specification is represented in CADSYN as a set of attribute-value pairs. For the structural design domain, the design specifications include the architectural specification (i.e., the functional attributes of a building; the layout and three-dimensional grid description), and environmental elements, such as load information.

Based on the complexity of the specifications of a structural design problem, a hierarchy of two layers is used to group the attribute-value pairs into functional sets. The more general level of specification is called the *overall problem description* and includes the architectural description, the functional use of the building, and the general layout of the spaces in the building. The second level in the hierarchical specifications provides information about the various geometric grids in the building. Each grid is specified by its geometric description, the relevant load information, and the layout of the functional spaces on the grid. The two layers of design specifications are illustrated in Figure 7.3.

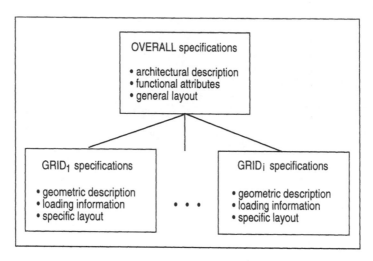

Figure 7.3. Two layers of design specifications.

In the problem specifications, a simplified grid representation is used in terms of grid labels and offsets of grid lines in two directions. One issue in adapting design cases in CADSYN is the difficulties arising from variations in geometry between the case and the new problem. A full geometric model is not necessary at the preliminary design stage, so a simplification of the geometry of the previous cases is used.

Figure 7.4 gives an example of a description of design specifications of a hotel. The problem specifications are represented in frames. Frame "problem-1" gives an overall specification of the hotel design problem. Frames "problem-1/parking," "problem-1/retail," and "problem-1/hotel" provide three different grid specifications for parking, retail, and hotel spaces, respectively.

Case retrieval in CADSYN can be based on a set of specifications for an entire building or on the set of specifications for a specific structural (sub)system. If a relevant case is not found for the entire building or for a structural subsystem, the specifications are expanded into subproblems. When considering the entire building, the subproblems are defined as each of the grid specifications. When considering the specifications of a structural subsystem, the decomposition knowledge in the general knowledge base is used to generate the specifications of the subproblems for the subsystem. Regardless of the level of abstraction of the design specifications, the specifications are represented as attribute-value pairs.

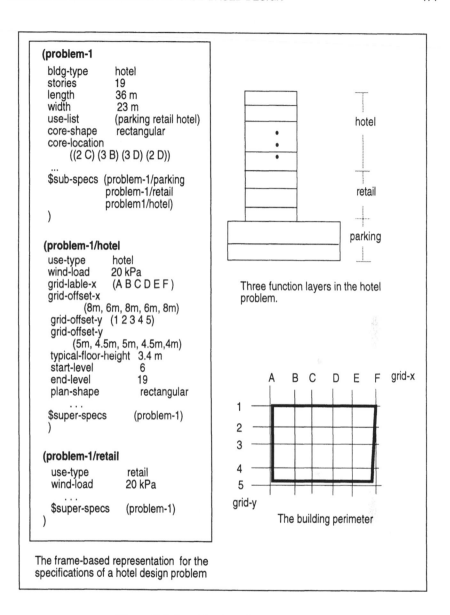

The frame-based representation for the specifications of a hotel design problem

Figure 7.4. Specifications for a hotel design.

Representation of Design (Sub)solutions

The design context is a dynamic representation of the intermediate states of a design solution, as well as a complete solution to a given design problem. During problem solving, solutions to subproblems are generated by the adaptation of relevant (sub)cases or by the synthesis of sets of design attributes and their values. These solutions are stored in a hierarchy in the design context. Once a subsolution is generated, it is attached to the set of specifications that were expanded into subproblems. Alternatively, the result of case adaptation can itself be a hierarchy of adapted subcases, where the solution to the design problem is a hierarchy. Regardless of the level at which a case is retrieved and adapted, the resulting design solution is represented as a hierarchy of sets of attribute-value pairs.

DESIGN CASE MEMORY IN CADSYN

Design case memory in CADSYN is a representation of previous structural design examples. Case memory is organized into two components: case hierarchies and case indexing information. As an organizational component, a case hierarchy is a representation of one case. The hierarchy of a structural design case is a description of structural design information relevant to a specific design situation and is organized as a hierarchy of functional subsystems. The case indexing information contains indices and attributes of (sub)cases for retrieval.

Contents of a Design Case in CADSYN

A design case in CADSYN is the description of the structural design of a specific building, consisting of the design requirements and design description of structural systems. Knowledge sources for design case data are design drawings, design documents, and design experts. Several categories of information about buildings are derived from structural design drawings and can be expanded on by discussions with designers. These categories include general information, geometric information, special architectural specifications, load information, and the functional subsystems: lateral, gravity, and transfer floor systems.

The following design information about a particular building design is stored as the contents of a design case in CADSYN:

- *General description:* building location, building type, building name, design construction date, occupancy category, wind exposure category, material, and total costs.
- *General geometric information:* length, width, height, plan aspect ratio, height aspect ratio, overall shape, and gross floor area.
- *Other architectural specifications:* number of stories below and above grade, floor-to-floor height, floor-to-ceiling height, grid systems,

number of architectural functions and general description of those functions' locations in the plan.

- *Load information:* dead load, live load, and wind load.
- *Lateral systems:* the structural type of systems, the construction material, and the directions in which they are placed.
- *Gravity systems:* types of floor systems, types of support systems, and construction material of the support systems.
- *Transfer system:* structural details of transfer floors, such as transfer type, material, cross section, and so on.
- *Beam information:* material and beam designation, such as beam type, shape, width, and so on.
- *Column information:* material and column designation, such as width, depth, and span.

Hierarchy of a Design Case

Each design case is stored declaratively in a hierarchical structure where each node in the hierarchy is comprised of a label and a set of attribute-value pairs. The information recorded in a structural design case has three layers, as shown in Figure 7.5: a problem specification as a global context, a grid representation for each geometric/functional use of the building, and descriptions of structural systems, stored in a hierarchy of subcases, as a design solution for each grid level. Each subcase describes the local context and the solution of a design (sub)system.

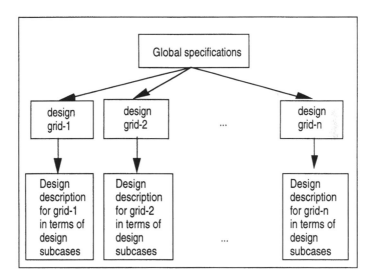

Figure 7.5. The layers of information in a structural design case.

The hierarchy of a design case is represented in multiple frames, where each subcase corresponds to a frame. The frame-based representation of a subcase is shown in Figure 7.6. In the frame of the subcase-i, slots "$name," "$system," "$supercase," and "$subcases" provide information about the identification of each frame and its relationship to other frames, and are treated as key features of the subcase. The remaining slots in the subcase represent the design description of the subcase in terms of attribute-value pairs.

```
(SUBCASE-i
    $name
        (name of  SUBCASE-i)
    $system
        (name of the system corresponding to SUBCASE-i)
    $supercase
        (name of the supercase of SUBCASE-i)
    $subcases
        (list of subsequent subcases of SUBCASE-i)
    attribute-value-1
    attribute-value-2
      •
      •
      •
    )
```

Figure 7.6. The description of a subcase node in the case hierarchy.

The hierarchical organization of a case is best illustrated through an example, as shown in Figure 7.7. The content of the design case is constructed in three layers: problem specifications as a global context, shown as Case1-bldg; a grid representation for each distinct architectural function of the building as a geometric context, shown as Case1/grid-parking, Case1/grid-retail, and Case1/ grid-office; and structural subsystems as subcases combined to provide a design solution for each grid.

The global specifications of the building in Figure 7.7 indicate that it is primarily an office building with 18 stories and a rectangular plan. The root frame of the hierarchy contains reference to the three subcases: These are the three functional grids; there is no supercase. The building has three functional grids, one each for parking, retail, and office space. Each grid is represented as a frame, with subcases representing the structural systems within the grid space.

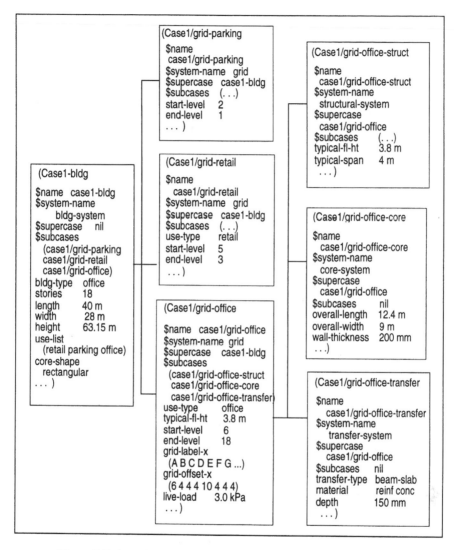

Figure 7.7. A partial description of a design case for an office building.

Figure 7.8 illustrates the 3-D envelope and a typical floor of the office building. Drawings are not part of the CADSYN case memory, they are shown here only to clarify the description of the case in Figure 7.7.

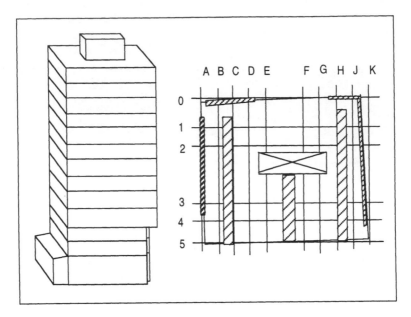

Figure 7.8. The 3-D envelope and a typical floor of Case1 in Figure 7.7.

Indexing Representation in CADSYN

CADSYN uses a feature-based indexing scheme. Structural design cases are indexed by a system list in terms of names of design subcases. The names of the subcases indicate their functionality. The system list in CADSYN consists of all structural (sub)system names used in the decomposition knowledge; for example, lateral-system, 2D-lateral-X-system, 2D-lateral-Y-system, gravity-system, transfer-system, and core-system. The system list provides pointers to all relevant design cases that contain the given subcase name.

The indexing representation in CADSYN is stored as a frame. A frame called 'system list' consists of a set of slots, each of which corresponds to a system name. Under each slot, a facet called SUBCASES contains a list of all subcases with this system name. The system list has a slot "index-system," indicating the names of the systems used as indices. For example, in Figure 7.9, slot "index-system" has a facet VALUE, which points to a list of all system names used as indices; the slot "lateral-system" contains a list of all subcases with lateral-system by the facet SUBCASES.

When the design cases are first loaded into the system, the frame "System-list" is loaded as a part of case memory. The frame system-list is changed or regenerated when a new design case is presented and case memory is updated.

All subcases of the new case are indexed in the system list by being added to the slot of the corresponding system.

```
(System-list
   index-systems
        VALUE          (lateral-system 2D-lateral-X-system
                        2D-lateral-Y-system
                        gravity-system transfer-system ...)

   lateral-system
        SUBCASES       (case0/grid-hotel-lateral
                        case0/grid-parking-lateral
                        case1/grid-residential-lateral ...)

   gravity-system
        SUBCASES       (case0/grid-hotel-gravity
                        case0/grid-parking-gravity
                           ...)
              •
              •
              •
   core-system
        SUBCASES       (case0/grid-hotel-core
                        case0/grid-parking-core
                        case0/grid-residential-core ...)
)
```

Figure 7.9. Feature-based indexing in CADSYN.

GENERALIZED KNOWLEDGE BASE

The generalized design knowledge base provides CADSYN with systems and subsystems definitions, including decomposition knowledge, structural design constraints, and procedural functions. These forms of generalized knowledge are stored in separate files and are implemented using a frame-based representation.

Decomposition Knowledge Representation

The decomposition paradigm in CADSYN can be shown as a hierarchy of multiple systems. Figure 7.10 shows a hierarchy of (sub)systems used in CADSYN for the decomposition of the structural design of buildings. At the top level, the building design system is broken into grid systems based on the number of architectural functions of a building. Each grid system is further decomposed into three subsystems: structural system, core system, and transfer system. The structural system leads the synthesis process to a further decomposition of the structural design solution.

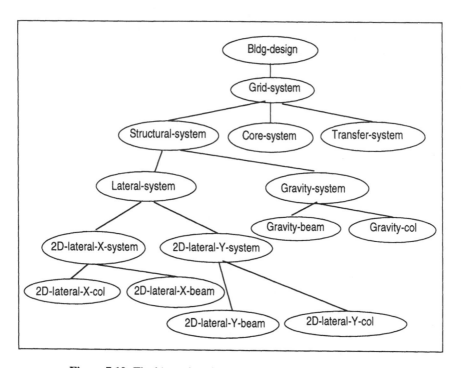

Figure 7.10. The hierarchy of structural (sub)systems in CADSYN.

The decomposition knowledge describes how the design of a problem is to be decomposed into separate (sub)systems that are eventually represented by a set of relevant attributes and their alternative values. An attribute is described in terms of various items:

- Name of the attribute, which specifies the design feature of the system.
- Identification of the attribute as a requirement specification or as a descriptive feature of the solution.
- Type of design method used to find the value for the attribute: "selection" or "procedure."
- A set of values or a procedural function corresponding to the design method.
- Name of the subsequent system, if the attribute is specified as a subsystem.

Gravity System Definition

```
SYSTEM  gravity-system
    max-aspect-ratio  req  procedure  (get-gravity-ratio)
    gravity-load      req  procedure  (get-gravity-load)
    typical-span-x    req  procedure  (get-span-x)
    support           des  selection    (cols-only 2-edges  4-edges)
    action            des  selection    (two-way one-way)
    beam              des  subsystem  beam-system
    column            des  subsystem  col-system
END-SYSTEM
```

Frame-Based Representation of Gravity System

```
(gravity-system
 $name
    VALUE       gravity-system
 $req-attributes
    VALUE       (max-aspect-ratio  gravity-load
                 typical-span-x  typical-span-y)
 $des-attributes
    VALUE       (floor-type  material  support action ...)
 $sys-attributes
    VALUE       (beam col)
 max-aspect-ratio
    METHOD    procedure
    VALUE       (get-gravity-ratio)
 support
    METHOD    selection
    VALUE       (cols-only 2-edges 4-edges)
 beam
    METHOD    subsystem
    VALUE       beam-system
 column
    METHOD    subsystem
    VALUE       col-system  )
```

Figure 7.11. The frame-based representation of gravity-system.

In the decomposition knowledge, a design system is represented in a frame by the name of the system. The definition and corresponding frame-based representation of a gravity-system is shown in Figure 7.11. The top part of the figure shows how the system is defined to CADSYN. The bottom part of the figure shows frame-based representation. In the frame-based representation, the slot "$des-attributes" indicates a list of descriptive attributes, slot "$req-attributes" shows the list of attributes as requirements, and slot "$sys-attributes" indicates the list of attributes that are further decomposed as separate subsystems. An attribute slot in the system frame has two facets: METHOD and VALUE, indicating how a value is assigned.

Constraints Representation

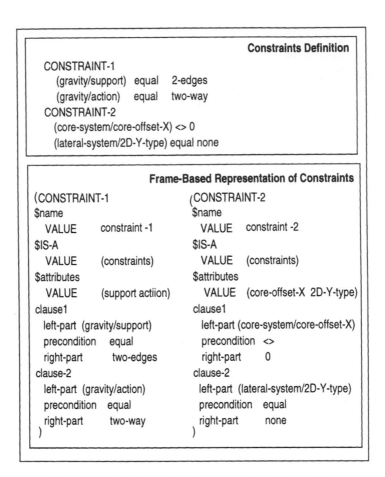

Figure 7.12. The frame-based representation of constraints.

A constraint is used to prune invalid design solutions; therefore, the "elimination" constraints specify invalid combinations of attribute-value pairs. A constraint consists of a set of clauses, where each clause represents a design attribute and its value. When all clauses of a constraint are satisfied, the constraint is violated. Constraints are represented in a frame by the name of the constraint. Each clause of the constraint is represented by three facets: "left-part," "precondition," and "right-part." Figure 7.12 shows the specification and frame-based representation of two constraints, corresponding to CONSTRAINT-1 and CONSTRAINT-2. CONSTRAINT-1 indicates that a floor supported by 2-

edges and two-way action in the gravity-system does not make sense. CONSTRAINT-2 indicates that an eccentric core location in the X direction is incompatible with a lateral system in the Y direction equal to none.

Function Representation

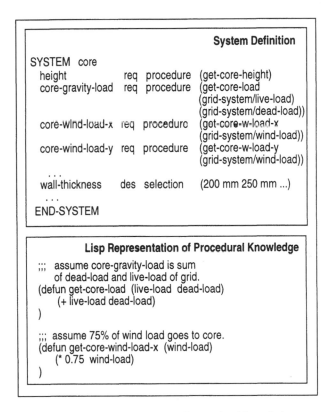

Figure 7.13. Representation of procedural knowledge.

Functions record procedural knowledge for finding values for the continuous attributes used in the decomposition representation. This procedural knowledge is represented by Lisp functions. In the decomposition knowledge, a continuous design attribute with the type of "procedure" design method has a value that is a function name with some input parameters in the design method column. Figure 7.13 shows an example of a core-system definition in the decomposition knowledge and two Lisp functions used in this system for the attributes "core-gravity-load" and "core-wind-load-x."

REASONING PROCESSORS

In addition to the representation of design case memory, CADSYN provides an implementation of the reasoning processes for case-based reasoning in design. In this section, the implementation of the following reasoning processes are described: retrieval mechanism, case adaptor, problem decomposer, solution combiner, and case-base updater. The two major reasoning processes are retrieval and adaptation. These are followed by a process specific to the way CADSYN has used generalized design knowledge, the *problem decomposer*. The *solution combiner* is a process in which solutions to different subcases are combined to form a consistent total solution. The *case updater* shows how a new solution is incorporated into case memory. Each reasoning process is described in terms of its input and output information, its function, and an English-like description of the algorithm used to implement the process. The development of the reasoning strategies for CADSYN is described in Chapter 5.

Retrieval Mechanism

The retrieval mechanism determines whether there are specific design (sub)cases sufficiently similar to the given (sub)problem, or whether the given subproblem needs to be further expanded before a relevant design case can be found. Case retrieval starts by searching case memory for a partial match with the new problem specifications. All partial matches are retrieved and presented to the user. The user determines, based on the matching information, which case/subcase is the best case for adaptation. The user may decide that none of the retrieved cases is suitable for adaptation. If a retrieved case is determined to be the best case, the adaptor is applied to produce a solution by modifying the case; otherwise, the decomposer is applied to decompose the current problem into subproblems.

The algorithm of the overall retrieval mechanism is outlined as follows:

```
Retrieval-mechanism
INPUT:
    current problem frame including design specifications.
OUTPUT:
    a case to adapt or a problem to decompose.
BEGIN
    retrieve a set of (sub)cases by the case retriever;
    select a best-case by the case selector;
    if best-case is available
        then adapt the best-case by the case adaptor
        else decompose current problem by the problem decomposer;
END
```

The retriever determines the subset of cases in case memory to be considered as possible best cases. The retriever takes as input a set of design problem specifications for the current problem. In CADSYN, the retrieval is performed based on direct symbolic matching between the labels of the system corresponding to the functionality of the current-problem and the systems used for indices to case memory. More specifically, the name of the subsystem being designed is used to directly identify those subcases that are examples of the specific subsystem. The retriever finds the matching subsystem in the system list that indicates all design cases and subcases with the same function label.

The algorithm of the retriever is:

```
Retriever
INPUT:
   current problem frame including design specifications.
OUTPUT:
   retrieved-cases.
BEGIN
   get the system-name from the current problem frame;
   use the system-name as an index-system;
   find a list of subcases for the index-system in the system list;
   output the list of subcases as retrieved cases;
END
```

The purpose of the selector is to rank the set of retrieved cases so as to identify the most relevant case. In CADSYN, all retrieved cases are ranked based on the number of specifications of the new problem that are matched by the cases. The selection of "best case" in the selector is determined by the user. The algorithm of the selector is:

```
Selector
INPUT:
   a list of retrieved-cases;
   the current problem frame.
OUTPUT:
   a best-case;
   or nil if no relevant case is selected.
BEGIN
   get the attribute-value pairs in the current problem frame;
   Repeat for each retrieved-case in the list of retrieved-cases
      compare the attribute-value pairs with a retrieved-case;
      get the number of matched attribute-value pairs;
   rank the retrieved-cases based on the number of matched pairs;
   display the ranked retrieved-cases;
   ask the user to select one case as the best-case;
END
```

Adaptor

The adaptor is an implementation of a structural adaptation and a constraint satisfaction approach that performs design adaptation (as described in Chapter 5). The adaptation includes three tasks: proposing a potential solution, verifying the potential solution, and modifying the solution. Accordingly, the adaptor is composed of three subsidiary processors: str-adaptor, constraint-checker, and modifier.

A case is first adapted structurally, so that all new problem attributes are represented in the potential solution and their values match those of the new problem. Then, the constraint checker tests this solution against design constraints, and the modifier removes inconsistencies detected in the constraint checker to reach a consistent and valid design solution. The adaptor performs as follows:

```
Adaptor
INPUT:
    the current problem frame including a set of specifications;
    a best-case consisting of multiple subcases.
OUTPUT:
    a new design solution.
BEGIN
    propose a potential solution by the str-adaptor;
    find the list of violated constraints by the constraint-checker;
    Repeat
        modify the potential solution by the modifier;
        find the list of violated constraints by the constraint-checker;
    Until the list of violated constraints is empty;
    output the potential solution as a feasible design solution.
END
```

The str-adaptor generates an initial potential design solution by adapting the best case from the selector. This stage of adaptation is characterized by eliminating differences between the problem specifications of the new problem and the best case by structurally adapting the previous solution of the best case.

The str-adaptor performs the adaptation based on the hierarchical representation of the best case. A potential design solution is generated by adapting the best case and its subsequent subcases, and so on. The adaptation requires a simple substitution of attributes and values from the new problem to the design case and a propagation of the effect of the new values on continuous variables with associated procedural attachments. The tasks of str-adaptor are:

- Change the values of attributes that have different values in the problem specifications of the best case and new problem. To do this, the str-adaptor checks each attribute in the top node of the best case hierarchy to see if the attribute is in the new problem specifications.

- Change the design description of the best case by considering the new problem specifications. This step includes two tasks: Make the names of subcases in the hierarchy of the best case consistent with the new problem, and replace the values of attributes in each node in the best case hierarchy by evaluating the procedures in the corresponding system.

The algorithm for the str-adaptor is described as follows:

```
Str-adaptor
INPUT:
    the current problem frame including a set of specifications;
    a best-case consisting of multiple subcases in a hierarchy.
OUTPUT:
    a potential solution consisting of multiple subcases in a hierarchy.
BEGIN
    Repeat for each attribute in the top node of the best-case hierarchy
        if attribute is in the new problem frame
            then replace the value by the value of the attribute in the
                new problem frame;
    Repeat for each node in the hierarchy of the best-case
        change the name of each subcase as a new name
                corresponding to the new problem;
        get the system name from the subcase;
    Repeat for each attribute in a subcase
        get the method of attribute in the system;
        if method is "procedure"
            then replace the value of the attribute by
                evaluating the procedure;
    output the adapted best-case as a potential solution;
END
```

The constraint-checker evaluates a potential design solution. Design constraints in the general knowledge base are used to identify the invalid attribute-value pairs and their systems. One task of the constraint-checker is to identify invalid systems within the potential solution. An invalid system is one that participates in a violated constraint.

In order to reason about invalid systems and their repair, each invalid system has an associated "system-cons" frame. The system-cons frame links the violated constraints to the invalid system and specifies the other systems that are part of the constraint definition. An example of the system-cons frame for the invalid lateral system is shown:

```
(System-cons-i
  system-name
        VALUE     lateral-system
  violated-cons
        VALUE     (constraint-1 constraint-3)
```

```
constraint-1
    VALUE      (beam-system)
constraint-3
    VALUE      (core-system)
```

The slot "system-name" provides the name of the invalid system. The slot "violated-cons" is a list of constraints violated by lateral-system. For each constraint in violated-cons, there is a slot by the name of the constraint that gives a list of other systems involved in the violated constraint, (e.g., slot "constraint-1" indicates that beam-system is another system involved in constraint-1).

The constraint-checker takes as an input a potential solution and tests it against design constraints. If all clauses of a constraint are true, the constraint is violated. Invalid systems are identified by checking each attribute involved in the constraint, only attributes that can be changed are considered further. For example, the attributes with procedural attachments cannot be changed unless the dependent attributes are changed. For each invalid system, if a "system-cons" frame already exists, relevant information is added; otherwise, a new "system-cons" frame is created and information about the violated constraint is added. The output of the constraint-checker is the list of violated constraints and a set of system-cons frames.

The algorithm of the constraint-checker is:

```
Constraint-checker
INPUT:
    a potential solution consisting of multiple subcases;
    design constraints.
OUTPUT:
    a list of violated constraints and a set of "system-cons" frames
        if constraints are violated;
    or true if all constraints are satisfied.
BEGIN
    Repeat for each design constraint
        get all clauses of constraint;
        if the potential-design matches all clauses
            then add the constraint to the list of violated constraints;
                Repeat for each attribute in the violated constraint
                    if attribute has a "procedure" method
                        then regard the systems in the dependency-attributes
                            as invalid systems;
                    if attribute has a "selection" method
                        then regard the system of attribute as an invalid
                            system;
                Repeat for each invalid system
                    if a system-cons frame exists for the system
                        then add this constraint to list of "violated-cons";
                            create a slot for this constraint;
                            add other systems to this constraint slot;
                    if a system-cons frame does not exist for the system
```

```
            then create a "system-cons" frame;
                create a slot "system-name";
                add the system into "system-name" slot;
                create a slot "violated-cons";
                add the constraint to the "violated-cons" slot;
                create a slot for this constraint;
                add other systems to the constraint slot;
        output the list of violated constraints;
    END
```

When constraints are violated, the invalid systems of the potential solution must be changed in order to reach a feasible solution. The modifier changes the description of an invalid system in the potential solution and propagates the effect of modification on the invalid system.

The modifier changes an invalid system through three major tasks:

1. Select an appropriate system to focus on. The modifier uses the procedure system-selector to select an invalid system. The system-selector applies the heuristic rules developed for the representation of design knowledge.

2. Find a substitution for the values of attributes in the selected system. The procedure synthesizer is applied in the modifier to generate a set of value combinations for the selected system. The modifier selects a value combination as the new description of the selected system based on global constraints satisfied by value combinations.

3. Propagate the effect of modification on the selected system in the potential solution.

The algorithm of the modifier is:

```
Modifier
INPUT:
    the system-cons frames for invalid systems;
    system sequence of problem solving by decomposition
            knowledge;
OUTPUT:
    a potential solution.
BEGIN
    get the selected system by the system-selector;
    get a set of value combinations for the selected system by
            the synthesizer;
    identify the global constraints of the system;
    Repeat for each value combination
        get the number of violated global constraints found by
            the constraint-checker;
    select a value combination which violates the least global
            constraints as the new system solution;
    replace the node corresponding to the system in the
            potential solution with the new solution;
    Repeat for each node below the new system
```

```
    evaluate the values of attributes whose method
            is "procedure";
END
```

In the system-selector, heuristic rules are applied based on "system-cons" frames created in the constraint-checker. The sequence of problem solving in terms of systems is also used in the application of heuristic rules. The systems sequence of problem solving is defined by a depth-first path through the decomposition hierarchy in the general knowledge base.

The rules for selecting a system to change are introduced in Chapter 5. The application of each heuristic rule in the system-selector is described as follows:

Rule 1. *Select the system that violates the most constraints.* This is done by counting the number of elements in the slot "violated-cons" in each "system-cons" frame. The system with largest number of "violated-cons" is selected.

Rule 2. *Select the system if it is the only adaptable system associated with a violated constraint.* This is done by listing the systems in the constraint slots in the "system-cons" frame. If there are no systems or only the "problem-system," the current system is the only adaptable system involved in this violated constraint.

Rule 3. *Select the system at the lowest level of the decomposition hierarchy when two or more systems violate the same constraint.* This is done by using the system-cons frames and the sequence of problem solving. The constraint slot in the system-cons shows other systems involved in this constraint. Among the systems involved in the same constraint violation, a system that appears earlier in the sequence of problem solving is regarded as the system at the lowest level of the decomposition hierarchy.

Rule 4. *Select systems appearing earlier in the sequence of problem solving.* This is done based on the sequence of problem solving. The system that appears earlier in the sequence than other systems is selected.

The algorithm of the system-selector follows. The heuristic rules are applied in the system-selector in the sequence of rules: 1, 2, 3, 4. Each rule is applied to the list of systems selected by the rule before.

```
System-selector
INPUT:
    a set of "system-cons" frames for invalid systems;
    systems sequence of problem solving.
OUTPUT:
    a selected invalid system.
BEGIN
; ; RULE 1:
    Repeat for each "system-cons" frame
```

```
        get the number of violated constraints in the slot
              "violated-cons" for the system;
        put the systems with largest numbers to selected list-1;
;; RULE 2:
        Repeat each system in selected list-1
          Repeat for each constraint slot in the "system-cons" frame of system
            get the list of other systems indicated by the constraint slot;
            if the list is empty or includes only problem-system
              then put this system to the selected list-2;
;; RULE 3:
        Repeat each system in selected list-2
          get the position of system in the system sequence of problem solving;
          Repeat for each constraint slot in the "system-cons" frame of system
            get the list of other systems indicated by the constraint slot;
            if position is less then the positions of other systems
              then put the system to selected list-3;
;; RULE 4:
        Repeat for each system in selected list-3
          get the positions of systems in the selected list-3;
        select the system with smallest number of position as the
              selected invalid system;
      END
```

The synthesizer generates a set of feasible value combinations for a specified system based on the corresponding generalized system in the knowledge base. All value combinations that satisfy the constraints are generated. Only the constraints associated with a specified system, called *local constraints*, are checked in the synthesizer. The algorithm of the synthesiser is given in Section 7.5.3.

Decomposer

When design cases are not available to solve a (sub)problem by case-based design adaptation, the decomposer is applied to expand the new problem specifications. The decomposer takes a given problem and breaks the problem into several subproblems using generalized system knowledge corresponding to the given problem.

The decomposer serves two functions. If the corresponding system of the given problem includes a number of descriptive attributes, the synthesizer is used to generate feasible value combinations for the problem. If the problem is decomposable (i.e., the system includes subsequent subsystems), the decomposer generates subproblems and expands the specifications for these subproblems. This is done by evaluating the values for the requirement attributes in the subsystem frame. The output of the decomposer is a set of attribute-value pairs for the given problem and/or a number of the subproblems with specifications expanded by the decomposer.

The algorithm of the decomposer is:

```
Decomposer
INPUT:
    a given problem frame including a set of specifications;
    the system frame corresponding to the problem;
    design constraints.
OUTPUT:
    a potential solution for the problem and/or a set of subsequent subproblems.
BEGIN
    get the list of des-attributes from the system frame;
    if the list is not empty
        then get a set of value combinations by the synthesiser;
                identify the global constraints of the system;
                Repeat for each value combination
                    get list of violated global constraints by the constraint-
                        checker;
                select a value combination which does not violate
                        constraints;
    get the list of sys-attributes from the system frame;
    if the list is not empty
        then
            Repeat for each system
                get the subsystem name from the method of attribute in the
                    system frame;
                create a new subproblem corresponding to the subsystem;
                get the list of req-attributes from the subsystem frame;
                evaluate the values of req-attributes in the new subproblem;
                put the new subproblem into the problem stack;
    END
```

The synthesizer is used to generate a set of alternative design solutions to the given system based on generalized knowledge. The local constraints of the system are used to prune the combination of design values for the attributes in the system.

The synthesizer uses a solution tree to represent the alternative combinations of feasible values for the attributes in the system. The synthesizer starts with a solution tree that only contains a root node. The root node contains the local problem specifications in terms of requirement attribute-value pairs. For each descriptive attribute in the system definition, the solution tree is extended by adding new leaf nodes in terms of the attribute and its values. Design constraints are used to verify the combinations of values for attributes in each path in the solution tree. During the creation of a new leaf node, if attribute-value pairs of nodes in the path between the new node and the root node violate constraints, the new node is removed. At the end of the synthesis process, attribute-value pairs of nodes in paths between leaf nodes and the root node are regarded as feasible value combinations for the system.

The algorithm of the synthesizer is shown as follows:

```
Synthesizer
INPUT:
    descriptive attributes with their domains in the system definition;
    design constraints.
OUTPUT:
    a set of feasible value combinations.
BEGIN
    Repeat for each descriptive attribute in the system definition
        Repeat for each leaf node in the solution tree
            if attribute has a "selection" method
                then get the number of alternative values: 'N';
                    create 'N' new leaf nodes under the node,
                        each of which contains the attribute and one value;
                        Repeat for each path between one new leaf
                            node to the top in the tree
                            check constraints by the constraint-checker;
                            if constraints are violated
                                then remove the new leaf node from the tree;
            if attribute has a "procedure" method
                then evaluate the value for the attribute in terms of
                the values of relevant attributes in the path between
                the node and top of the tree;
                    create a new leaf node using attribute and its value;
                    check the path from the new node to top by constraint-checker;
                    if constraints are violated
                        then remove this new node from the tree;
            if the node has no new leaf node
                then remove this node from the tree;
    Repeat for each leaf node in the tree
        collect attribute-value pairs in the path from the leaf node
        and the top of the tree to form a set of feasible attribute-value pairs;
END
```

Combiner

The adaptor and decomposer are two processors that help produce the solution to a given subproblem. To produce a complete design solution to the overall problem, the processor combiner adds a subsolution into the hierarchy of subsolutions in the design context when the subsolution is generated from the adaptor or the decomposer.

Because the subsolutions are generated independently of each other, the consistency of the combined solution must be verified. Constraint satisfaction is used to maintain the consistency of the combined solution. The combiner calls on the processors constraint-checker and modifier to do this.

The algorithm of the combiner is as follows:

```
Combiner
INPUT:
    a new subsolution for the new subproblem;
    a hierarchy representing a partial solution to the overall problem
            consisting of multiple subsolutions.
OUTPUT:
    a combined solution.
BEGIN
    add the new subsolution into the hierarchy of subsolutions
            in the design context;
    check constraints by the constraint-checker;
    Repeat
        modify the combined solution by the modifier;
        check constraints by the constraint-checker;
    Until all constraints are satisfied
END
```

Updater

Once a new design solution is generated, it is stored in the case memory for future use. The two tasks involved in the updater are:

1. Storing a new design description as a new case file.
2. Recording subcases in the case in the system list.

This is done using the following algorithm:

```
Updater
INPUT:
    a new design description consisting of multiple subcases;
    the "system-list" frame.
OUTPUT:
    an updated system list.
BEGIN
    save the new design description as a case file;
    get all nodes of subcases in the new case;
    get the list of index systems from slot 'index-system' in the
        "system-list" frame;
    Repeat for each subcase
        get the system-name from the subcase frame;
        if the system-name is included in the list of index-systems
            then add the subcase to the list of subcases in the slot
                by system-name;
        if the system-name is not included in the list of index-system
            then add the system-name to the list of index-systems;
                add a new slot by system-name in the system-list;
                put the subcase as a list in the filler of the new slot;
END
```

SYSTEM CONTROL

CADSYN is comprised of several design process modules. To generate the design solution to a given problem, a control mechanism is needed to coordinate these processes. The system manager serves as a central control mechanism, controlling the commencement and termination of problem solving by coordinating various processors. Figure 7.14 illustrates the control of reasoning processors by the system manager. Basically, the control is hierarchical, where the system manager calls the top-level processors, and each processor has subprocessors. For each problem presented to CADSYN, the system manager calls the retrieval mechanism, the combiner, and the updater. The retrieval mechanism is responsible for finding a solution to the subproblem by calling the retriever, the decomposer, and/or the adaptor. The hierarchy of calls continues as shown in Figure 7.14. The loop between the constraint-checker and the modifier is called by both the adaptor, when making changes to a selected case, and the combiner, when incorporating a subsolution into the total solution.

When the design problem is broken into subproblems by the decomposer, the system manager needs to maintain a representation of unsolved subproblems. A problem stack is used to store the subproblems generated during problem solving, where the last subproblem placed in the stack is the next problem to be solved. Initially, the design problem specifications from the user are stored as a new problem in the problem stack. As the design process proceeds, the subproblems with relevant specifications expanded by the decomposer are stored in the problem stack. The system manager checks the problem stack to determine when to terminate the design process. If the problem stack is empty, a complete design solution is generated.

If there is a design problem stored in the problem stack, the behavior of CADSYN can be generalized as follows: The system manager takes the latest problem in the stack as the current problem. The retrieval mechanism is activated, and it queries the retriever for a set of relevant design cases and the selector for identifying the best case. If the best design case is found by users, the adaptor is used to generate a solution to the current problem by calling the str-adaptor, constraint-checker, and modifier. If no best case is available, the decomposer is applied to synthesize a solution to the problem. If necessary, the decomposer divides the current problem into a set of subproblems and sends them to the system manager. These new subproblems are stored in the problem stack. The combiner is then activated by the system manager to integrate the solution with the available design subsolutions generated before. The control then returns to the system manager. These processes iterate until the problem stack is empty. When the problem stack is empty, the updater is then activated to store the complete solution in design context in the case memory.

A user interface is monitored by the system manager. A simple user interface provides users with a communication channel to the system manager. Through the interface, users can interact with the system and review and revise design decisions. The user initiates a design problem by storing the design specifications in a specification file. CADSYN reads the file, starts the retrieval processor, and then displays the similar design cases and numbers of matched attribute-value pairs between the current problem and each retrieved case. The user then chooses one case among the retrieved cases as the best case, based on the similarity information.

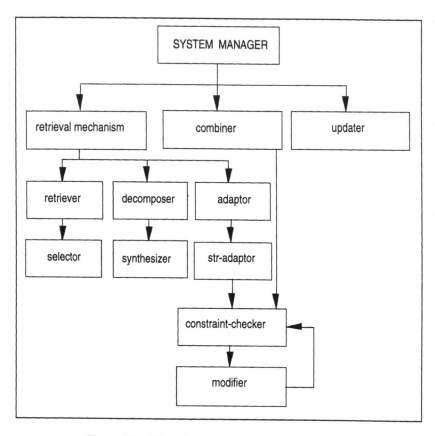

Figure 7.14. Hierarchy of procedure calls in CADSYN.

The interface also displays information about decisions made in the generation of a new design solution. In other words, it provides users with a trace of the design processes in CADSYN. For example, in the course of adaptation, the system outputs relevant information on modification and verification of the adapted design case. This information includes violated constraints, invalid systems in the potential design, selected invalid system to modify, and new design description for the invalid system. If none of the retrieved cases is selected as the best case to a given (sub)problem by users, the (sub)problem is decomposed. The (sub)solution for the (sub)problem generated by using decomposition knowledge and the further decomposed subproblems are displayed in the interface.

SUMMARY

This chapter describes the implementation of a hybrid design process model using case-based reasoning with generalized decomposition and constraint satisfaction. The implementation of the retrieval mechanism, adaptor, decomposer, combiner, and updater are described as reasoning processes. The representation of case memory and generalized design knowledge as a frame-based implementation is described. CADSYN demonstrates the combination of a CBR approach with a general decomposition approach and the incorporation of specific and generalized design knowledge.

GLOSSARY OF TERMS

Adaptor: a constraint satisfaction process in which a case is adapted to fit the new context.

CADSYN: a hybrid case-based design system using decomposition and constraint satisfaction.

Case memory: a representation of specific design situations.

Combiner: a process in which subsolutions are combined with the hierarchy of the design context.

Constraint: a representation of invalid attribute-value pairs.

Decomposer: a process in which design specifications are decomposed into functional subproblems.

Decomposition: a hierarchical representation of generalized systems and subsystems.

Design context: a dynamic representation of the intermediate states of a design solution, as well as a complete solution to a given design problem.

EDESYN: a domain-independent knowledge-based system for design by decomposition.

Generalized design knowledge: a representation of generalized design systems and constraints in a specific domain (e.g., structural design).

Hybrid case-based design: an approach to design using more than one reasoning paradigm and/or more than one knowledge representation paradigm.

Retriever: a process in which a subset of cases is retrieved from case memory for further consideration.

Selector: a process in which retrieved cases are ranked to determine the best case.

Updater: a process in which a new design solution is added to case memory.

SUGGESTED READING

Maher, M. L., and Zhang, D. M. (1991). CADSYN: Using case and decomposition knowledge for design synthesis, in J. S. Gero (Ed.), *Artificial Intelligence in Design '91*. Oxford, UK: Butterworth-Heinemann.

> Design synthesis is a part of the design process during which alternative design solutions are generated. Two distinct process models of design synthesis, case-based reasoning, and decomposition are described. Combining the two approaches allows previous experience to be used directly when available and relevant, and generalized knowledge to be used when direct experience is not appropriate. This hybrid approach to knowledge-based design has been implemented as an extension of an existing knowledge-based design environment, EDESYN. To develop a combined case-based design process model, EDESYN has been extended to accommodate case-based reasoning by adding a case base of design examples and providing a pattern matching algorithm to locate relevant cases.

Maher, M. L., and Zhang, D. M. (1993). CADSYN: A case-based design process model. *Artificial Intelligence for Engineering Design, Analysis and Manufacturing* 7(2): 97-110.

> Design synthesis presents challenges to current methodologies of CBR in the application of the various approaches to case memory organization, indexing, selection and transformation. The focus of this paper is on the adaptation process. Multiple types of design knowledge are essential to derive new design solutions. CADSYN, as a hybrid case-based design process model, integrates specific design situations and generalized domain knowledge. Case adaptation is treated as a constraint satisfaction problem, where a specific design case provides a starting point for a new design problem and constraints are used to revise the case for consistency with the new context.

Zhang, D. M. (1994). *A Hybrid Approach to Case-Based Design*, Ph.D. Thesis, University of Sydney, Australia: Department of Architectural and Design Science.

> This thesis investigates the incorporation and flexibility of using multiple types of knowledge in design synthesis. A hybrid framework of a case-based design model is explored as a vehicle for achieving this incorpora-

tion and flexibility. CADSYN, as an implementation of a hybrid case-based design process model, is developed in the structural design of buildings. The relevant issues are addressed, including specific design case representation, design case memory organization, generalized design knowledge representation, and design case adaptation. An adaptation model using an ontology of generalized design systems and design constraints is developed. A design-specific constraint satisfaction approach is developed to achieve the design subgoals in the adaptation process.

APPENDIX A:
Lisp Programs of CASECAD

INTRODUCTION

In this appendix, the Lisp programs developed as part of the CASECAD system are presented. In developing CBR systems using CASECAD, the case base can be created using generalized classes and specific cases. CASECAD supports FBS model-based hierarchical case representation using multimedia information. The current implementation provides three modalities for representing case data:

1. Text.
2. FBS attributes.
3. 2-D graphics and 3-D drawings.

The programs support case representation, case memory organization and indexing, case retrieval and ranking, and case browsing and viewing functions. In CASECAD, classes are represented as FBS models, and the contents of cases are organized based on those classes. Both classes and cases are implemented as frames. CASECAD has been developed using FRAMEKIT, a hierarchical frame-based knowledge representation language, developed at Carnegie Mellon University (Nyberg, 1988). In using FRAMEKIT, frames are represented as abstract data types comprised of slots, facets, views and fillers. In general, the user may create as many slots, facets, and views as he or she wishes within a single frame. FRAMEKIT provides the basic mechanisms of frames, inheritance, demons, and defaults. The current version of CASECAD is written in Common Lisp and Xview programming languages under UNIX on SUN Microsystems workstations.

The remainder of this appendix describes the following aspects of the CASECAD system.

- Global variables.
- Case creation functions.
- Loading functions.
- Listing functions.
- Case retrieval functions.
- Case ranking functions.
- Case viewing functions.
- Pretty print functions.
- Miscellaneous functions.

GLOBAL VARIABLES

A number of global variables have been utilized in the system. Each global variable is given a name surrounded by asterisks. Although this is not absolutely necessary, it is a good programming practice, because the special names remind us of the global nature of the variables.

- *project-directory* holds the project name that is used for an application.
- *library-directory* holds the library name that is being used at a particular time.
- *frame-list* holds a list of the names of all the frames in the system.
- *case-list* holds a list of the names of all the root-cases in the system.
- *class-list* holds a list of the names of all the root-classes in the system.
- *case-name* holds the name of the case currently being loaded.
- *class-name* holds the name of the class currently being loaded.
- *case-id* represents the identification number assigned to a case.
- *subcase-id* represents the identification number assigned to a subcase.
- *index-frame* holds the name of the frame that stores indices of cases and classes.
- *retrieval-frame* holds the name of the frame that stores retrieved cases and classes.
- *default-category* is used by retrieval functions when no category is given.
- *default-view* is used by frame functions when no view is given.
- *default-inherit* is used by the frame access functions, and its value t indicates the use of inheritance.
- *indent-factor* controls the indentation. It indicates the number of spaces that the output stream is indented at each level of embedding in a case.
- *acad-pipe-stream* represents the pipe stream between CASECAD and AutoCAD.
- *inheritance-link* represents the slot name that is used for inheritance: currently, is-a.

```
;Define global variables
(defvar *project-directory* nil)
(defvar *library-directory* nil)
(defvar *frame-list* nil)
(defvar *case-list* nil)
(defvar *class-list* nil)
(defvar *case-seed* 0)
(defvar *case-name* nil)
(defvar *class-name* nil)
(defvar *subcase-id* 0)
```

```
(defvar *default-category* 'function)
(defvar *index-frame* 'case-index)
(defvar *retrieval-frame* 'case-retrieval)
(defvar *default-view* 'common)
(defvar *default-inherit* t)
(defvar *indent-factor* 3)
(defvar *acad-pipe-stream* nil)
(defvar *inheritance-link* 'is-a)
```

CASE CREATION FUNCTIONS

Each application developed using CASECAD must be given a project name. This name is assigned to the global variable *project-directory*. Each such project directory has two subdirectories, CASELIB and CLASSLIB. The directory CASELIB contains information about cases, whereas CLASSLIB contains information about classes or models. Information about individual cases or classes is organized into separate directories within the CASELIB directory and CLASSLIB directory, respectively. Each case/class directory contains four types of files, as indicated by their extensions. The file extensions and their contents are as follows:

> .lsp file   - FBS attributes of a case/class in Lisp.
> .sld file   - AutoCAD slide files representing the structure.
> .fig file   - XFIG drawing files representing the behavior.
> .pty file   - Pretty print version of a case/class.

The user creates a case base by developing .lsp, .sld, and .fig files. The system creates .pty files automatically during the loading of a project. Before presenting the case/class creating functions, we must define the syntax, or allowable format, of the case/class entities that form the case memory. A class is a generalized design entity; a case is a specific design entity. In CASECAD, cases are defined to the system by the call MAKE-CASE, which places the case in the memory. Classes are created by the call MAKE-CLASS, which places the class in the memory. Both MAKE-CASE and MAKE-CLASS use MAKE-NODE to store their contents as a frame. MAKE-NODE creates a multilevel data structure that is used to store information about classes/cases. In this section, the top-level creation functions, along with other related subfunctions, are described.

Function MAKE-CLASS is the top-level class creation function. It accepts two required arguments: <class name>, <class body>. It returns the name of the class (a symbol). MAKE-CASE is the top-level case creation function. It accepts two required arguments: <case name>, <case body>. MAKE-CASE returns the name of the case (a symbol). MAKE-NODE creates a frame structure to store a case/class node. Each case/class node is described by any number of slots, each slot can have any number of facets, each facet can have any number of views, and each view can have any number of fillers. MAKE-NODE then returns the name of the node (a symbol). In CASECAD, cases and classes are indexed using FBS attributes. MAKE-NODE stores these indices separately, in a frame with pointers to the cases/classes that have these attributes. During case retrieval, only those cases that have the attributes of the new design problem need to be searched. Case indices are stored in a frame called "case-index," and class indices are stored in a frame called "class-index."

```
; Make a class
(defun make-class (class-name class-body)
      ; Update subnodes
      (add-filler *class-name* 'relation 'subnodes class-name :view 'value)
      ; Create frame for the subclass
      (make-node class-name class-body))

; Make a case
(defun make-case (case-name case-body)
      ; Update subnodes
      (add-filler *case-name* 'relation 'subnodes case-name :view 'value)
      ; Create frame for the subcase
      (make-node case-name case-body))

;Make a subnode
(defun  make-node (name body)
      ; Create frame in the name
      (create-frame name)
      ; Create the slots one by one
      (dolist (slot body)
         (create-slot name (first slot))
         ; Create the facets one by one
            (dolist (facet (rest slot))
            (create-facet name (first slot) (first facet))
         (if (FBS-slot-p (first slot))
            (add-filler *index-frame* (first slot) (first facet) name))
            ; Create the views one by one
         (dolist (view (rest facet))
               (create-view name (first slot) (first facet) (first view))
               ; Add fillers to a view
            (add-fillers name (first slot) (first facet)
                  (rest view) :view (first view)))))

      name)
```

Here is an example use of make-class:

```
(make-class 'floor-system '(
    (relation
       (part-of
          (value  building)))
    (function
       (transmit-dead-load
          (type  numeric)
```

```
        (dimension (F)))
    (transmit-live-load
        (type numeric)
        (dimension (F))))
(behavior
    (fire-resistance-level
        (type numeric))
    (deflection
        (type numeric)
        (dimension (L)))
    (shear-stress
        (type numeric)
        (dimension (F L -2))))
(structure
    (structural-material
        (type symbolic))
    (start-level
        (type integer))
    (end-level
        (type integer))
    (floor-framing
        (type symbolic))
    (span-type
        (type symbolic))
    (maximum-span
        (type numeric)
        (dimension (L)))
    (typical-span
        (type numeric)
        (dimension (L)))
    (floor-depth
        (type numeric)
        (dimension (L)))
    (span-to-depth-ratio
        (type numeric))
    (maximum-aspect-ratio
        (type numeric)))))
```

Here is an example use of make-case:

```
(make-case (setq fcn (get-subcase-name)) '(
    (general
        (text
            (value
    "The floor system used consisted of a combination of standard
    Rescrete precast 'Formplank' panels supported by custom-made
    precast beam shells and by facade wall panels. The ends of the
    Formplank' panels rested on either corbels on the facade wall units or the
    upturned edges of the precast beam shells. These precast elements were
    used to produce a one-way slab, one-way beam system with structural detailing
    providing continuity between beams, precast columns and facade panels.")))
```

```
(relation
    (instance-of
        (value floor-system)))
(function
    (transmit-dead-load
        (value 3)
        (units kPa))
    (transmit-live-load
        (value 3)
        (units kPa)))
(behavior
    (fire-resistance-level
        (value 2)
        (units hrs))
    (deflection
        (value 18)
        (units mm))
    (shear-stress
        (value 0.98)
        (units Mpa))
    (xfig-file
        (value "floor-system.fig")))
(structure
    (material
        (value precast-concrete))
    (start-level
        (value 1))
    (end-level
        (value 17))
    (span-type
        (value one-way))
    (maximum-span
        (value 11)
        (units m))
    (typical-span
        (value 9 )
        (units m))
    (floor-depth
        (value 250)
        (units mm))
    (span-to-depth-ratio
        (value 44))
    (acad-file
        (value "floor-system.sld"))
    (maximum-aspect-ratio
        (value 4.2)))))
```

LOADING FUNCTIONS

The function LOAD-PROJECT loads a given project and builds both case memory and class memory. If the file "specifications.lsp" exists in the *project-directory*, it is also loaded. The function LOAD-PROJECT accepts one argument: <project name>. The function LOAD-CASES loads all cases in the CASELIB directory in the *PROJECT-DIRECTORY*. The file "cases.lsp" in the *project-directory* contains the names of cases in the CASELIB. The function LOAD-CLASSES loads all classes in the CLASSLIB directory in the *PROJECT-DIRECTORY*. The file "classes.lsp" in the *project-directory* contains the names of classes in the CLASSLIB directory. The function LOAD-SPECIFICATIONS loads and interprets the specifications for a new problem. Specifications are stored as a frame in the file "specifications.lsp" in the *project-directory*. It returns t if loading is successful; otherwise, nil. The CommonLisp function PROBE-FILE returns t if its argument is an existing file; otherwise, nil. The function MAKE-FRAME creates a complete frame and is part of FRAMEKIT.

An example of cases.lsp file is shown below.

```
(setq cases '(
    "130Elizabeth"
    "370Pitt"
    "NovotelHotel"
    "ParkInnHotel"
    "145ClaranceSt"))
```

Here is an example of classes.lsp file:

```
(setq classes '(
    "building"
    "high-rise-building"
    "low-rise-building"
    "medium-rise-building"
    "core-structure"
    "floor-system"
    "grid-system"))
```

Here is an example of "specifications.lsp":

```
(make-frame 'specifications
    '((function
        (support-grid-geometry
            (common (= rectangular)))
        (support-building-type
            (common (= office))))
    (behavior
        (cost-of-construction
            (common (<= 20 $millions))))
    (structure
    (number-of-stories
        (common (= 20)))
```

```lisp
    (material
      (common (= reinforced-concrete)))))
    ))

;Load a project
(defun load-project (project-name)
    (setq *project-directory* project-name)
      (format t "Loading project ~a ...~%" *project-directory*)
      ;Load class library
    (load-classes)
      ; Load case library
    (load-cases)
    ;Load problem specifications
    (load-specifications)
      (format t "Loading project ~a is completed~%" *project-
        directory*))

;Load all cases that belong to a project
(defun load-cases ()
    (let ((file (format nil "~a/cases.lsp" *project-directory*)) out-file)
      (load file)
      ; Set value to *index-frame*
      (setq *index-frame* 'case-index)
      ; Load cases one by one
      (dolist (case cases t)
          (setq *case-name* case)
          ; Initialize *case-seed*
          (setq *case-seed* (+ *case-seed* 100))
          (add-filler 'global *case-name* 'seed *case-seed*)
          ; Initialize *subcase-id* to zero
          (setq *subcase-id* 0)
          (load (format nil "~a/CASELIB/~a/~a.lsp" *project-directory*
    case case))
          ; Write pretty-print version of the case
            (setq file (format nil "~a/CASELIB/~a/~a.pty"
          *project-directory* case case))
            (setq out-file (open file :direction :output))
            (pretty-print-case case :stream out-file)
          ; Write all the subcase names to a file
            (write-subcases case)
          ;Update the value of *case-list*
          (setq *case-list* (append2 *case-list* *case-name*)))))

;Load all classes that belong to a project
(defun load-classes ()
    (let ((file (format nil "~a/classes.lsp" *project-directory*)) out-file)
      (load file)
      ; Set value to *index-frame*
      (setq *index-frame* 'class-index)
      ; Load classes one by one
      (dolist (class classes t)
          (setq *class-name* class)
          (load (format nil "~a/CLASSLIB/~a/~a.lsp"
          *project-directory* class class))
          ; Write pretty-print version of the class
```

```
        (setq file (format nil "~a/CLASSLIB/~a/~a.pty"
        *project-directory* class class))
        (setq out-file (open file :direction :output))
            (pretty-print-class class :stream out-file)
        ; Write all the subclass names to a file
            (write-subclasses class)
        ;Update the value of *class-list*
        (setq *class-list* (append2 *class-list* *class-name*)))))

;Load all specifications
(defun load-specifications ()
        (let ((file (format nil "~a/specifications.lsp" *project-directory*)))
            (if (probe-file file) (load file))))
```

LISTING FUNCTIONS

CASECAD provides a set of functions to list the names of cases, classes, subcases, subclasses, and specifications. The function LIST-CASES lists the names of all the root-cases in the system. The function LIST-SUBCASES lists names of all the subcases in the system. The function LIST-SUBCLASSES lists names of all the subclasses in the system. The function FIND-ALL-SUBNODES returns a list of subnodes of a case/class. The function LIST-SPECIFICATIONS lists all the specifications of the new problem. The macro frame-p returns its argument if it is a frame, otherwise nil. The function FIND-ALL-SUBNODES returns a list of subnodes of a case/class. The function FIND-SUBCASE-TYPE returns the type of its argument.

```
;List the names of all cases of a project
(defun list-cases()
        (cond    (*case-list*
                    (format t "~%The cases are: ~%~%")
                    ;List cases one by one
                    (dolist (case *case-list* t)
                    (format t "   ~25a~%" case)))
                (t  (format t "Cases not found~%"))))

;List the names of all subcases of a case
(defun list-subcases(case)
        (let    (subcase-list)
                (format t "~%THE SUBCASE NODES OF ~a~%~%" case)
                (setq subcase-list (find-all-subnodes case))
                ; List subcases one by one
                    (format t "   ~25a~a~%~%" "node" "type")
                (dolist (subcase subcase-list t)
                        (format t "   ~25a~a~%" subcase (find-subcase-type
                subcase)))))

;List the names of all classes of a project
```

```
(defun list-classes()
     (cond   (*class-list*
               (format t "~%The classes are: ~%~%")
                   ;List classes one by one
               (dolist (class *class-list* t)
                   (format t "   ~25a~%" class)))
               (t (format t "Cases not found~%"))))

;List the names of all subclasses of a class
(defun list-subclasses(class)
     (let   (subclass-list)
               (format t "~%THE SUBCLASS NODES OF ~a~%~%" class)
               (setq subclass-list (find-all-subnodes class))
               ; List subclasses one by one
                   (format t "   ~40a~a~%~%" "node" "type")
               (dolist (subclass subclass-list t)
                       (format t "   ~40a~a~%" subclass (find-subclass-type
                   subclass)))))

;List all specifications
(defun list-specifications ()
     (cond   ((frame-p 'specifications)
           (pretty-print-node 'specifications))
                   (t (format t "Specifications not found~%"))))

;List class indices
(defun list-class-index ()
     (cond   ((frame-p 'class-index)
               (pretty-print-node 'class-index))
               (t (format t "Class-indices not found~%"))))

;List case indices
(defun list-case-index ()
     (cond   ((frame-p 'case-index)
               (pretty-print-node 'case-index))
               (t (format t "Case-indices not found~%"))))
```

CASE RETRIEVAL FUNCTIONS

Given a description of a problem's requirements, retrieval functions must find a small set of useful similar cases. Case retrieval involves two important subprocesses: matching and ranking. Matching is the process of comparing two cases or case attributes to each other and determining their match. Ranking is the process of ordering partially matching cases according to the number of matches.

The function RETRIEVE-CASES is the top-level case retrieval function. This function retrieves cases using a particular category of specifications, for example, function, behavior, or structure. The default category is function. Both RETRIEVE-CASES and RETRIEVE-CLASSES use RETRIEVE-NODES to retrieve relevant subnodes. The function RETRIEVE-NODES does all the work.

The function RETRIEVE-NODES finds cases based on a given category of problem specifications. Retrieved cases are stored in a frame "case-retrieval" and a slot "category-name." It returns nil if no specifications found for the category; otherwise it returns t. The function RETRIEVE-NODES identifies all the nodes that match partially or completely with the specifications of the problem. It takes two arguments: <entity type> and <category name>. The entity type argument indicates whether the node is a class or case. The macro %slot-facet-names returns all facet names of a given slot.

```
(defun retrieve-cases (&key (category *default-category*))
    (setq *retrieval-frame* 'case-retrieval)
    (setq *index-frame* 'case-index)
    (cond    ((equal category 'all)
                (retrieve-nodes 'function)
                (retrieve-nodes 'behavior)
                (retrieve-nodes 'structure))
             (t (retrieve-nodes category))))
    (rank-retrieved-nodes category))

(defun retrieve-classes (&key (category *default-category*))
    (setq *retrieval-frame* 'class-retrieval)
    (setq *index-frame* 'class-index)
    (cond    ((equal category 'all)
                (retrieve-nodes 'function)
                (retrieve-nodes 'behavior)
                (retrieve-nodes 'structure))
             (t (retrieve-nodes category))))
    (rank-retrieved-nodes category))

(defun retrieve-nodes (category)
    (prog (attribute-list constraint-list constraint attribute matches)
             ; Check to see if there are specifications of given category
            (cond    ((null (setq attribute-list (%slot-facet-names
                                 'specifications category)))
                       (format t " No %s specifications found~%" category)
                       (return nil)))
            (format t "~%~a USING ~a SPECIFICATIONS~%" *retrieval-frame*
category)
                (format t "~%    ~30a~20a~a~%" "attribute" "constraints" "no-
                       of- matchings")
            ; Consider attributes one by one
            (dolist (attribute attribute-list)
                    (cond ( (setq constraint-list (%view-fillers 'specifications
                    category attribute 'constraint))
                            ; Set no of matches to zero
                            (setq matches 0)
                            (format t "~%    ~30a~20a" attribute constraint-list)
                    ; Consider nodes that include the attribute one by one.
                            (dolist (node (reverse (%view-fillers *index-frame*
                    category attribute *default-view*)))
                                    ; Check to see if the attribute matches the
                                            constraint.
```

```
        (cond ((match-attribute node category attribute
        constraint-list)
                (setq matches (+ 1 matches))
        ; If match succeeds store the attribute and
        the node
                (add-filler *retrieval-frame* category node
                attribute))))
                (format t "~5a" matches))))
    (return t)))
```

MATCHING AND RANKING

The function MATCH-ATTRIBUTE is the top-level case attribute matching
function. The function MATCH-RANGE checks to see if the value of a slot is
in the appropriate range. The function MATCH-VALUE checks to see if the
value of a slot satisfies specified constraints. The function RANK-RETRIEVED-
SUBNODES ranks all retrieved subnodes according to the number of matches and
prints out the ordered subnodes, along with their numbers of matches.

```
(defun match-attribute (node category attribute constraints)
    ; A constraint is specified as a list of triplets: (relation value units)
    ; Relation is a relational operator or a verb such as 'equal-to' or
'include'
    (prog (range values relation value units)
        (setq values (get-fillers node category attribute :view 'value
        :inherit t))
            (setq range (first (get-fillers node category attribute :view
                'range :inherit t)))
        (dolist (constraint constraints)
            (setq relation (first constraint))
            (setq value (second constraint))
            (setq units (third constraint))
            (if values
                (if (not (match-value value relation values))
                    (return nil)))
            (if range
                (if (not (match-range value range))
                    (return nil))))
        (return t)))

(defun match-range (value range)
    ; Range for an attribute is specified in  class nodes as a list.
    ; For example, (10  to  15), (steel rc pc)
    (cond    ((and (numberp (first range))
                (numberp (third range))
                (equal (second range) 'to))
                (and (=> value  (first range)) (<= value  (third range))))
            (t (member value  range))))

(defun match-value (value relation val-list)
```

```
(cond   ((null val-list) nil)
        ((or  (equal relation 'is) (equal relation '=)
              (equal relation 'equal-to))
         (equal value (first val-list)))
        ((equal relation 'include) (subsetp value val-list))
        (t (funcall relation (first val-list) value ))))

(defun rank-retrieved-nodes (category)
   (let  (subnode matches matched-nodes ranked-nodes entity num
          category-list)
      (setq file (format nil "~a/~a-~a.lsp" *project-directory* category
   *retrieval-frame*))
      (setq out-file (open file :direction :output))
      (if  (equal category 'all)
           (setq category-list '(function behavior structure))
           (setq category-list (list category)))
      (dolist (category category-list t)
         (format t "~%~% ~a BASED ON ~a SPECIFICATIONS~%"
   *retrieval-frame* category)
         (format t "~%~20a~30a~10a~%" "sub-node" "entity" "no of
   matches")
         (dolist (subnode (reverse (%slot-facet-names *retrieval-frame*
            category)))
            (setq num (length (%view-fillers *retrieval-frame* category
         subnode *default-view*)))
            (setq matched-nodes (cons (list subnode  num) matched-
         nodes)))
            (setq ranked-nodes (sort matched-nodes '(lambda (p q)
            (cadr p) (cadr q))))))
      (terpri)
      ; Print ranked nodes one by one
      (dolist (ranked-node ranked-nodes)
         (setq subnode (car ranked-node) num (cadr ranked-node))
         (setq entity (find-entity-name subnode))
            (format t "~20a~30a~10a~%" subnode entity num)
            (format out-file "~20a~a~%" subnode entity )))
      (close out-file)))
```

PRETTY PRINTING FUNCTIONS

The function PRETTY-PRINT-CLASS pretty prints a class and PRETTY-PRINT-CASE pretty prints a case. Both of these functions call PRETTY-PRINT-NODE to print their subnodes.

```
;Pretty print a class
(defun pretty-print-class (class &key (stream t) (indent 0))
   (format stream "~a~%" "--------------------------------------------")
   (format stream "           Class: ~a~%" class)
   (format stream "~a~%" "--------------------------------------------")
   ; Print nodes one by one
   (dolist (node (find-all-subnodes class))
```

```
        (pretty-print-node node :stream stream :indent indent))
        (if (not (equal stream t)) (close stream)))))

;Pretty print a case
(defun pretty-print-case (case &key (stream t) (indent 0))
        (format stream "~a~%" "------------------------------------------------")
            (format stream "                     Case: ~a~%" case)
            (format stream "~a~%" "------------------------------------------------")
            ; Print nodes one by one
            (dolist (node (find-all-subnodes case))
                (pretty-print-node node :stream stream :indent indent))
            (if (not (equal stream t)) (close stream)))))

;Pretty print a subnode
(defun pretty-print-node (name &key (stream t) (indent 0))
        (terpri stream)
        (terpri stream)
        (indent-stream indent stream)
        ; Pretty print the node-name
        (format stream "~a~%" name)
        (underline-stream (atoml name) indent stream)
        ; Print slots one by one
        (dolist (slot (reverse (%frame-slot-names name)))
            ; Pretty print the slot
                (pretty-print-slot name slot stream (+ indent *indent-factor*)))
        (terpri stream)
        (terpri stream))

;Pretty print a slot
(defun pretty-print-slot (name slot stream indent)
        (terpri stream)
        (indent-stream indent stream)
        ; Pretty print the slot name
        (format stream "~a~%" slot)
        (underline-stream (atoml slot) indent stream)
        ; Print facets one by one
        (dolist (facet (reverse (%slot-facet-names name slot)))
            ; Pretty print the facet
            (pretty-print-facet name slot facet stream (+ indent
            *indent-factor*))))

;Pretty print a facet
(defun pretty-print-facet (name slot facet stream indent)
        (terpri stream)
        (indent-stream indent stream)
        ; Print the facet
        (format stream "~a: " facet)
        ; Print views one by one
        (dolist (view (reverse (%facet-view-names name slot facet)))
            (if (not (equal view 'common))
                ; Pretty print the view
                (pretty-print-view name slot facet view stream (+ indent
        *indent-factor*))
                ; Pretty print the fillers
                (print-fillers (%view-fillers name slot facet 'common) stream))))
```

```
;Pretty print a view
(defun pretty-print-view (name slot facet view stream indent)
        (terpri stream)
        (indent-stream indent stream)
        ; Print the view
        (format stream "~a: " view)
        ; Print the fillers
        (print-fillers (%view-fillers name slot facet view) stream))

;Pretty print fillers
(defun print-fillers (filler-list stream)
        (let ((count 0))
            (dolist (x filler-list)
                (setq count (1+ count))
                (if (> count 1) (format stream ", "))
                (format stream "~a" x))))
```

VIEWING FUNCTIONS

Viewing Functions

Once a set of partially matched cases has been retrieved, the user can view the retrieved cases in order to select the most applicable or "best case" for the current problem. The case retriever provides a list of cases or subcases after searching the case memory. For each retrieved case, the rank and number of matching features are shown. The user can then view the contents of any of the retrieved cases. The function VIEW-SUBCLASS displays a given subclass. The function VIEW-SUBCASE displays a given subcase. The function VIEW-NODE displays a given node showing text, FBS attributes, and drawings.

```
;View a subclass
(defun view-subclass (subclass &key (stream t) (indent 0))
      (setq *library-directory* "CLASSLIB")
    (view-node subclass))

;View a subcase
(defun view-subcase (subcase &key (stream t) (indent 0))
      (setq *library-directory* "CASELIB")
    (view-node subcase))

;;View a subnode representing either a subcase or a subclass
(defun view-node (node &key (stream t) (indent 0))
      (prog (slide-file xfig-file entity-name)
          (cond  ((not (frame-p node))
                    (format t "VIEW-NODE - node has no definition! ~a" node)
                    (return nil)))
          (setq entity-name (find-entity-name node))
```

```
        ;Pretty print the node
     (pretty-print-node node)
        ;Check to see if there is an acad drawing file
     (if (setq slide-file (first (%view-fillers node 'structure 'acad-file
'value)))
    ; If drawing file exists, send a command to ACAD to display it
        (write-acad-pipe (format nil "~a/~a/~a/~a" *project-directory*
*library-directory* entity-name slide-file)))
        ;Check to see if there is a XFIG drawing file
     (if (setq xfig-file (first (%view-fillers node 'behavior 'xfig-file
'value)))
        ; If drawing file exists, send a command to XFIG to display it
        (system (format nil "xfig ~a/~a/~a/~a &" *project-directory*
*library-directory* entity-name xfig-file)))))
```

AutoCAD communication functions

The function OPEN-ACAD-PIPE establishes a pipe connection between the
CASECAD environment and the AutoCAD environment. It uses the UNIX
function MKNOD for this purpose. The function WRITE-ACAD-PIPE sends a
command through the pipe to the AutoCAD system. The function CLOSE-
ACAD-PIPE closes the pipe connection between the CASECAD environment
and the AutoCAD environment. The function READ-PIPE is used by the
AutoCAD system to read commands forwarded by the CASECAD system. The
function VIEW-SLIDE displays a slide file in a graphics window.

```
; Establish a pipe connection to AutoCAD
(defun open-acad-pipe ()
     (system "/usr/etc/mknod .acad p")
     (format t "Please enter the command (read-acad-pipe) in the acad window~%")
     (setq *acad-pipe-stream* (open ".acad" :direction :output))
     (format t "A pipe connection with ACAD has been established~%"))

; Write a command to the AutoCAD  pipe
(defun write-acad-pipe (string)
     (cond   (  *acad-pipe-stream*
             (format t "~%~a" string)
             (format *acad-pipe-stream* "~a~%" string)
             (format *acad-pipe-stream* "~a~%" "") t)
        (t     (format t "~%A pipe connection with acad has not been
        established~%") nil )))

; Close the pipe connection to AutoCAD
(defun close-acad-pipe ()
        (cond   (  *acad-pipe-stream*
             (write-acad-pipe "finish")
             (close *acad-pipe-stream*)
             (system "rm .acad")
             (setq *acad-pipe-stream* nil)
             "The pipe connection with AutoCAD has been terminated~%")
```

```
        (t      (format t "~%A pipe connection with acad has not been
        established~%") nil)))

; Read from the AutoCAD pipe
(defun read-acad-pipe ()
        (let  ((command nil))
                (setq in-pipe (open ".acad" "r"))
                (format t "read-pipe-mode established~%")
                (while (not (equal msg "finish"))
                (setq command (read-line in-pipe))
                (cond    ((not (and (equal command "finish") (equal command "")))
                  (view-slide msg) t)))

; View a AutoCAD slide
(defun view-slide (slide)
        (let  (file)
                (setq file (findfile slide))
                (if file (command "vslide" slide)
                        (format t "~%~a~%" (strcat "Could not find file " slide ".")))))
```

MISCELLANEOUS FUNCTIONS

```
;Save the current project into a file
(defun save-project()
        (format t "~%Saving project ~a ... ~%" *project-directory*)
        (save (format nil "~a.exe" *project-directory*)))

;Find the type of a given subclass
(defun find-subclass-type (subclass)
                (first (%view-fillers subclass 'relation 'is-a 'value)))

;Find the type of a given subcase
(defun find-subcase-type (subcase)
                (first (%view-fillers subcase 'relation 'instance-of 'value)))

;Find the root of a given subcase
(defun find-entity-name (subcase)
                (first (%view-fillers subcase 'relation 'subnode-of 'value)))

;Find all the subnodes of a given case/class
(defun find-all-subnodes (name)
                (reverse (%view-fillers name 'relation 'subnodes 'value)))

;Check to see if its arg is a relation attribute
;If so, it returns its reverse link
(defun get-inverse-link (name)
        (cond ((equal name 'instance-of) 'instances)
                ((equal name 'instances) 'instance-of)
                ((equal name 'parts) 'part-of)
                ((equal name 'part-of) 'parts)
```

```lisp
            ((equal name 'subnode-of) 'subnodes)
            ((equal name 'subnodes) 'subnode-of)
            ((equal name 'subclasses) 'is-a)
            ((equal name 'is-a) 'subclasses)))

; Generate a new name for a subcase/subclass
(defun get-subcase-name ()
        ; If *subcase-id* has zero value, then case-name is the root subcase
        (if (zerop *subcase-id*)
        ; Initialize *subcase-id*
        (setq *subcase-id* *case-seed*))
        (setq *subcase-id* (+ 1 *subcase-id*))
        (read-from-string (format nil "SUBCASE~d" *subcase-id*)))

;Write all the current specifications to a file
(defun  write-specifications ()
        (let (file out-file)
            (cond   ((frame-p 'specifications)
                    (setq file (format nil "~a/specifications.lsp"
                    *project-directory*))
                        (setq out-file (open file :direction :output))
                        (print-frame 'specifications :stream out-file)))))

; Write the names of all subcases of a case into a file
(defun  write-subcases (case)
        (let   (subcase-list file)
                (setq file (format nil "~a/CASELIB/~a/subcases.lsp"
            *project-directory* case))
                (setq subcase-list (find-all-subnodes case))
                (setq out-file (open file :direction :output))
                (dolist (subcase subcase-list)
                (format out-file "~25a~a~%" subcase
                (find-subcase-type subcase)))
                (close out-file)))

; Write the names of all subcases of a case into a file
(defun  write-subclasses (class)
        (let   (subclass-list file)
                (setq file (format nil "~a/CLASSLIB/~a/subclasses.lsp"
            *project-directory* class))
                (setq subclass-list (find-all-subnodes class))
                (setq out-file (open file :direction :output))
                (dolist (subclass subclass-list)
                (format out-file "~25a~a~%" subclass
                (find-subclass-type subclass)))
                (close out-file)))

;Indent a stream by a specified number of spaces
(defun indent-stream (num &optional (stream t))
        (dotimes (loopvar num)
            (write-char #\Space stream)))

;Underline a stream by a specified length
(defun underline-stream (length indent &optional (stream t))
        (indent-stream indent stream)
```

```
    (dotimes (loopvar length)
        (write-char #\- stream)))

;Find the length of an atom
(defun atoml (x)
    (length (format nil "~a" x)))

; Append an element to the end of a list
(defun append2 (l e)
        (append l (list e)))
```

APPENDIX B:
A Sample Case From CASECAD

CASECAD was implemented using a case base developed from a collection of medium- to high-rise buildings in Sydney, Australia. The design data for the building cases were collected through the cooperation of the engineers in Acer Wargon Chapman Associates. The case base currently contains five building cases. Each case in the case memory is a single building design. A subcase is a structural component of the building, for example, a rigid frame or a floor system component. In this Appendix, we illustrate the case 370-PITT-ST. The 370-PITT-ST building is a 17-story office block incorporating two retail floors with arcades linking into adjacent properties. It uses precast concrete elements for major structural and architectural components. The building is complicated by being located partly over railway tunnels, requiring special footings and innovative solutions to vibration isolation. An eccentric core required specific facade elements to be designed as a wind-shear frame. The hierarchical organization of the case 370-PITT-ST is shown in Figure B.1.

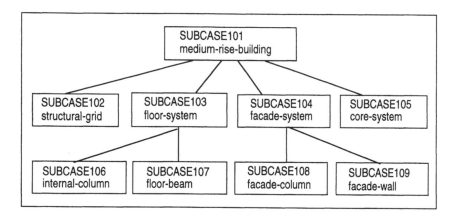

Figure B.1. The hierarchical organization of the case 370-PITT-ST.

CASE: 370-PITT-ST

Node: SUBCASE101
  GENERAL
    text:
    value:

"370-PITT-ST is a $20 m office building
completed in 1989. Its 17 stories rest partly
over tunnels forming a link in Sydney's
underground railway system. Retail outlets
and car parking facilities are located on
ground and upper-ground levels, while each
typical floor provides approximately 1000
m^2 of office space. There is no basement,
due to the presence of the underground city
circle rail loop immediately below the
building. The building's outstanding design
features include its utilization of precast
concrete elements for major structural and
architectural components. These elements
include load-bearing facade panels,
columns, floor system beam and slab
shells, stairs, and wall panels. Lateral
stability is provided by the eccentric core
and the western facade panels."

    RELATION
        subnode-of:
            value: 370-PITT-ST
        instance-of:
            value: medium-rise-building
    FUNCTION
        support-building-type:
            value: office
        resist-wind-load:
            value: 1.5
            units: kPa
        resist-gravity-load:
            value: 6
            units: kPa
        support-grid-type:
            value: rectangular
        maximum-span:
            value: 10
            units: m
    BEHAVIOR
        net-area-of-usable-space:
            value: 15000
            units: m^2
        construction-cost:
            value: 20

            units: millions
        core-area-as-a-percent-of-
            total-floor-area:
            value: 10.8
STRUCTURE
    acad-file:
        value: building.sld
    building-location:
        value: 370-Pitt-Street-
            Sydney
    date-of-construction:
        value: 1989
    overall-shape:
        value: rectangular
    overall-length:
        value: 38
        units: m
    overall-width:
        value: 29
        units: m
    overall-height:
        value: 70
        units: m
    floor-system-type:
        value: beam-slab
    wind-system-type:
        value: core-and-frame
    location-of-core:
        value: eccentric
    gross-area-of-core:
        value: 121
        units: m^2
    overall-length-of-core:
        value: 11
        units: m
    overall-width-of-core:
        value: 11
        units: m
    material:
        value: precast-concrete,
            insitu-concrete
    number-of-floor-levels-above-
            grade:
        value: 17
    number-of-floor-levels-below-
            grade:
        value: 0
    number-of-stories:
        value: 17
    height-to-width-ratio:
        value: 2.42
    length-to-width-ratio:
        value: 1.84
    floor-to-floor-height:

value: 4
units: m
floor-to-ceiling-height:
value: 3.5
units: m

SUBCASE: STRUCTURAL-GRID

Node: SUBCASE102
GENERAL
text:
value:

"The structural grid is a rectangular arrangement consisting of parallel grids to assist with the placement of vertical supporting elements of the building and to express how the building is functionally zoned."

RELATION
subnode-of:
value: 370-PITT-ST
instance-of:
value: structural-grid
part-of:
value: SUBCASE101
FUNCTION
support-building-type:
value: office
support-spanning-type:
value: one-way
STRUCTURE
grid-geometry:
value: rectangular
acad-file:
value: grid-system.sld
x-grid-labels:
value: (a b c d)
x-grid-locations:
value: (0 9 18 27)
y-grid-labels:
value: (1 2 3 4 5)
y-grid-locations:
value: (0 10 19 28 38)

SUBCASE: FLOOR-SYSTEM

Node: SUBCASE103
GENERAL

text:
value:

"The floor system used consists of a combination of standard rescrete precast 'formplank' panels supported by custom-made precast beam shells and by facade wall panels. The ends of the 'formplank' panels rested on either corbels on the facade wall units or the upturned edges of the precast beam shells. These precast elements were used to produce a one-way slab, one-way beam system with structural detailing providing continuity between beams, precast columns, and facade panels."

RELATION
subnode-of:
value: 370-PITT-ST
instance-of:
value: floor-system
part-of:
value: SUBCASE101
FUNCTION
transmit-dead-load:
value: 3
units: kPa
transmit-live-load:
value: 3
units: kPa
BEHAVIOR
fire-resistance-level:
value: 2
units: hrs
deflection:
value: 18
units: mm
shear-stress:
value: 0.98
units: Mpa
xfig-file:
value: floor-system.fig
STRUCTURE
material:
value: precast-concrete
start-level:
value: 1
end-level:
value: 17
span-type:
value: one-way
maximum-span:
value: 11
units: m
typical-span:

value: 9
    units: m
floor-depth:
    value: 250
    units: mm
span-to-depth-ratio:
    value: 44
acad-file:
    value: floor-system.sld
maximum-aspect-ratio:
    value: 4.2

SUBCASE: FACADE-SYSTEM

Node: SUBCASE104
    GENERAL
        text:
        value:

"The preglazed load-bearing perimeter panels measured up to 10 m in length, 3.5 m in height and weighed up to 15 tonnes. All joints were open and drained with vented baffle strips between the precast panels and horizontal flashings at the base. Continuity was provided between the facade columns and the beams by means of connecting reinforcing bars to the columns with alpha splices. Along the top of each facade unit, a corbel was cast, which served both as a stiffening element and as a seat for the slab panels."

    RELATION
        subnode-of:
        value: 370-PITT-ST
        instance-of:
        value: facade-system
        part-of:
        value: SUBCASE101
    STRUCTURE
        acad-file:
        value: facade-system.sld
        number-of-stories:
        value: 17
        number-of-sides:
        value: 4
        material:
        value: precast-concrete
        storey-height:
        value: 4.0
        units: m
        plan-shape:

value: rectangular

SUBCASE: CORE-SYSTEM

Node: SUBCASE105
    GENERAL
        text:
        value:

"The building's resistance to wind forces was designed to be provided by the core structure walls and by the western facade panels. Architectural requirements for the building made it necessary for the core to be eccentric to wind forces in the east-west direction. The precast panels on the western elevation were designed to act as a wind-shear frame in order to provide torsional rigidity. The core walls were built in-situ using slipform construction techniques. All the walls around the lifts (elevators), stairs, and service functions were incorporated to form a core approximately 11 m square."

    RELATION
        subnode-of:
        value: 370-PITT-ST
        instance-of:
        value: core-system
        part-of:
        value: SUBCASE101
    FUNCTION
        resist-gravity-load:
        value: 70
        units: MN
        resist-wind-load:
        value: 1.5
        units: kPa
    BEHAVIOR
        lateral-displacement:
        value: 35
        units: mm
        overturning-moment:
        value: 1
        units: MNm
        bending-stress:
        value: 1.25
        units: Mpa
        compressive-stress:
        value: 9.19
    STRUCTURE
        acad-file:

value: core-system.sld
overall-shape:
    value: square
material:
    value: reinforced-concrete
overall-length:
    value: 11
    units: m
overall-width:
    value: 11
    units: m
height:
    value: 70
    units: m
thickness-of-walls:
    value: 200
    units: mm
height-to-width-ratio:
    value: 6.4
width-to-thickness-ratio:
    value: 55

SUBCASE: INTERNAL-COLUMN

Node: SUBCASE106
 GENERAL
    text:
    value:

"Three basic square column sizes were
used 800 mm, 700 mm, and 600 mm. In
keeping with the concept of off-site work,
electrical conduits and power switch
cavities were cast into the columns. The
precast columns were designed to achieve
a rigid moment connection with the
supported beams, this being achieved by
the extension of the column reinforcement
some 400 mm into slab beams. Internal
columns carry only vertical loads."

    RELATION
        subnode-of:
            value: 370-PITT-ST
        instance-of:
            value: column
        part-of:
            value: SUBCASE103
 FUNCTION
    resist-axial-load:
        value:
        units: kN
    resist-bending-moment:

value:
    units: kNm
resist-shear-force:
    value:
    units: kN
BEHAVIOR
    axial-compressive-stress:
        value:
        units: Mpa
    bending-compressive-stress:
        value:
        units: Mpa
    combined-compressive-stress:
        value:
        units: Mpa
    shear-stress:
        value:
        units: Mpa
STRUCTURE
    plan-location:
        value: interior
    acad-file:
        value: typical-column.sld
    start-level:
        value: 1
    finish-level:
        value: 17
    design-height:
        value: 4.0
        units: m
    section-shape:
        value: square
    section-width:
        value: 800
        units: mm
    section-depth:
        value: 800
        units: mm

SUBCASE: FLOOR-BEAM

Node: SUBCASE107
 GENERAL
    text:
    value:
"The system uses wide and shallow beams,
as its floor-to-floor height is critical. The
beam shells were designed with all positive
beam reinforcement and shear reinforcement cast in place."

    RELATION
        subnode-of:

value: 370-PITT-ST
instance-of:
  value: beam
part-of:
  value: SUBCASE103
FUNCTION
  resist-shear-force:
  value:
    units: kN
  resist-bending-moment:
  value:
    units: kNm
BEHAVIOR
  deflection:
  value:
    units: mm
  bending-stress:
  value:
    units: Mpa
  shear-stress:
  value:
    units: Mpa
STRUCTURE
  acad-file:
    value: typical-beam.sld
  maximum-span:
    value: 9
    units: m
  type:
    value: continuous
  plan-location:
    value: interior
  spacing:
    value: 10
    units: m
  number-of-spans:
    value: 4
  shape:
    value: rectangle
  width:
    value: 1200
    units: mm
  depth:
    value: 500
    units: mm
  span-to-depth-ratio:
    value: 20

SUBCASE: FACADE-COLUMN

Node: SUBCASE108
  GENERAL

text:
  value:

"External columns are integrated into the facade precast wall units, leaving just 4 free-standing columns per floor. All exterior columns are rectangular except at corners where L-shaped columns are located. External columns carry both lateral and vertical loads."

RELATION
  subnode-of:
    value: 370-PITT-ST
  instance-of:
    value: column
  part-of:
    value: SUBCASE104
FUNCTION
  resist-axial-load:
    value:
    units: kN
  resist-bending-moment:
    value:
    units: kNm
  resist-shear-force:
    value:
    units: kN
BEHAVIOR
  axial-compressive-stress:
    value:
    units: Mpa
  bending-compressive-stress:
    value:
    units: Mpa
  combined-compressive-stress:
    value:
    units: Mpa
  shear-stress:
    value:
    units: Mpa
STRUCTURE
  plan-location:
    value: exterior
  acad-file:
    value: typical-column.sld
  start-level:
    value: 1
  finish-level:
    value: 17
  design-height:
    value: 4.0
    units: m
  section-shape:
    value: rectangular
  section-width:

value: 1200
units: mm
section-depth:
value: 600
units: mm

SUBCASE: FACADE-WALL

Node: SUBCASE109
RELATION
subnode-of:
value: 370-PITT-ST
instance-of:
value: rigid-frame
part-of:
value: SUBCASE104
FUNCTION
resist-gravity-load:
value:
units: kN
resist-lateral-load:
value:
units: kN
BEHAVIOR
total-drift:
value:
units: mm
story-drift:
value:
units: mm

xfig-file:
value: facade-wall.fig
STRUCTURE
number-of-stories:
value: 17
number-of-bays:
value: 4
material:
value: precast-concrete
acad-file:
value: typical-frame.sld
storey-height:
value: 4.0
units: m
panel-height:
value: 3.5
units: m
panel-length:
value: 10
units: m
panel-weight:
value: 15
units: tonnes
wall-height:
value: 70
units: m
wall-width:
value: 29
units: m
wall-location:
value: (5 a), (5 d)

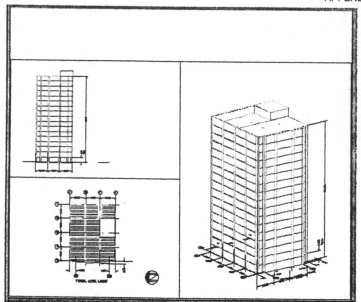

Figure B.2. Structure — subcase 101.

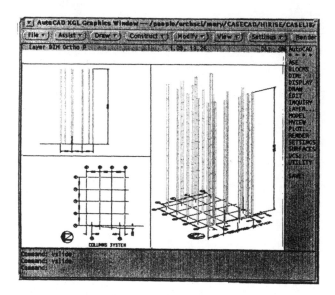

Figure B.3. Structure — subcase 102.

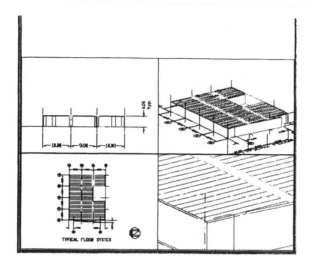

Figure B.4. Structure (a) — subcase 103.

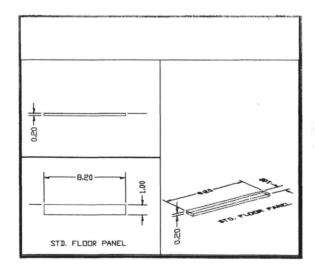

Figure B.5. Structure (b) — subcase 103.

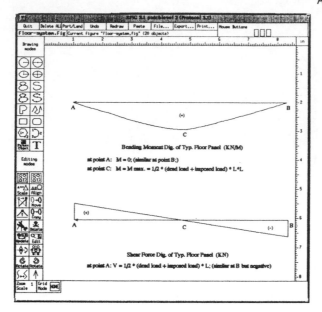

Figure B.6. Behavior — subcase 103.

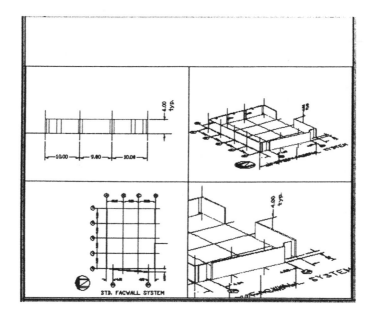

Figure B.7. Structure — subcase 104.

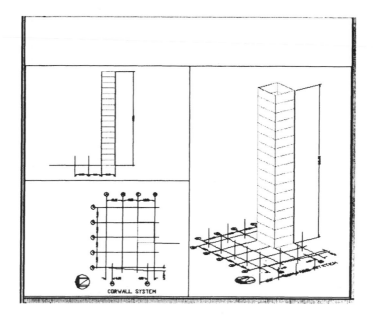

Figure B.8. Structure (a) — subcase 105.

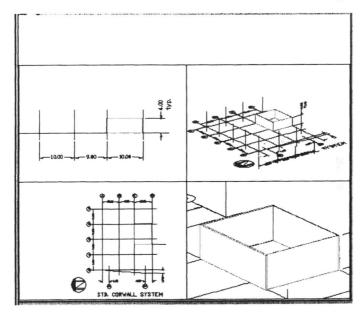

Figure B.9. Structure (b) — subcase 105.

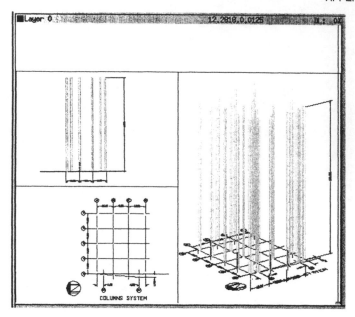

Figure B.10. Structure — subcase 106 and 108.

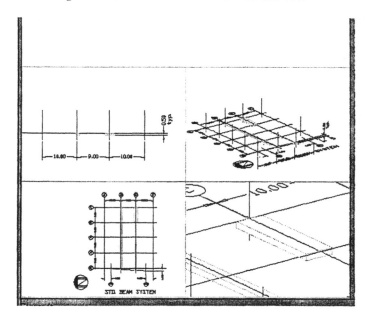

Figure B.11. Structure — subcase 107.

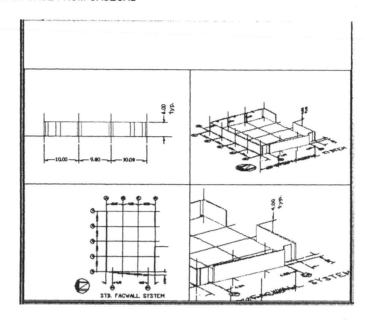

Figure B.12. Structure — subcase 109.

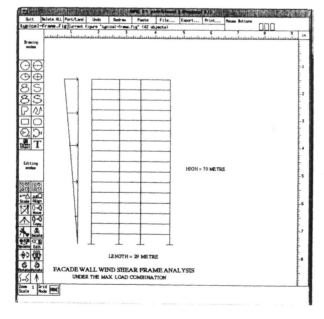

Figure B.13. Behavior — subcase 109.

References

Acorn, T., and Walden, S. (1992). SMART: Support management cultivated reasoning technology for Compaq customer service, *Proceedings of AAAI-92.* Cambridge, MA: AAAI Press/MIT Press.

Alberts, L. K. (1992). The use of primitive generic components for the structuring of design cases, in P. Pu (Ed.), *Unpublished Proceedings of the AID'92 Workshop on Case-Based Design Systems,* pp. 5-8.

Alterman, R. (1986). An adaptive planner, *Proceedings of AAAI-86.* Cambridge, MA: AAAI Press/MIT Press.

Autodesk (1992). *AutoCAD Reference Manual.* Sausalito, CA: Autodesk, Inc.

Barber, J., Bhatta, S., Goel, A., Jacobsen, M., Pearce, M., Penberthy, L., Shanker, M., and Stroulia, E. (1992). AskJef: Integrating case-based reasoning and multimedia technologies for interface design support, in J. S. Gero (Ed.), *Artificial Intelligence in Design '92.* Dordrecht: Kluwer Academic.

Bariess, E. R. (1989). The experimental evaluation of a case-based learning apprentice, *Proceedings of the DARPA Workshop on Case-Based Reasoning.* San Mateo, CA: Morgan Kaufmann.

Brown, D., and Chandrasekaran, B. (1985). Expert systems for a class of mechanical design activity, in J. S. Gero (Ed.), *Knowledge Engineering in Computer-Aided Design.* Amsterdam: North-Holland, pp. 259-282.

Buchanan, B., and Shortliffe, E. (1984). *Rule-Based Systems.* Reading, MA: Addison-Wesley.

Buhl, H. R. (1985). *Creative Engineering Design.* Ames, IA: The Iowa State University Press.

Carbonell, J. G. (1981). A computational model of analogical problem solving, *Proceedings of the Seventh International Joint Conference on Artificial Intelligence* **1**: 147-152.

Carbonell, J. G. (1983). Learning by analogy: Formulating and generalizing plans from past experience, *Machine Learning: Volume 1. An Artificial Intelligence Approach.* Palo Alto, CA: Tioga, pp. 137-161.

Carbonell, J. G. (1986). Derivational analogy: A theory of reconstructive problem solving and expertise acquisition, *Machine Learning: Volume 2. An Artificial Intelligence Approach*. San Mateo, CA: Morgan Kaufmann, pp. 371-391.

Chandrasekaran, B. (1990). Design problem solving: A task analysis. *AI Magazine* **11**(4): 59-71.

Coyne, R. D., Rosenman, M. A., Radford, A. D., Balachandran, M., and Gero, J. S. (1990). *Knowledge-Based Design Systems*. Reading, MA: Addison-Wesley.

Domeshek, E. A., and Kolodner, J. L. (1992). A case-based design aid for architecture, in J. S. Gero (Ed.), *Artificial Intelligence in Design '92*. Dordrecht: Kluwer Academic.

Domeshek, E. A., and Kolodner, J. L. (1993). Finding the points of large cases. *Artificial Intelligence for Engineering Design, Analysis and Manufacturing* **7**(2): 87-96.

Duffy, A. H. B., and MacCallum, K. J. (1989). Computer representation of numerical expertise for preliminary ship design. *Marine Technology* **26**: 289-302.

Falkenhainer, B., Forbus, K. D., and Gentner, D. (1990). The structure-mapping engine: Algorithm and examples. *Artificial Intelligence* **41**: 1-63.

Faltings, B., Hua, K., Schmitt, G., and Shih, S. (1991). Case-based representation of architectural design knowledge, *Proceedings of the DARPA Workshop on Case-Based Reasoning*. San Mateo, CA: Morgan Kaufmann, pp. 307-316.

Flemming, U. (1987). More than the sum of parts: the grammar of Queen Anne houses. *Environment and Planning B, Planning and Design* **14**.

Gero, J.S. (1990). Design prototypes: A knowledge representation schema for design. *AI Magazine* **11**(4): 26-36.

Goel, A., and Chandraskaran, B. (1989). Use of device models in adaptation of design cases, *Proceedings of the DARPA Workshops on Case-Based Reasoning*. San Mateo, CA: Morgan Kaufmann, pp. 100-109.

Goel, A., and Kolodner, J. L. (1991). Toward a case-based tool for aiding conceptual design problem solving, *Proceedings of the DARPA Workshop on Case-Based Reasoning*. San Mateo, CA: Morgan Kaufmann, pp. 109-120.

Goodman, M. (1989). CBR in battle planning, *Proceedings of the DARPA Workshop on Case-Based Reasoning*. San Mateo, CA: Morgan Kaufmann.

Hammond, K. (1986). CHEF: A model of case-based planning, *Proceedings of the AAAI'86*. Philadelphia, PA, pp. 237-258.

Hammond, K. (1989). *Case-Based Planning*. New York: Academic Press.

Hennessy, D. H., and Hinkle, D. (1992). Applying case-based reasoning to autoclave loading. *IEEE Expert* **7**(5): 21-26.

Hinrichs, T. R. (1988). Towards an architecture for open world problem solving, *Proceedings of the DARPA Workshop on Case-Based Reasoning*. San Mateo, CA: Morgan Kaufmann, pp. 105-119.

Hinrichs, T. R. (1991). *Problem solving in open worlds: a case study in design*, Ph.D. Thesis, Atlanta, GA: Georgia Institute of Technology, Department of Computer Science.

Hinrichs, T. R., and Kolodner, J. L. (1991). The role of adaptation in case-based design, *Proceedings of the DARPA Workshop on Case-Based Reasoning*. San Mateo, CA: Morgan Kaufmann, pp. 121-132.

Hua, K., Schmitt, G., and Faltings, B. (1992). Adaptation of spatial design cases, in J. S. Gero (Ed.), *Artificial Intelligence in Design '92*. Dordrecht: Kluwer Academic, pp. 559-575.

Hughes, J. (1991). *Object-Oriented Databases*. New York: Prentice-Hall International.

Jackson, P. (1990). *Introduction to Expert Systems* (2nd ed.). Reading, MA: Addison-Wesley.

Kambhampati, S., and Hendler, J. A. (1992). A validation structure based theory of plan modification and reuse. *Artificial Intelligence Journal* **55**: 193-258.

Keane, M. T. (1988). *Analogical Problem Solving*. Chichester: Ellis Horwood.

Kolodner, J. L. (1984). *Retrieval and Organizational Strategies in Conceptual Memory: A Computer Model*. Hillsdale, NJ: Lawrence Erlbaum Associates.

Kolodner, J. L. (1988). Retrieving events from a case memory: A parallel implementation, *Proceedings of the DARPA Workshop on Case-Based Reasoning*. San Mateo, CA: Morgan Kaufmann.

Kolodner, J. L. (1993). *Case-Based Reasoning*. San Mateo, CA: Morgan Kaufmann.

Kolodner, J., and Mark, W. (1992). Using history: Case-based reasoning [Special issue]. *IEEE EXPERT: Intelligent Systems and Their Applications* **October**.

Kolodner, J. L., and Riesbeck, C. K. (1986). *Experience, Memory, and Reasoning*. Hillsdale, NJ: Lawrence Erlbaum Associates.

Koning, H., and Eizenberg, J. (1981). The language of the prairie: Frank Lloyd Wright's prairie houses. *Environment and Planning B* **8**: 295-323.

Koton, P. (1988). Integrating case-based and causal reasoning, *Proceedings of the Tenth Annual Conference of the Cognitive Science Society.* Hillsdale, NJ: Lawrence Erlbaum Associates.

Maher, M. L. (1987). Engineering design synthesis: A domain independent representation. *Artificial Intelligence for Engineering Design, Analysis and Manufacturing* **1**(3): 207-213.

Maher, M. L. (1990). Process models for design synthesis. *AI Magazine* **11**(4): 49-58.

Maher, M. L., and Balachandran, M. B. (1994a). Flexible retrieval strategies for case-based design, in J. S. Gero and F. Sudweeks (Eds.), *Artificial Intelligence in Design '94.* Dordrecht: Kluwer Academic, pp. 163-180.

Maher, M. L., and Balachandran, M. B. (1994b). A multimedia approach to case-based structural design. *ASCE Journal of Computing in Civil Engineering* **8**(3): 359-377.

Maher, M. L., and Zhang, D. M. (1991). CADSYN: Using case and decomposition knowledge for design synthesis, in J. S. Gero (Ed.), *Artificial Intelligence in Design '91.* Oxford, UK: Butterworth-Heinemann, pp. 137-150.

Maher, M. L., and Zhang, D. M. (1993). CADSYN: A case-based design process model. *Artificial Intelligence for Engineering Design, Analysis and Manufacturing* **7**(2): 97-110.

Minsky, M. (1975). A framework for representing knowledge, in P. H. Winston (Ed.), *The Psychology of Computer Vision.* New York: McGraw-Hill, pp. 211-277.

Mitchell, W., and Stiny, G. (1978). The palladian grammar. *Environment and Planning B* **5**: 5-18.

Navinchandra, D. (1988). Case-based reasoning in CYCLOPS, a design problem solver, *Proceedings of the DARPA Workshop on Case-Based Reasoning.* San Mateo, CA: Morgan Kaufmann, pp. 286-301.

Nyberg, E. H. (1988). *FrameKit: A Hierarchical Frame-Based Knowledge Representation Language Handbook.* Pittsburgh, PA, Carnegie Mellon University, Center for Machine Translation.

Owens, C. (1993). Integrating feature extraction and memory search. *Machine Learning* **10**(3): 311-340.

Pearce, M., Goel, A. K., Kolodner, J. L., Zimring, C., Sentosa, L., and Billington, R. (1992). Case-based design support: A case study in architectural design. *IEEE EXPERT* 14-20.

Prieditis, A. (1988). *Analogica.* San Mateo, CA: Morgan Kaufmann.

Pu, P. (Ed.) (1993). Case-based reasoning in design [Special issue]. *Artificial Intelligence for Engineering Design, Analysis and Manufacturing* 7(2).

Qian, L., and Gero, J. (1992). A design support system using analogy, in J. S. Gero (Ed.), *Artificial Intelligence in Design '92.* Dordrecht: Kluwer Academic.

Riesbeck, C.K., and Schank, R.C. (1989). *Inside Case-Based Reasoning.* Hillsdale, NJ: Lawrence Erlbaum Associates.

Roderman, R., and Tsatlouis, C. (1993). PANDA: A case-based system to aid novice designers. *Artificial Intelligence for Engineering Design, Analysis and Manufacturing* 7(2): 125-134.

Rosenman, M. A., Gero, J. S., and Oxman, R. E. (1991). What's in a case? The use of case bases, knowledge bases and databases in design, in G. N. Schmitt (Ed.), *CAAD Futures '91.* Zurich: ETH, pp. 263-277.

Russell, S. (1989). *The Use of Knowledge in Analogy and Induction.* San Mateo, CA: Morgan Kaufmann.

Schank, R. C. (1982). *Dynamic Memory.* London: Cambridge University Press.

Simon, H. A. (1969). *The Sciences of the Artificial.* Cambridge, MA: MIT Press.

Simon, H. A. (1973). The structure of the ill-structured problems. *Artificial Intelligence* 4: 181-201.

Simoudis, E. (1992). Using case-based retrieval for customer technical support. *IEEE Expert* 7(5): 7-13.

Stanfill, C. (1987). Memory-based reasoning applied to English pronunciation, *Proceedings of the Sixth National Conference on Artificial Intelligence, AAAI'87.* San Mateo, CA: Morgan Kaufmann.

Steinberg, L. (1987). Design as refinement plus constraint propagation: The VEXED experience, *Proceedings of the Sixth Annual Conference on Artificial Intelligence, AAAI'87.* San Mateo, CA: Morgan Kaufmann, pp. 830-835.

Stroulia, E., Shankar, M., Goel, A., and Penberthy, L. (1992). A model-based approach to blame-assignment in design, in J. S. Gero (Ed.), *Artificial Intelligence in Design '92.* Dordrecht: Kluwer Academic, pp. 519-537.

Sycara, K. P., and Navinchandra, D. (1989). Integrated case-based reasoning and qualitative reasoning in engineering design, in J. S. Gero (Ed.), *Artificial Intelligence in Design.* New York: Springer-Verlag, pp. 231-250.

Sycara, K. P., and Navinchandra, D. (1991). Index transformation techniques for facilitating creative use of multiple cases, in J. S. Gero and F. Sudweeks (Eds.), *Preprints of the Artificial Intelligence in Design Workshop of IJCAI-91.* Sydney: Key Centre of Design Computing, University of Sydney, pp. 15-20.

Sycara, K. P., Navinchandra, D., and Narasimhan, S. (1992). Parametric adaptation case based design, *Proceedings of the Case-Based Design Workshop, AID'92,* pp. 113-125.

Voβ, A., Coulon, C.-H., Gräther, W., Linowski, B., Bartsch-Spörl, B., Börner, B., Tammer, E. C., Dürschke, H., and Knauff, M. (1994). Retrieval of similar layouts, in J. S. Gero and F. Sudweeks (Eds.), *Artificial Intelligence in Design '94.* Dordrecht: Kluwer Academic, pp. 625-640.

Wang, J., and Howard, H. C. (1989). Design-dependent knowledge for structural engineering design, in J. S. Gero (Ed.), *Artificial Intelligence in Engineering: Design.* Dordrecht: Kluwer Academic, pp. 267-277.

Wang, J., and Howard, H. C. (1991). A design-dependent approach to integrated structural design, in J. S. Gero (Ed.), *Artificial Intelligence in Design '91.* Oxford, UK: Butterworth-Heinemann, pp. 151-170.

Wang, W., and Gero, J. S. (1991). A model for the organization of design prototype and design case memories, *Proceedings of IJCAI-12 Workshop on Artificial Intelligence in Design.* Sydney: Key Centre of Design Computing, University of Sydney, pp. 301-307.

Zacherl, A. L., and Domeshek, E. A. (1993). Indexing evaluations of buildings to aid conceptual design, *Proceedings of AAAI Workshop on Case-Based Reasoning.* Menlo Park, CA: AAAI Press.

Zhang, D. M. (1994). *A Hybrid Approach to Case-Based Design,* Ph.D. Thesis, University of Sydney, Australia, Department of Architectural and Design Science.

Zhao, F. (1991). *A Knowledge-Based Representation For Creative Design,* Ph.D. Thesis, Pittsburgh, PA, Carnegie Mellon University, Department of Civil Engineering.

Author Index

A

Acorn 14
Alberts 151
Alterman 14
Autodesk 143, 146, 155

B

Balachandran 16, 75, 81, 107, 131,
    163, 164
Barber 16, 18
Bareiss 15
Bhatta 16, 81
Billington 16
Brown 29, 131
Buchanan 3
Buhl 131

C

Carbonell 1, 2, 35, 114
Chandrasekaran 16, 29, 30, 42, 74,
    131, 150
Coyne 131

D

Domeshek 16, 81, 84, 88, 163
Duffy 61
Dym 24

E

Eizenberg 31

F

Falkenhainer 2
Faltings 30, 41, 125, 140
Flemming 31
Forbus 2

G

Gentner 2
Gero 43, 44, 62, 71, 84, 131, 150
Goel 16, 30, 42, 74, 81, 150
Goodman 15

H

Hammond 13, 116
Hendler 14
Hennessy 15
Hinkle 15
Hinrichs 30, 39, 125, 140
Howard 30, 40
Hua 30, 41, 125, 140
Hughes 60, 150

J

Jackson 3, 16, 81

K

Kambhampati 14
Keane 2
Kolodner 1, 2, 16, 21, 30, 39, 59,
    81, 84, 87, 96, 105, 106, 107,
    110, 125, 140, 163

Subject Index